MAN'S VISION OF GOD

MAN'S VISION OF GOD

and the Logic of Theism

By
CHARLES HARTSHORNE

ARCHON BOOKS
HAMDEN, CONNECTICUT
1964

Reprinted 1964 in an unaltered and
unabridged edition by arrangement with
HARPER & ROW, INCORPORATED

LIBRARY OF CONGRESS CATALOG CARD NUMBER: 64-24714
PRINTED IN THE UNITED STATES OF AMERICA

We all know the nature of life and the real, though only with exquisite care can we tell the truth about them.

C. I. LEWIS, in *Mind and the World Order*

Can I see another's woe
And not be in sorrow too? . . .
Can a father see his child
Weep, nor be with sorrow filled?

And can he who smiles on all
Hear the wren with sorrows small,
Hear the small bird's grief and care,
Hear the woes that infants bear,

And not sit beside the nest,
Pouring pity in their breast,
And not sit the cradle near,
Heaping tear on infant's tear . . . ?

O, no! never can it be!
Never, never can it be!

O! he gives to us his joy,
That our grief he may destroy;
Till our grief is fled and gone
He doth sit by us and moan.

WILLIAM BLAKE, in *Songs of Innocence*

PREFACE

To the mountainous — I had almost said, monstrous — mass of writings devoted to "philosophical theology," what can there be to add? I answer simply, if without apparent modesty, there is exactitude, logical rigor. Beyond question, of those who have dealt with the problem of God, some, including both theists and atheists, have possessed abundant capacity for rigorous analysis. But many causes have prevented them from making full use of this capacity in their treatment of theism. Such causes include the state of logic in general at the time when they were writing, the belief that the main logical outlines of the problem had already been discovered by great, not to mention saintly, predecessors, or the belief that theism is too essentially irrational to deserve or require more than hasty analysis. The purpose of this book is to show that and how the question, Is there a supreme, or in any sense perfect, being, a God? can be answered by secular or philosophic reason operating according to strict canons of procedure. It is all too likely, if not beyond doubt, that I too have deviated at times from these canons. But it may not seem altogether surprising that one who has by chance been rather intimately associated, as pupil, colleague, or editor, with several of the most competent logicians that ever lived, including C. I. Lewis, H. M. Sheffer, A. N. Whitehead, Charles Peirce, should find his thought about the problem which has preoccupied him for twenty-five years falling more and more into sharply logical patterns. If there is any use for logic in reflection upon the religious object, there should be some value in these patterns (and perhaps in others which have not yet occurred to anyone).

The conclusion at which this book arrives, in harmony with a rather widespread belief of recent times, is that secular knowledge supports the religious idea of God if, and only if, by religion is meant something quite distinct from, and partly incompatible with, what has passed as orthodox theology. It is coming to be seen that the meaning which "God" had for the prophets and their most sensitive followers is philosophically more defensible than the definitions of the term which (until recently and with inconspicuous exceptions) were given by theological and philosophical technicians, even when they were also religious men. In other words, religious people have held philosophically justifiable beliefs about God thanks rather to their religious superiority than to their scientific or philosophical skill — somewhat as, before the discovery of vitamins, common practice was a better guide to some aspects of dietetics than was physiological chemistry. Theology appears now to have reached the vitamin stage; it now sees in precise technical terms what was somehow felt to be true all along — a secret told to babes and withheld from the wise and understanding.

Not religion alone, but philosophy as well, is concerned in this result. All the great philosophical systems do something about the problem of God, but only some of the most recent show accurate grasp of the religious idea which is the historical source of the problem. Of late the partly irreligious character of the traditional theologico-philosophical concept of God has been recognized by a number of writers. What has still to be realized, I think, is the philosophical power inherent in the truly religious conception. When we compare Aquinas or Spinoza with James or Bergson, it may perhaps seem that new trends in philosophical theology are relatively weak in logical cogency, in philosophical power. Also, it may seem to many that James's or Bergson's idea of God is a radical religious heresy. Or again, Whitehead is not only thought to lack the intellectual clarity of, say, Thomas, but is sometimes accused of not meaning by " God " what religion means by the word. I believe, nevertheless, that the main drift of thought at work in these men, and in many others of our time, is in the direction of greater fidelity both to religious experience and to the canons of philosophical rigor.

The ground then for this book is the conviction that a magnificent intellectual content — far surpassing that of such systems as Thomism, Spinozism, German idealism, positivism (old or new) — is implicit in the religious faith most briefly expressed in the three words, God is love, which words I sincerely believe are contradicted as truly as they are embodied in the best known of the older theologies, as they certainly have been misunderstood by atheists and skeptics. Various pioneers have already marked out some of the main lines of the doctrine I have in mind, with a genius for discovery which I admire rather than hope to emulate. But somehow the scholarly world has not yet been made aware of the extent and exact nature of the revolution which has in principle been effected. This is partly because the movement is split into theological specialists on one side and philosophical specialists on the other, and because both groups are still further split into various schools whose divergencies on other matters tend to conceal their considerable agreement as to the idea of God, especially their negative agreement concerning what God, if he exists, assuredly cannot be. But the main reason, I suspect, is that no one has quite made the *logic* of the new theism his special province. A great logician, Whitehead, is profoundly aware of many aspects of this logic, but his thought is for many readers inaccessibly intricate and entangled in the technical problems of science, and he has not had the leisure to develop and expound the theological aspect of his philosophy. I think too he has fallen into some fairly serious errors, or at least faults of exposition. As for Bergson, his ultra-simplicity and anti-logicism serve to conceal the depth of some of his insights, insights by no means dependent upon anti-intellectualism.

Then there is the influence of those theologians, some of them among the most spectacular of our time, who maintain that philosophical theology is in principle of no use to religion. They deduce this from the doctrine of the Fall and the corruption of human reason. The deduction might be more convincing did one not know that these theologians — e.g., Barth or the Upsala school — are chiefly familiar with those forms of philosophical theology which philosophers like Whitehead would agree with them in rejecting, and that there are even signs that such theologians are not themselves free from the influence of the erroneous philosophies referred to.

The rational way to inquire into the truth of religion is first to allow religion to assert what its claims are, and to avoid the error of supposing that these claims can only be such as are statable in terms of a given, say Neo-Platonic or Aristotelian, philosophy. For unless such philosophy is as infallible as religion could possibly claim to be, this procedure runs the risk of making religion responsible for errors with which it has nothing to do. The only way to avoid such question-begging procedure and yet to furnish a philosophical scheme in terms of which the religious idea can be rationally formulated is to discover a *logically complete* classification of possible ideas about God, a non-controversial statement of what the theistic controversy might conceivably be about. Classifications of different kinds of theism are commonly couched in conceptions so vague as to be almost meaningless — such as pantheism, deism, transcendence, immanence, the supernatural — or with reference to contrasts that do not exhaust the possibilities, e.g., Is God in *all* respects or in *no* respects perfect (not usually stated so baldly as to make the non-exhaustiveness obvious)? Again, it is not generally realized that "perfection" has two fundamentally distinct meanings, only one of which receives the slightest consideration in the older works, although it can be shown that both meanings are required to define God. Thus religion or philosophy is asked to commit itself as between doctrines both of which may be false, or so loosely expressed as to have no determinate content. Even if this process endures for fifteen hundred years (as it has) it is logically inadmissible to claim that the truth about religion could be reliably ascertained by it. A fallacy becomes no less one through being many times repeated, even though thereby it reaches the status of the great tradition. This is the answer to those who reject recent thought with the assertion that religious and metaphysical truth being eternal, progress is out of place in theology. If only certain errors did not threaten to be eternal — or at least immortal! To root these out is assuredly progress. Nor is it impossible to explain how the errors were made and why they were persisted in. Rather, the known traits of the human mind make it seem only natural that religious people should have felt more truth than they were able for long centuries to analyze, and that Greek logic and ontology should have taken some false turns which made them inadequate to the higher values, as they certainly were to more than set ajar the door to the exploration of nature. Initial and long-lasting error is as natural in metaphysics as in science.

It turns out that a definite and by logical necessity complete classification of concepts of deity is easily possible, though apparently it has been hitherto overlooked. This classification assumes no peculiarly religious and no partisan philosophical notions, but turns upon a few simple ideas which inevitably occur in everyday life (far more plainly and unambiguously than such notions as cause, form, matter, and the like) as well as in every philosophy, and which yet have manifest relevance to what practically every theology has asserted about God. The issue then becomes that of choosing among a number of special cases, or rather special combinations, of elements whose meaning is scarcely a subject of controversy. And it seems almost as certain as arithmetic that some one of the combinations (among which atheism is included) is the truth.

This book also seeks to throw new light upon the types of evidence to which the rival theistic (and atheistic) doctrines may appeal. Thus the cosmological and ontological arguments are given a form which at once fits the religious idea of God and does justice to the criticisms of the older forms of these arguments. The older doctrine possessed its (incomplete and imperfect) rationale, which was elaborated most fully by Aquinas. Any significant alternative must also have its rationale — indeed, if it is the truth, a uniquely convincing and beautiful one.

Concerning method — that acute contemporary problem — I have something to say in chapter 2. "Empiricism" in theology as it is usually conceived is there shown to be an insufficient procedure; and I also attempt to show that the metaphysical method of the Schoolmen and of Spinoza and Leibniz calls for neither mere rejection nor mere acceptance, but for transformation in the light of modern logic. A long discussion of the positivistic objections to metaphysics has been deleted. But I may remark here that since expert opinion (by any reasonably neutral test of expert) is deeply divided on the question, the hypothesis that a sound metaphysics is possible cannot be ruled out. Even the recognized logical authority, C. I. Lewis, who is sometimes classed with positivists, affirms such a possibility (in his *Mind and the World Order*). If a scientific metaphysics is possible, it will never be actual until we cease to wallow in confusion in regard to the religious aspect of philosophy, in which all the metaphysical questions come to a focus.

The new theism agrees roughly with the positivistic critique of theism as theism is generally conceived, but denies that this critique is relevant to theism as recently revised — in part, just to remove the defects which positivists allege. The revision seems unknown to positivism, and to leading non-theists generally, for example, Dewey.

Those who wish religion to be spoken of only in religious, or, as they suggest, poetic or mythical or devotional or (in Barth's sense) dialectical terms, should then conscientiously refrain from making *any* statements about God which suggest a prosaic logical interpretation, such as the bald statement that God does not change, an assertion which precisely such persons ought not to suppose intended by the biblical " in whom there is no shadow of turning," since this phrase means that God is changeless *in some sense required by religion,* but not necessarily in every sense of importance to metaphysics. Tillich, a thinker I deeply admire, likes to insist that descriptions of God are symbolic not literal, since God is the " unconditioned," and language deals literally only with the conditioned. But the term unconditioned is itself a term, and not a religious one either. How does Tillich know but that God is only conditionally, or *in some but not in every sense,* unconditioned? Just this we shall find to be a reasonable conclusion.

The validity of revelation, or of religious experience as furnishing knowledge, is not a necessary assumption of the argument of this book. I assume only that the most obvious and central implications of religion deserve not less than the compliment of careful examination by philosophy.

For a theology which builds frankly upon revelation, but which appears for the most part consistent with the doctrines developed hereinafter, I point to two writers, Berdyaev and Garvie, representing the Greek Orthodox and the Congregational churches, respectively. These men may believe more than I am at present able to do, but they do not believe most of the doctrines I am explicitly attacking. The same could be said of some leading writers in other churches, including the Anglican — all the great churches indeed but the Roman Catholic. This may make it clear that it is the philosophical not the truly theological element in the Christian tradition that I as a philosopher venture to attack. Is it not time Christianity should be judged in its own terms, not in terms of its borrowed Greek garments, however good a fit these may have long appeared to exhibit? As a personal confession I could say little more, or less, than that I believe that the fundamental (and true) religious insight (into the essentially social character of the supreme or cosmic being) was more vividly present to the Jews than to any other ancient people, and to Jesus than to any other man. But the question I propose for discussion is only this: Were the early Christians right — is anyone right — from the standpoint of secular philosophy, in believing that *deus est caritas?*

To those who feel that the chief equipment necessary for the discussion of such questions is ability to refer to documents composed, say, in the thirteenth century, a few remarks may be directed. First, there are very learned theologians and philosophers who on the main point accept the "new" theology. Moreover, the new doctrine is also in some measure an ancient tradition, though one so inconspicuous that it was not even refuted by most of the great system-makers, but largely overlooked, although logically it is one of the chief possibilities for philosophical thought. Its history has yet to be made conveniently available.

Moreover, the view which is offered in the place of traditional theism involves a hearty acceptance of many tenets of the latter when these have been subjected to certain rather drastic and scarcely traditional qualifications. (I do not deny, for example, that God is in some sense simple, immutable, complete and perfect, but I affirm that there is a sense, no less important, in which he is complex, changeable, ever incomplete and growing in value.) Whatever the weaknesses of my exposition, the basic issue itself — whether there is a defensible mean between the merely absolute and immutable deity of the classical theologians, and the merely imperfect and indefinitely unstable one of some recent thinkers — is something larger than the eccentricities of any man or any generation. The human race obviously must explore it as thoroughly as any other issue. The only questions are, When? and How?

Under present world conditions it may seem peculiarly difficult to conceive of divine love. More than ever, one feels the force of the old dilemma: either divine power or divine goodness must be limited. But the now rather popular solution of accepting the first horn of the dilemma (denying omnipotence) is too crude to give general satisfaction. The real trouble is not in attributing too much power to God, but in an oversimple or too mechanical conception of the nature of power in general. The problem of evil in its traditional sense disappears for one who sees, on the one hand, that even the greatest conceivable or "perfect" power could not guarantee complete harmony among other individuals (and upon what except such individuals could the perfect power be exercised?) since these as such must have some individuality of action of their own, some freedom however slight; and who sees, on the other hand, that divinity is not the privilege of escaping all sufferings but the exactly contrary one of sharing them all. *Unlimited companionship in the tragedies which freedom makes more or less inevitable* is the theologically most neglected of divine prerogatives. This companionship does not by any means imply that all is for the best, even for God. It only implies that all is as nearly best *as any one will could conceivably insure,* and that all is expressive of a love which both as benevolent influence and as the will to companionship is unlimited, perfect, when measured by the utmost that is conceivable.

Thus careful analysis, crudely sketched here, shows that both horns of the famous dilemma are false or at least ambiguous. We need not, in this dark time, inquire why God has not arranged all things for the best, since this notion of " arranging " applies only so far as things are not genuine individuals with their own modicum of initiative. (The notion is really an illusion when taken absolutely, and seems to derive from the deceptive appearance of complete passivity of some physical substances to our manipulation, a passivity which physics shows to be a statistical effect of the behavior of numerous individuals which individually cannot ever be strictly manipulated or arranged.) In their ultimate individuality things can only be influenced, they cannot be sheerly coerced. Power is influence, perfect power is perfect influence, over *individuals* which as such only very imperfect power would even try to reduce to mere echoes or mechanical executors of its own decisions. There is a perfect way, as there are imperfect ones, of allotting to others the amount of good and evil they shall have within reach of their own decisions. There is neither an imperfect nor a perfect way of dealing with individuals as totally without power of their own over good and evil.

I should like also, again in view of world conditions, to state that I entirely disagree with those who hold that the theological conception of love implies the doctrine of absolute pacifism or non-participation in war. This too, I must think, is due to a crude analysis of the meaning of love, that is to say, social awareness. Those pacifists in England and France whose simultaneous occurrence with extreme bellicosity in Germany and Italy helped to make the current tragedy so devastating exhibited to my mind a deficiency of social awareness, of sympathy in the religious sense, not an excess of it. (I have discussed this question briefly toward the end of chapter 4.) Faith in love is not belief in a special kind of magic whereby refusal to use violence against violence automatically results in the least harm, still less in appeasing the violent. There is nothing in exact theology to indicate that the result may not often be worse than that of resistance — indeed indefinitely worse if enough good men accept pacifism, leaving violence, the most dangerous of all means, to be employed only by those whose lack of scruples will maximize not minimize its dangers. Nor does it contradict the proposition that social awareness is the essence of God and the ideal for man to hold that refusal to resist by violence may actually greatly encourage and intensify the will to violence on the other side, so that either the conflict must break out on a larger scale and with less hope of the more scrupulous party's winning, or else the world must be enslaved and all high ideals, even pacifism, be largely driven out by brutal control of all the organs of opinion and education.

I should like to recall my debt to my first teacher in philosophical theology, Professor William Ernest Hocking, who introduced me to the idea of a God not in every sense absolute, and yet in the religious sense perfect; and to Professors C. I. Lewis and H. M. Sheffer, also of Harvard University, who introduced me to logical exactitude, though whether the introduction was effective in this case is for the reader to judge. I am also much obligated to my colleagues in the department of philosophy and the divinity schools of the University of Chicago for providing an exacting critical environment for reflections upon the philosophical aspects of religion, or the religious aspects of philosophy. I recall also those teachers of my childhood and youth who led me to look upon intellectual integrity as a religious virtue rather than an impiety. These are: my father, the Reverend F. C. Hartshorne; my school science teacher, also a clergyman, who saw divine beauty in the atom and in the process of evolution, not because he thought he ought to see it but because he did; and Professor Rufus M. Jones, who sees beauty in nearly everything.

My wife, as always, has suggested numerous improvements in the style and reasoning.

This book is intimately related to a preceding volume, *Beyond Humanism,* published in 1937, and to a sequel, largely completed and soon to be published, *The Universal Orthodoxy.* Certain topics touched on hereinafter are more fully dealt with in these other works. Such topics are the case for panpsychism, or social idealism as a theory of all existence (see both of the works mentioned, especially the first), the case for indeterminism, or the theory of open alternatives within the temporal process (see *Beyond Humanism*), the relations of theology to physics and biology (see both of the above), and the following topics dealt with chiefly in *The Universal Orthodoxy:* the goodness and omnipotence of God in relation to the facts of evil, the relations of philosophical to revealed theology, "the synthesis of philosophical extremes in current theism," "the formula of immanence and transcendence." Any of the three books can be read independently, but the present one is probably the most convenient introduction to the system of ideas expressed in all.

As an effort to introduce more strict modes of thought into philosophical theology, the book cannot be altogether easy reading. Not — I venture to hope — that it is obscure, but that in the nature of its goal it is worth reading only if, in crucial passages at least, it deserves careful study. Today, if ever in history, it is upon the competence of readers, more than of writers, that the religious question in its philosophic aspect depends. The past hundred years of freedom from religious persecution have witnessed the vigorous exploration of the logically possible types of theistic and atheistic thought, so that probably not a great deal of such exploration remains to be done. What is now needed is judgment in evaluation — the overcoming of such rigid prejudices, or such laziness or dishonesty of thought, as must make selection among the views offered arbitrary and of no general or permanent validity.

C. H.

CONTENTS

MAN'S VISION OF GOD

I

THE FORMALLY POSSIBLE DOCTRINES

It seems strange to me, said Cleanthes, that you, Demea, who are so sincere in the cause of religion, should still maintain the mysterious, incomprehensible nature of the Deity, and should insist . . . that he has no manner of likeness or resemblance to human creatures. The Deity, I can readily allow, possesses many powers and attributes, of which we can have no comprehension: But if our ideas, so far as they go, be not just and adequate I know not what there is in this subject worth insisting on. . . . Those who maintain the perfect simplicity of the Supreme Being, to the extent in which you have explained it, are complete Mystics . . . in a word Atheists, without knowing it. . . . A mind, whose acts and sentiments and ideas are not distinct and successive; one, that is wholly simple and totally immutable; is a mind which has no thought, no reason, no will, no sentiment, no love, no hatred; or in a word, is no mind at all. . . .

Pray consider, said Philo, whom you are at present inveighing against. You are honoring with the appellation of Atheist all the sound orthodox divines almost, who have treated of this subject. . . .

DAVID HUME, in *Dialogues Concerning Natural Religion,* Part IV

FOR NEARLY two thousand years European theology staked its fortunes upon a certain conception of divinity. In spite of the seeming variety of doctrines, one basic principle was accepted by almost all philosophical theists. Only in the last few decades has a genuinely alternative type of theology been at all widely considered — so unobtrusively, however, that many opponents of theism, even some of the most distinguished, are still fighting the older conception exclusively, convinced that if they can dispose of it the theological question will be settled. And many of those who find the idea of a godless universe incredible suppose that it is to traditional theology that they must turn. Both parties are mistaken. Today the theistic question, like many others, is a definitely new one. Many of the old controversies, in their old forms, are antiquated.

As traditional theology was a relatively well defined system, the same in certain basic respects—despite all sorts of philosophical and ecclesiastical differences—in Augustine, Thomas Aquinas, Maimonides, Leibniz, Calvin, Immanuel Kant, and some schools of Hindu thought, so the new theology which may be contrasted with the old is found more or less fully and consistently represented in thinkers as far apart as William James, the American of over a generation ago, James Ward, his English contemporary, Henri Bergson, F. R. Tennant, W. R. Matthews, dean of St. Paul's, A. N. Whitehead, Berdyaev, the Orthodox Russian thinker, and in numerous others of every brand of Protestantism, besides a few (officially opposed and obstructed) Roman Catholics. I have also heard a clear statement of some aspects of it from a leading Hindu thinker, Radhakamal Mukerjee. Of course, there are interesting differences between these theologians, just as there were between Bonaventura and Calvin; and in some writers now, as of old, the logical implications are more adequately and rigorously worked out than in others. But there are some fundamental points of agreement which are rapidly becoming standard among non-Roman Catholic theologians.

To be aware of these points of convergence is essential to a liberal education today. They are as characteristic of our time as relativity physics and logical positivism are, or as medieval theology was of the thirteenth century. Ideas which until about fifty years ago were almost wholly neglected, never clearly worked out and systematized, and perhaps passed over for centuries with scarcely a mention, are now to be met in scores of theological works and in philosophical works that deal carefully with theology. The time seems at hand for attempts to state clearly the revolution of thought through which we have been passing.

What is the " new " doctrine? We shall see presently that it *must* be an expression of one of the three and only three formally possible views (including atheism and positivism as special cases of one of the three) regarding the supreme being, and that there are reasons for characterizing the new view as that one of the three which is related to the main line of the tradition as a carefully qualified assertion is to an unqualified one, and related to atheism (and certain heretical extremes of theism) as to an unqualified denial. In other words, it is related to the two other possible views as a " higher synthesis " to its " thesis " and " antithesis," as embraced and corrected in a " higher unity," or as a balanced whole truth to its two contrasting half-truths. From this standpoint traditional atheism and traditional theism are two sides of the same error, one of the most characteristic errors of human thought.

An immediate objection to the suggestion of a new idea of God will doubtless be that the term God as defined by usage properly means the God of the religious tradition. But we must distinguish, in the tradition, between religion and theology. Granting that " God " is a religious term, and that theology attempted to describe the object of religious devotion, it is one of the principal questions at issue whether or not this attempt was wholly successful. It is a belief of many today that the " new " theology is more, not less, religious than the old,[1] at least if religion means " devoted love for a being regarded as superlatively worthy of love," which is the Christian conception and to some extent the conception of the higher religions generally.

Of course theologians do not now regard as worthless and merely wrong the entire vast structure of historic theology, any more than Einstein so regards Newton's physics — to use an analogy which could easily be pressed too far, but whose value could also be underestimated. What is now being done is to distinguish two strands in the theological tradition which were not clearly held apart in the past, and to argue that they are not only distinguishable, but so related that only one of them can be true, and so related also that which one, if either, is true can be ascertained from the logical relations between the two strands alone, since one of the strands is incompatible alike with the assertion and the denial of the other, and hence, by recognized logical principles, is incompatible with itself and necessarily false. It is somewhat — to use another imperfect analogy — like the discovery in geometry of the independence of the parallel postulate from the other assumptions of Euclid; though in the theological case it is not really independence but inconsistency which is involved. Thus it is not a question of the logical possibility, merely, of what might be called a "non-Euclidean theology," but of its logical necessity, at least if there is to be any theology at all. (Unfortunately, there is no individual name which can conveniently serve as the theological parallel to Euclid; but Philo, a Jewish scholar of the first century, might be taken as the first man to give relatively complete expression to the postulate in question, and so we might speak of the current doctrine as non-Philonian theology, in a sense in which Aquinas, Spinoza, Royce, and orthodox Hinduism are all Philonian.[2])

The "strand" which theologians, on the whole, still propose to retain, and which is alone self-consistent, as judged by its relations to the other strand, is the popularly familiar definition of God as everlasting, all-controlling, all-knowing, and ethically good or "holy" to the highest possible degree. It may seem that this is just traditional theology and must involve the whole time-hallowed system. The extraordinary fact is that this has been found not to be the case. None of the older theologians (unless the neglected — and persecuted — Socinians, and the neglected Jew Gersonides, in the sixteenth and fourteenth centuries respectively, be exceptions) were content with this popular definition of God and the consequences which genuinely follow from it. They invariably adopted other conceptions as even more fundamental; and rather than attempt seriously to deduce these other conceptions from the popular definition, they treated the latter as a more or less dangerously loose or anthropomorphic equivalent of the more fundamental definition. This more fundamental definition turns upon such terms as perfection, infinity, absoluteness, self-dependence, pure actuality, immutability. God, for all the church writers, and for many others, including Spinoza, was the "absolutely infinite," the altogether maximal, supreme, or perfect, being. All his properties, including the popular religious ones so far as philosophically valid, were to be deduced from this absoluteness or perfection, as is so beautifully explained by Thomas Aquinas.

It might seem, therefore, that the only alternative must be the now somewhat fashionable conception of a "finite" God. Fortunately this is not the case. I say fortunately, because the notion of a purely finite or imperfect deity seems to have all the weaknesses that overwhelmed primitive polytheism, plus a lamentable lack of variety. Of simply imperfect deities we can hardly have too many, in order that the virtues of one may make amends for the defects of another.

It is true that the expression "finite (or 'imperfect') God" has various meanings. Some who employ it mean perhaps only this: the traditional idea of infinity (or perfection) is erroneous, and the empirical method (which such writers are likely to profess) cannot establish any sort of perfection in God. Only if these authors assert that they *know* God to be in *no respect* perfect, or that it is impossible to know that he is in any respect perfect, is there much need to quarrel with them. They are seeking the minimal conception of God, and that is a useful attempt.

If theology is capable of rejuvenation, its hope lies rather, I believe, in a re-examination of the idea of infinity or perfection. Perhaps this idea is ambiguous, perhaps there is a sense in which God should be conceived as perfect, another sense in which perfection cannot apply to God, because (it may be) this sense involves an absurdity or, in other words, is really nonsense. Perhaps God is perfect in whatever ways perfection can really be conceived; but some among the traditional theological ways of trying to conceive perfection are capable of producing only pseudo-concepts devoid of consistent meaning.

To discuss God is, by almost universal usage, to discuss some manner of " supreme " or " highest " or " best " individual (or superindividual) being. As a minimal definition, God is an entity somehow *superior* to other entities. Now such superiority may be merely with respect to other actual entities, or with respect to all entities whether actual or possible. The second or more complete superiority seems to give the appropriate meaning of " perfection," and was defined long ago by Anselm in his description of God as " that than which none greater can be conceived." This definition presupposes only the ideas of *something* (" that ") , *greater* or more or better (more in value) *than, negation* or none, and the conceivable or *possible,* and these ideas are secular as well as religious. Indeed, no ideas are more elementary and unavoidable in philosophy; hence it is clear that religion and philosophy can and must meet on common ground, provided the

Anselmian definition successfully defines the religious object. But before we can decide whether the secular terms employed can apply to the God of religion we must be clear as to what the terms mean. Astonishingly enough, the simple phrase "none greater" involves two major equivocations, not indeed as Anselm used the phrase, but as it might reasonably be used, even though the possibility of such usage seems not to have been clearly seen by Anselm or anyone else. The neglected usages constitute, together with Anselm's usage, a complete set of possible meanings of "perfect being," choice between which meanings *is* the theistic problem, a problem not fully stated until the neglected meanings are made explicit.

"None" may mean "no entity other than *that* (the being said to be perfect) *as it actually is,"* or it may mean "no entity other than *that as it either is or else could be or become."* According to the first meaning (which follows automatically if one assumes that the perfect can have no potential states — an assumption not deducible from the mere idea of "none greater," because of the latter's equivocal connotation) the perfect is *unsurpassable in conception or possibility even by itself;* according to the second meaning it is *unsurpassable except by itself.* The first or absolute unsurpassability may be called *absolute perfection,* the second may be called *relative perfection.* (We shall see in the appendix to this chapter, and the reader may have noted, that there is still a third possibility, though apparently it is of no great importance.)

"Greater" has as many meanings as there are dimensions or *respects* of more and less (or better and worse). But from a purely formal point of view (important because it is exact and non-controversial) there are just three possibilities, two positive and one negative. By "greater" we may mean, "in *some* (but not all) respects" (say in size or in ethical goodness); or we may mean, "in *all* respects whatever "; while the joint negative of these two, " in *no* respect," gives the third possibility.

Combining the two meanings of " none " with the three meanings of " greater " we derive seven possible cases, only one of which is the unequivocal negation of " none greater," or of " unsurpassability even by the conceivable." Thus it is proved that the question, Is there a perfect being? is six distinct questions rather than one. Has anyone a right to assure us, in advance of exploration of the other five, that the Anselmian (unconscious) selection of one among the six — as the faithful rendering either of the religious question or of the most fruitful philosophical one — is safely established by the fact that the choice has been repeated no less unconsciously by multitudes of theologians? If anyone asserts this, I must doubt his understanding of the elementary requirements of good reasoning.

The seven cases can be arranged, in several different ways, into three main groups. The following of the possible triadic arrangements seems the most useful:

GROUP	SYMBOL	CASE	SYMBOL	INTERPRETATION
I	(A)	1	A	Absolute perfection in *all* respects.
II	(AX)	2	AR	Absolute perfection in *some* respects, relative perfection in all others.
		3	ARI	Absolute perfection, relative perfection, and "imperfection" (neither absolute nor relative perfection), each in *some* respects.
		4	AI	Absolute perfection in *some* respects, imperfection in all others.
III	(X)	5	R	Absolute perfection in *no* respects, relative in all.
		6	RI	Absolute perfection in *no* respects, relative in some, imperfection in the others.
		7	I	Absolute perfection in *no* respects, imperfection in all.

EXPLANATION OF SYMBOLS: A stands for absolute perfection, R for relative perfection, I for the joint negative of A and R, X for the negative of A (and thus for the disjunction of R and I), and (A) or (X) for the factors occurring throughout a group.

NOTE: It will be shown in the appendix to this chapter that imperfection can be subdivided into two possible forms, making fifteen cases in all, though the additional eight seem of little importance—despite the fact that all eight express modes of unsurpassability, and so of perfection in the most general sense!

In a different mode of presentation we have:

GROUP	I		II			III		
A in	*all*		*some*			*no*		respects
	(A)		(AX)			(X)		
CASE	1	2	3	4	5	6	7	
	A	AR	ARI	AI	R	RI	I	

NOTE: It might be thought that God's "supremacy" requires not only that he cannot conceivably be surpassed, but that he cannot even be equaled. Anyone who wishes to experiment with this conception of the *unrivaled as well as unsurpassed* is of course at liberty to do so. My reason for neglecting the concept—which might be called "incomparability"—is that I agree with the usual verdict of theologians that the unsurpassable is bound to be unique, so that if superiority is out of the question, equality is also. If good reason for doubting this verdict can be found, then "incomparability" should be substituted, at least experimentally, for "unsurpassability" in the definition of perfection.

So far as I know, this is the only rigorous *formal* classification (which as formal and a mere classification is beyond intelligent controversy) of possible doctrines about God—except mere dichotomies (e.g., God is or is not eternal, one with all reality, etc.), which are never very helpful because only one of the two classes has positive content. Yet, though formal, the classification is relevant to religion, if religion believes in an unsurpassable being. And it certainly is relevant to philosophy; for the seven cases (as formal possibilities) follow automatically from concepts which philosophy is bound to use.

At least the classification serves this purpose: it shows how hopelessly ambiguous are phrases like "perfect being," "finite God," "absolute," and the like. Six of the seven cases come under the phrase, "perfect being," if perfection means unsurpassability. At least four are compatible with the description, "finite." Four are definitely included in the class of "absolute" beings. Yet within each classification the differences are at least as important as the resemblances, indeed much more so. For it can be shown that the difference between absolute perfection in all, in some, and in no respects is the crucial difference, and yet it is neglected by all the concepts mentioned and by most generally current ones. (Some exceptions are Brightman's phrase, "finite-infinite God," and similar expressions used by W. P. Montague.)

Take, for example, the term pantheism. By any usual definition of this term, it should be possible to give a plausible interpretation of *all seven* of our cases as conforming to the definition. Thus pantheism means literally almost anything you please, and so nearly nothing. That is probably the chief reason for its popularity as a label for opponents. And it ought to be clear that to say, "God is the all," means whatever one's view of the all implies, perhaps nothing definite whatever, for offhand we have no clear notion of the all.

It is impossible to think effectively about seven possibilities at once. We think best in threes. As has been shown, the seven possibilities fall logically into three groups. God, if he exists, is *absolutely* (not relatively) perfect in all, in some, or in no respects. The usual view has been the first. Atheism is a special case of the third, in which man or some wholly imperfect thing is regarded as the nearest thing to a "supreme being" that exists. So here is the primary issue: Which group contains the truth? One of them, by absolute logical requirements, must do so. (If perfection is meaningless, this only makes case seven, that is, group three, true a priori.) When we know the answer to this question, we shall at least know whether or not the usual view of God (" usual " in philosophy and theology, perhaps not really usual in religion) is sound, and whether or not atheism or something close to it is sound, or whether, finally, the truth lies in a less explored region, the second group.

It must in all this discussion be understood that certain doubtful or trivial meanings of " perfect " or " unsurpassable " are excluded (merely to save time and energy), such as that a squirrel is perfect if it has all that is demanded by the concept (whose concept?) of a squirrel, or that a nail is as good as any other could be if it holds the building together as long and as well as is wanted. Such merely subjective or merely instrumental perfection is not what is meant by the perfection of God. It is not for this or that special purpose or point of view that God is unsurpassable. Rather it is his purpose and point of view themselves which are thought to be unsurpassable and the very standard of all other purposes or perspectives. Everything is good merely *for* something except persons, or at least sentient beings, but these are good in themselves. God (if he be an individual) must be at least sentient, or he is anything but unsurpassable.

These things being understood, it follows that *one, and only one, of the following propositions must be true:*

I. There is a being in *all* respects absolutely perfect or unsurpassable, in no way and in no respect surpassable or perfectible. (THEISM OF THE FIRST TYPE; absolutism, Thomism, most European theology prior to 1880.)

II. There is no being in all respects absolutely perfect; but there is a being in *some* respect or respects thus perfect, and in some respect or respects not so, in some respects surpassable, whether by self or others being left open. Thus it is not excluded that the being may be relatively perfect in all the respects in which it is not absolutely perfect. (THEISM OF THE SECOND TYPE; much contemporary Protestant theology, doctrines of a " finite-infinite " or perfect-perfectible God.)

III. There is no being in *any* respect absolutely perfect; all beings are in all respects surpassable by something conceivable, perhaps by others or perhaps by themselves in another state. (Doctrines of a merely finite God, polytheism in some forms, atheism.)

This division is exclusive and exhaustive. To prove any two of these propositions false is to establish the truth of the remaining proposition; there can be no " higher synthesis " which combines the truth of any two or of all three of them, except as this synthesis amounts to accepting some one of the three as it stands and contradicting some part of each of the other two; that is, one of the three must be the higher synthesis. One may subdivide the three cases, but one cannot evade the necessity for rejecting some two and affirming some one of them as a whole, or else giving up the theistic question, the latter option being not an additional objective possibility but merely a subjective attitude toward the three possibilities. Of course one might say that there are two Gods, one corresponding to the first proposition, the other to the second proposition without the initial negative clause. But this would merely be a special case under Proposition One, and would have importance only if Proposition One is acceptable as it stands and Proposition Two false as it stands. After we have decided, if we do so decide, that there is one God wholly, partially, or not at all absolutely perfect, it will then be time enough to ask if there is also another God with another of the three characteristics.

Would it not be satisfying if the debate between atheism and theism turned out to have been so stubborn because the truth was in neither, as traditionally conceived, but in a middle ground not by any means a weak compromise between them but a clear-cut alternative as definite and legitimate, formally regarded, as any other? Without pretending here to anything like conclusiveness, I will give some reasons for taking this possibility seriously.

First of all, what does religion (not theology) say as to the three groups? Suppose the usual religious ideas of omniscience, omnipotence, and holiness or supreme righteousness be accepted. This seems to mean that God is absolutely perfect in knowledge, power, and ethical goodness. Does it follow that he is absolutely perfect in all respects? What about happiness or bliss? Surely religion is not, at any rate, so emphatic here. Is not God displeased by sin, and so something less than purely happy in beholding it? Does he not love us and therefore sympathize with our sufferings, wish that they might be removed? Do we not wish to "serve" God, carry out his purposes, contribute to his life somehow? All this must be explained as extremely misleading, if not indefensible, if God enjoys absolute bliss in eternity. But, you say, would not perfect power, wisdom, and goodness insure perfect bliss? Not at all, I answer with all the conviction I can feel about anything. To be happy is not a mere function of these three variables. For to know all that exists is not to know all that might exist, except as potentialities, and if potentialities are as good as actualities, then let us all cease to exist and be done with it. It is not even true that the omniscient must know details of the future, unless it can be proved, against Bergson, Whitehead, Peirce, James, and many others, that the future has any details to know.[3] (Of course it *will be detailed,* but this does not imply that it has detailed will-be's as parts of itself now. See chapter 3.)

Thus there is no reason why perfect knowledge could not change, grow in content, provided it changed only as its objects changed, and added as new items to its knowledge only things that were not in being, not there to know, previously. Again, to have perfect power over all individuals is not to have all power in such fashion as to leave the other individuals none. For to be individuals and to have some power are two aspects of the same thing. So even the greatest possible power (and that by definition is " perfect " power) over individuals cannot leave them powerless, and hence even perfect power must leave something to others to decide. And if one loves these others, and their decisions bring conflict and suffering, how can one, as loving toward them, escape a share in this sorrow? We know nothing of the nature of benevolence in ourselves if it is not a sharing, at least imaginative, in the interests of others, so that the partial defeat of these interests becomes in a real sense a partial defeat for us. Thus, perfect goodness is not a sufficient condition of all possible bliss. Rather, the good person suffers more than the bad at the spectacle of the badness and suffering of others. The dilemma appears final: *either value is social,* and then its perfection cannot be wholly within the power of any one being, even God; *or it is not social at all,* and then the saying, " God is love," is an error. It may be said, however, that I have confused love with desire. I reply, Love *is* desire for the good of others, ideally all others, or I have yet to be told what it is.

So religion does not decide clearly in favor of group one, and seems rather to support group two. God is absolutely perfect (and in so far "without shadow of turning") in those things that depend by their nature upon one's own excellence alone. There is, for instance, nothing in the idea of knowledge to imply that God could not know all that goes on in the bad man as well as in the good; but if he equally derives (or equally does not derive) bliss from the two, so much the worse for his alleged goodness!

Inspection of the table of seven cases reveals also interesting implications for philosophy. If there is a being corresponding to case one, then there is a being totally exempt from the possibility of decrease or increase in value, hence of *change* in any significant sense. In such a being time is not, or at least is not time, which implies certain well known philosophical paradoxes. If, on the other hand, there is no being corresponding to any of the cases except those in the third group, if, that is, even the highest being is in all respects without absolute unsurpassability, then there is no individual being not capable of change (at least improvement) in any and every respect whatever; and in that case there is no enduring individual whose identity through all time is assured, for self-identity is incompatible with "change in all respects whatever." This threatens the intelligibility of time from the opposite point of view, for time must have some identity as well as differences. And it threatens religion, for the service of a God whose permanence is not assured fails to add anything essential to the service of men; and, moreover, the perfection of God is the heart of religious thought and feeling.

From another point of view one may reach the same result. Absolute and relative are polar concepts and seem to require each other, yet only group two makes this polarity affect the nature of the basic substance or individual.

In religious terms, God, according to group two, is not just the creator opposed to the creatures, nor is he just another creature, but he is the creator-with-the-creatures, his reality is not in all respects as it would be did the creatures not exist. In doctrines of incarnation this is in a fashion recognized, but the point to weigh is whether any concept of God is philosophically or religiously defensible that does not make logical place for such a union of absolute and relative by rejecting case one as simply an error, not at all, as tradition affirms, the rationally knowable, as distinct from the revealed (incarnate), nature of God.

As among the three cases under group two, it might appear that case three (ARI) is the most promising of all, since it alone combines all three fundamental categories (surpassability by nothing, surpassability by self only, surpassability by others than self). But the third category is in a sense derivative. God can very well embrace surpassability by others, but as his property only in so far as it is that of relative beings united to him by virtue of his relative aspect. Thus if x comes to be surpassed by y, then God in his total value, as first including the value of x and then the value of y, will surpass himself in a manner which will be the reality of the x and y relation as enjoyed by him. But if God were incapable even of self-surpassing, then no surpassing could contribute anything whatever to his value or mean anything to him, for to him there would be no more or less but just sheer value.

On the other hand, as between cases two and four (AR and AI), the apparent choice is in favor of two. For AI implies that a being consists exclusively of an absolute fixed perfection plus a purely changeable and surpassable imperfection; or in other words, in so far as the being changed at all there would be no ultimate limit of any sort to this change, and no guarantee that the being which in some respects was absolutely perfect would remain even superior to others in his non-absolute aspects. Even supposing that two such pure opposites could constitute one individual or entity, this entity seems to have little to do with anything that has been meant by God.

Thus we have some reason for suspecting that the second case, AR, the farthest removed from atheism or pure relativism, the closest to the theological tradition, is the truth of the whole question. Since it is five steps away from atheism out of a possible six, lovers of the letter of orthodoxy who might feel inclined to attack case two as little better than atheism, or as a blasphemous or at best a crudely inept doctrine, might pause, before indulging in such judgment, long enough to consider — and I am confident they will not have done so before — what the five steps really mean. They mean, in fact, that most of traditional theology is acceptable to AR theorists as a description of one aspect of God, the A aspect. Yet since, on the other hand, the single step separating case two from the older theory involves the entire difference between admitting and not admitting real change, growth, possibility of profit, suffering, true sociality, as qualities of the divine, along with radical differences (as we shall see) in the meanings ascribed to creation, the universe, human freedom, and in the arguments for the existence of God, those inclined to think that any view that is intimately connected with theological traditions must have been disposed of by this time should also beware lest they commit a *non sequitur*. And finally, those who think that the modern experiments with a " finite " God have proved abortive might take heed of the radical ambiguity of all such phrases, and of the logical independence of case two from all of the four or five doctrines which could most reasonably be meant by them.

It is not even to be assumed that case one, at the opposite

extreme seemingly from atheism, is really in every sense " farther " from it than is case two. For the " line " connecting the seven cases may be self-returning, if more than one dimension be involved. And this condition is here fulfilled. Case one makes God no more superior than does case two in the dimensions covered by A in AR, and it makes him infinitely *less* perfect in the R dimensions, if any, for these are such as to imply change, self-transcendence, for their value — as, for instance, does novelty as a dimension of value. Also, as we have seen, trying to treat these R dimensions under A might destroy even the dimensions to which A is appropriate. So the God of A might really and consistently have even less perfection than the human race, or whatever the atheist regards with such reverence as he may feel. Hume's *Dialogues* (Part IV) are one of the earliest expressions of insight into this meeting of extremes.

The formal analysis of perfection makes evident the absurdity of supposing the theistic question to be a mere product of superstition or of some " complex." The notions which define perfection are logically inevitable in philosophy. Either these notions admit consistent combination as required for the definition of perfection (in one or more of the six senses) or they do not. This depends solely upon the meanings of " greater," " none," and " possible." Hence if we do not know whether or not perfection is conceivable, and in what sense or senses, we do not know what we mean by concepts than which none could be more elementary in philosophy.

As to whether or not — supposing that perfection is conceivable — a perfect being exists, the ontological argument is involved, since this argument holds that from the conceivability of God his existence can be inferred. Whether or not the argument is valid depends partly upon whether or not the relation of properties to existence is governed by a law, admitting no exceptions, that this relation is always contingent. Such a law must spring from the meanings of " existence " and of " property " as such. Hence if we do not know the validity or invalidity of the law, we do not know altogether what we mean by these fundamental conceptions. But on the other hand, since the ontological argument derives the exceptional relation of God to existence from his perfection, it is clear that the law to which appeal is made in order to refute the ontological argument has no priority over the latter, both resting upon a similar basis of insight into elementary meanings. Any supposedly axiomatic insight we may have into the possibility or impossibility that " essence " should " imply existence " must be balanced against our insights, equally entitled to the role of axioms, into the meanings of the concepts which define perfection, and which either do or do not imply a necessary relation of perfection to existence. If they do imply it, then we know that the law is not valid except for imperfect existence, and even in relation to imperfect existence the exact meaning of the law may depend upon the exceptional role of perfect existence, since although exceptional the perfect being must also be universally relevant, the immanent ground of all existence. Thus we see that the other aspects of philosophy depend upon the solution of the theistic question just as truly as that solution depends upon the other aspects of philosophy.

For example, Kant's alleged refutation of the theistic arguments merely shows the principles of his philosophy to be incompatible with the validity of any proofs for the forms of theism which Kant knew. These forms are not the only possible ones, and if the others are also incapable of proof in terms of Kant's philosophy it may be just as significant that Kant's philosophy would perhaps appear incapable of proof in terms of some form of theism. There is no unique starting point in philosophy, and the nearest we can come to avoiding begging the question is to embrace all the possibilities under a rational classification. Kant is so certain that God and the soul are not ultimately in time that he never explores the extent to which a temporal idea of God might affect the problems with which the *Critique* is concerned. (Clearly his doctrine that we know positively only the temporal would be entirely compatible with the assertion of knowledge of God if God be temporal. But then there would be no thing in itself behind changing phenomena. And also Kant's deterministic theory of time would have to be dropped, because the divine creative action must be given a place within change. One side of two at least of Kant's antinomies would, it could be shown, disappear.)

Exact thinking, it is rather generally agreed among those noted for it, is mathematical, or rather has at least a mathematical aspect, however complex or simple. (In very simple cases, mathematical symbols may scarcely be required.) It will have been observed that the formally possible modes of unsurpassability are simply the mathematically possible combinations of the ideas required to render "unsurpassable" univocal in meaning. This is an application of mathematics to the greatest of human problems, an application not less legitimate or important because so elementary and simple that it seems prodigious talent must have been required, and certainly was in fact expended, to overlook it for so many centuries. As in all cases of *applied* mathematics, truth cannot be certified by the mathematics alone. What can be certified is the definiteness and completeness of the possibilities among which the truth, so far as statable through the concepts initially proposed, must lie. There is no other way whatever of insuring that the truth does lie between given alternatives, rather than in some alternative not even consciously considered. Those who may fear that the use of exact formal concepts must somehow be hostile to religion will in so far be true enemies of knowledge as well as doubtful friends of religion. But just as Bradley affected to quarrel with arithmetic, so we should expect that some will dislike the attempt to arithmetize theology. Exact thought has its enemies.

It will be noted that unsurpassability is verbally a pure negative. It can be correlated with a positive idea by the notion of totality. If a being has " all " the values that exist, then it is in all respects unsurpassed by anything actual. If it has all the values that are possible, then it is unsurpassable by anything possible. But if all values are not " compossible," cannot all coexist, as seems an almost obvious truth, then a purely final or static perfection possessing all possible values is impossible. We must then conceive perfection as partly dynamic, in some such manner as follows:

A being may have a relation to all actual values which, as a relation, has all the value possible, or as much value as possible, *in view of the relata* (the values given as actual), and the being may have a relation to all possible values as such which, as a relation to possibilities, could not be superior. Such a highest possible relation to actual and possible value might consist in this: that all possible values *would,* if and when actualized, belong to the being in question, that is, the being would always be unsurpassable, except by itself as it actualized more and more of the possibilities confronting it. Yet as possessing thus at all times the highest possible abstract *type of relation* to actuality and possibility the being would, in one aspect of itself, enjoy absolute or static perfection, be not only unrivaled but even incapable of improvement. All that is necessary to reconcile this with the religious idea is to show that such absolutes as omnipotence or omniscience or perfect righteousness or loving-kindness are abstract relational absolutes in the manner just indicated, and thus not only compatible with but inseparable from a qualitative, concrete aspect of perfection which is dynamic, since it involves inexhaustible possibilities for achievement. Is it not almost obvious, again, that the religious terms mentioned are abstract and relational precisely in the manner outlined?

One might try to make perfection positive in another way, by using the notion of surpassing all things rather than of being surpassed by none. But the reader will, I think, if he experiments with this idea, find that it leads to the same result. The importance of assuring a positive content for perfection is that otherwise one cannot well deny the contention of atheism that the word God is merely a word for what is left when we deny all that we know; that is, it represents what we know when we know nothing. This "negative theology" has often been praised, on the ground that all our knowledge is so inadequate to God that we must indeed negate it to arrive at God. But why not to arrive at non-being? Some positive content to the former idea there must be to distinguish it from the latter, and why not the utmost positive content, infinite, indeed? Surely a little dose of positivity will not suffice here. And the dilemma remains even in the negative theology, that either all value is compossible — which seems certainly untrue, for values conflict — or else God must fail to possess some values which yet are possible — and how then can he be incapable of growth in value? Possibilities which to God represented no possible achievements would be the same to him as no possibilities. True, one can recognize values for others, say their joys, without fully possessing or expecting to possess these as one's own, but what one cannot do is to fail in such a case to derive at least some value from the joys through the act of recognition itself, and precisely the most perfect mind would derive most from the satisfactions of others. It is the imperfection of man that compels him to admit that some of the joy which he wishes others to possess may when it comes contribute nothing to him, since he may be absent, dead, or somehow cut off from participation in the joy. Only the perfect can participate perfectly, gain for himself the entire sum of all actual gains.

If all values are compossible, and are all actual in God, then it is meaningless to say that some values are only possible. Possibility in that case ceases to have any distinctive meaning. Even if you say that God has not the actuality of what *for us* are possible values but rather a value above all our possibilities, you are only saying that what we call possibility is nothing from the ultimate standpoint. It is at least a serious thing to make the idea of God the destruction of a category without which it is doubtful that we can think at all.

The question is sometimes asked, Is God a concrete individual or is he an abstraction? If there is anything in the ontological argument, it may be that God must be concrete. For that argument may perhaps amount to this, that perfection is conceivable only as the property of an existing individual, and not of merely possible individuals (whereas we may conceive the nature of Mr. Micawber, for example, as *not* in fact the nature of an existing man). But even if we grant that God is an abstraction or a Platonic form or something somehow superindividual, still this does not obviate our trichotomy of doctrines (see the appendix to this chapter). The form is in all respects, in some respects, or in none an absolute ideal, the ideal of an unsurpassable maximum. The question then is, Are the dimensions of value alike in admitting, or in not admitting, an upper limit, or are there some which do and some which do not and which yet must apply to all things having value?

Our classification of doctrines depends only upon the four following assumptions:

p. There is a difference between actual and possible (or conceivable) things.

q. There may be a difference between actual and possible states of an individual. (Not that God is assumed to be an individual in this sense, but that it is not assumed that he is not, in the statement of the classification, whose purpose is to state, not to answer, controversial questions.)

r. It is meaningful to say that one thing is higher or better than, or superior to (or has more of some variable property not a mere deficiency than), another; but this meaning is not simply univocal, since *x* may be better than *y* in one respect, say in ethical goodness, and not better in another, say in happiness. Thus " better than " is multidimensional. (The doctrine of the tradition that God is not simply better than other even possible beings, but is better than goodness itself, better than " best," since he transcends the concept of goodness altogether, does not alter the necessity that he be better-than-best in some, in none, or in all dimensions of value; or negatively, that he be surpassable in all, some, or no dimensions. The tradition spoken of clearly elected the first of the three formal cases, making God unsurpassable by anything conceivable, even by potential states of himself.)

s. The notions of " all," " some," and " none " exhaust the possible divisions of a plurality, hence of a plurality of respects of higher and lower. (Logicians distinguish between " all " and " every," but this seems of no importance here.)

These assumptions (except the last, which is clearly self-evident) are not posited absolutely. It may, you may believe, turn out that actual and possible coincide, or that the different dimensions of value or superiority are really one. The point is, we must not assume this at the outset. What we certainly must assume at the outset is that the question of such distinctions requires discussion, and that therefore every type of doctrine implied as formally possible *if* the distinctions are genuine must be given full and fair hearing. If two views formally distinguished turn out to be the same (since some alleged distinction separating them proves equal to zero), then that will be the conclusion reached; but it must be a conclusion, and not in any sense a formal premise, of the argumentation. There can be no harm in setting a terminological locus for alleged distinctions, admitting that they may assume every value of significance from zero to infinity; but there is very definite harm in depriving apparent distinctions of terminological and systematic locus, since their value is then determined as zero by fiat. Now the distinctions between " superior to actuality " and " superior even to possibility," or between " superior to other possible individuals " and to " other possible states of oneself " (as an individual identical in spite of changes or alternate possible states), or again, between " superior in all," " in some," or " in no " respects of value — these distinctions are urged upon us by universal experience and common-sense modes of thought. They may be overruled in the outcome, they can never validly be overruled before the outcome, of technical procedure. And we have painfully learned (all but one or two groups of philosophers) that the way to evaluate ideas is to deduce their consequences and compare these with the relevant data of experience. So we have no rightful alternative to the systematic development of the consequences of the distinctions mentioned. The discussion of the resulting doctrinal classifications is the bottleneck through which alone we can arrive, if ever, at a rational treatment of the theistic question.

This question can, it is true, be put in other initial terms than those we have used. For instance, it can be put in terms of causality. Has the world a cause, or is it self-sufficient? But this formulation is not precise. It suggests that God is nothing but causation, and the world nothing but effect; in other words, that God is in *no* sense affected by other individuals, and the world in *no* sense causal in relation to God. But the idea of God in its common-sense or religious meaning may not require this. God is of course the *supreme power* in existence, the causal influence superior to all others. It remains to be seen, however, whether superiority of power implies a purely one-way causal action, an action without reaction or interaction. That is a basic technical question, not to be decided near the beginning of discussion but toward the end. Perhaps the supreme action is also, necessarily, the supreme interaction. Nor can words like " creator " and " creation " dispose of the matter. Religion is not prima facie committed on such technicalities as the relation of creativity to various causal concepts.

In terms of causality there are, rather, three formal possibilities, corresponding to, indeed coinciding with, our basic trichotomy. The highest cause may be (1) in *every* sense or aspect " uncaused," in no sense or aspect the effect of anything else; or it may be (2) in *some* aspects uncaused, and in others causally influenced, but its manner of both acting and receiving influences may be the highest conceivable, hence absolutely " perfect," although even so its whole being *may* not in every sense be perfect, because the influences as coming from other causes, say human beings, may be less admirable than they might be; or the supreme cause may be (3) in *no* sense or aspect uncaused, independent of other powers, hence in no way wholly exempt from the imperfections of the latter.

Again, if we use Aristotelian concepts of matter and form, power and actuality, still the same three cases have to be considered. The supreme being may be (1) the absolute non-potentiality, an actuality whose " purity " from unrealized potency has no conceivable superior; it may be (2a) supreme as compared to other conceivable beings and yet also itself supremely capable of being what it actually is not, as a man not only *is* more than an insect but has, in any actual state, a greater range of unused potentialities to choose from, or (2b) supreme over other conceivable entities in potency only (as is Santayana's " Realm of Essence ") ; or finally (3) there may be no being supreme either in actuality or in potency over other conceivable individuals and other states of itself (that is, no being that is A with respect to actuality *or* potency). These are our three friends again, and the second of them (2a and 2b) can be ruled out from systematic consideration only by arbitrarily limiting the apparent possibilities as suggested by concepts derived from universal experience.

It makes no difference what concepts are used, whether " self-existent," " necessary being," " unity," " final cause," or what you will to describe the divine individuality; there are always three formally possible cases (though the boundaries between them could be variously located, and they can be subdivided) among which choice must be made openly and carefully, not surreptitiously nor by a short and easy appeal to self-evidence. A being may, for instance, be necessary in all its aspects, or not in all but in some, or, finally, in none. So with all the other concepts mentioned above. Nothing can result but endless debate (and bad feeling) from the attempt to short-cut the exploration of an irreducibly triadic situation. Dyadic formulations of the theistic problem are question-begging through and through.

The almost complete overlooking of the second of the three main types of doctrine has some title to be called the greatest intellectual error mankind has ever made, since it affects the most basic of all ideas, and since it escaped widespread detection for nearly the whole period of recorded philosophico-scientific development, at any rate for well over two thousand years. The only error perhaps surpassing it is indeed closely connected with it. This is the misconception of the nature and function of mathematics, the notion that mathematical knowledge is the model of all knowledge instead of merely the model of one aspect of knowledge, radically incomplete in itself, that therefore what mathematics knows is independent of everything else, pure "being" above "becoming," and that therefore all thought about high matters should follow the mathematical pattern of deduction from easily established axioms, settled once for all, and should see as its ideal object some timeless essence, or sheer perfection, devoid, in Plato's memorable words, of motion and life and power. These words are all the more memorable because Plato is partly responsible, as he is usually interpreted, for the error. It is a great mathematico-philosophical mind, perhaps the nearest to Plato in combination of interests that our time has produced, Alfred North Whitehead, who has most effectively criticized this mistake.[4] The whole modern era has seen the increasing emancipation of natural science from false mathematicism or deductivism; it is not surprising that theology has also been learning the lesson, though more quietly and with inferior publicity. It is also not surprising that in both cases reaction has sometimes gone too far, and the role of the merely empirical has been exaggerated at the expense of the formerly exalted a priori element. The balance is, I believe, being found in both fields of thought.

One sometimes speaks of an "empirical" theology as characteristic of our time. If this means that the relations of abstractions to the concrete, of meaning to perception, feeling, and action, are much more carefully traced in current than in medieval theology, it is one of the merits which may be claimed for contemporary theological thinking (or some of it). But if it means that theology is an inductive science, similar to astronomy, that it commits the logical fallacy of trying to prove or disprove an eternal truth like the existence (or non-existence) of God (as in any respect perfect) by examining the details of experience in the manner of the inductive sciences, then I hold this to be an error, characteristic rather of the last than of the present century. There is, in fact, a trichotomy of views concerning method, of which the usual conceptions of a priori and empirical represent but two of the three possibilities (see chapter 2).

What is striking in theology today is that it has discovered improvements upon the older theology precisely as a metaphysics, as an a priori analysis (which does not mean analysis unrelated to experience, but analysis related to the strictly general traits of experience). Some of the conclusions (in accordance with AR) are that God is all-knowing, and yet not in every sense "above time" or aware of the details of the future; that he is the most powerful possible being, yet not in every sense "impassive," incapable of being acted upon; that he is the necessary being as to his essence, and yet has accidents which are contingent; that he is ethically perfect, yet aesthetically perfectible without limit.

Naturally any view which ascribes ethical perfection and yet the "greatest possible power" to God must face the problem of evil. In its appeal to the imagination this problem will no doubt always be the most troublesome one in theology. But in pure logic it is not true that there is sheer contradiction between the joint admission of divine perfection of goodness and divine perfection of power, on the one hand, and the fact of real evil on the other, for the simple reason that the greatest possible power (which by definition is "perfect" power) may not be the same as "all the power that exists united into one individual power." For such union of "all" power may be impossible. Had God "all the power there is," he must be responsible for all that happens. But why assume that all real power could *possibly* belong to one individual? If it could not — and there is ground for this negative — then even the perfect or (by definition) greatest possible power is not all-power. Omnipotence (alas, our only word for perfection of power!) is power to the highest degree possible and over all that exists, it is "all" the power that *could* be exercised by any *one* individual over "all" that is; but it remains to be shown how much power *could* be exercised in this fashion. The minimal solution of the problem of evil is to affirm the necessity of a division of powers, hence of responsibilities, as binding even upon a maximal power. But this solution seems to imply the passivity of the supreme power, and hence not to be available to first-type theists.

Undoubtedly, "ethical" needs careful defining, but roughly it means action issuing from the fullest realization available to the individual of all the interests affected by the action. It does not necessarily mean observing the rules or codes recognized in any human society, except in so far as these represent the attempt of that society to make actions express the nearest thing to full realization of affected interests which is possible to the average human being. Being ethical does not mean never injuring anyone; for the interests of others may require such injury. Still less does being ethical mean never permitting any agency to bring injury to anyone; for not permitting this might be possible — owing to the division of power — only at the cost of greater injury through interference with other powers. Being ethical means acting from love; but love means realization in oneself of the desires and experiences of others, so that one who loves can in so far inflict suffering only by undergoing this suffering himself, willingly and fully. Those who think God cannot mean well toward us because he " sends " us suffering can prove their point only by showing that there is a way to run the universe, compatible with the existence of other real powers than just the supreme power, which would be more fully in accord with the totality of interests, or by showing that God sends us the suffering while himself remaining simply outside it, in the enjoyment of sheer bliss. Theologians themselves (first type) seem generally to have made a present of the latter notion to atheists; but the former view has its plausibility for all of us. I wish only to say here that I think neither is put beyond reasonable doubt by metaphysical necessity or empirical facts. It is poor method to try to estimate facts, especially such as are hard to measure with any accuracy, without careful survey of the logical structure of the ideas we bring to bear upon these facts. Therefore the facts of evil are not sufficient to justify dismissal of theology prior to the adequate exploration of its three main formal possibilities. Facts will never render decisions between ill-conceived alternatives; and the meaning of such terms as omnipotence or goodness depends in second-type theism upon a number of conceptions which have not been clearly considered in the classic discussions (such as the marvelous one in Hume's *Dialogues*) of the relations of such terms to the facts of evil.

One way of trying to escape a decision among the three

possible views concerning God as a perfect being would be to say that perfection as "that than which nothing higher or better in a given respect is conceivable" is a meaningless concept, itself inconceivable. This, however, besides seeming tolerably dogmatic, would only be to say that Proposition Three is true by necessity; for if a predicate is nonsense, then of course nothing exists having that predicate. Hence no form of positivism can provide an evasion of the decision to be made.[5] Nor can any other doctrine do so. What we have is a non-controversial statement of what the theistic controversy is. In general, I believe, all stubborn controversies in philosophy have involved questions the very existence of which as such is itself controversial, because they have not been formulated in neutral terms, terms that avoid arbitrarily limiting the prima facie possibilities.

In particular, most philosophico-theological controversies have amounted to one of the following procedures:

A. To considering reasons for preferring one or the other of Propositions One and Three, or more probably, some special variety of One to some variety of Three;

B. To considering reasons for preferring some one variety of One (such as "theism" or "absolutism") to some other variety of One (such as "pantheism" or "deism").

A is bound, sooner or later, to involve the fallacy of inferring the truth of One from the falsity of Three, or vice versa; whereas it is formally possible, and should be held really possible, until the contrary has been shown, that both One and Three are false because Two is true. The fallacy is bound to occur so long as Two is neglected, for the reason that men do not adopt a philosophy because its proofs are beyond question and its conclusions completely satisfactory — this being never the case — but because its proofs seem to them stronger and its conclusions more satisfactory than would be true of what they regard as the alternative. It is a question of preference, not of absolute sunclear evidence and perfect understanding. In so far as this is the case, almost everything depends upon the adequacy of the philosopher's survey of the possibilities. Now there is no more rigorous trichotomy than that of "all, some, none"; hence the question, *Is God absolutely perfect in all, in some, or in no respects?* is as rigorous a division of the theological problem as can be given if any use at all is to be made of the idea of perfection — and what theology has avoided its use? Moreover, if all the formal possibilities are not controlled, we not only run the risk of fallaciously inferring the truth of one view from the difficulties of some only of its possible rivals, but also we run the risk of trying to answer a perhaps meaningless question, namely, Which of two falsehoods (or absurdities) is more false? The falsehoods may be extremes (and One and Three are clearly such), and hence one may be as false as the other, by any objective standard. In that case, the choice between them will be on subjective and variable grounds, and no agreement is to be anticipated. If then, under these circumstances, complete agreement is not reached, it does not follow that agreement could not be at least greatly increased by the accurate, exhaustive statement of the doctrines open to us, arranged in a reasonably small number of exclusive groups or types.

B is an attempt to decide upon the details of a type of theory whose admissibility as a type has not been shown, owing to the role of the fallacy mentioned (which is implicit both in traditional proofs for God's existence and in atheistic criticisms of these proofs). This does not mean that such discussions have accomplished nothing, but it does mean that no exact and reliable estimate of *what* they have accomplished (though it is, I believe, a great deal) is possible until we have granted full " belligerent rights " to second-type theism, as a no less qualified contender than either of the others. True, this type of theism has already had a good many defenders; but taking philosophers as a whole and theologians as a whole it is still far from true that the theological problem is seen in terms of its fundamental trichotomy, systematically investigated.[6]

In general it is clear that, while dyadic divisions of opinion may easily be made exhaustive by the simple device of confronting an assertion with its denial — for example, " everything is mental " and " some things are not mental," or " there is a God " and " there is no God " — such divisions of opinion are ideal devices for securing endless debate. For they throw no light on alternative ways of conceiving the positive idea underlying the assertion. They limit one to a single definition of God (or else leave the term utterly vague) or to a single conception of " mental." Nothing is shown more clearly by the history of thought than that disagreements are typically more complex and subtle than such dyadic issues can possibly make explicit. Of course one can employ a number of dyadic issues, but the only way to make their interrelationships explicit is by a triadic or polyadic division. This has the psychological advantage of enabling a third person to adjudicate a stubborn dispute without having to say that either party to it was simply wrong in comparison to the other, which is what one must say with dyadic disputes taken at face value. Somebody must be insulted, and without effective compensation.

If perfection is defined as " excluding, on every dimension of better and worse, values other than maximal," then of course God is either perfect or not-perfect. But " not-perfect " here conceals alternatives exactly as profound logically as the one it states, for the difference between "maximal in all dimensions" and "maximal not in all but in some," or that between "maximal in some" and "maximal in none," is as worthy of consideration as that between "maximal in all" and "not maximal in all." The formally correct thing to do is simply to state the three cases which exhaust the issue. We should put some part of the problem of definition (we cannot put all of it) into our division of doctrines, and use as assumed definitions only such ideas as are put most nearly beyond controversy or need of further analysis by unambiguous experiences, a description no man in his senses would apply to perfection as "maximal value on all dimensions of value."

Our basic trichotomy of doctrines may be put in still another way, which also gives a clue as to the possible validity of the neglected second type. If we define a "closed" dimension of value as one of which there can exist a supreme or maximal case, and an "open" dimension as one of which no supreme case is possible, then one of three things is true: *all* dimensions of value are closed, *some* dimensions are closed and some are open, or *none* are closed and all are open. It is indeed not formally evident that the first proposition defines first-type theism; for we have not specified or shown that the maximal case of the different dimensions must be found in the same real individual. But at least it is clear that if, and only if, the first of the dimensional propositions is true, first-type theism *may* be true; and that if the second dimensional proposition is true, second-type theism may be true, for then there may be a real case of perfection on some dimension which will not be a case of perfection upon all, because — by the assumptions — not all admit of perfection. (If the ontological argument were shown to be valid, the "may be true" would in both cases imply "is true.")

Now, is it particularly obvious that all dimensions of value must be closed dimensions, assuming some of them are? Consider the dimensions of goodness, knowledge, power, and duration. A being may perhaps be the maximal case of goodness if he guides his action by concern for *all* the interests affected by his actions. This " all " is the universe (up to the present, at least) so far as it contains values. Or, a being may be omniscient if he knows all there is to know: that is, again, the cosmos as a totality. A being may, similarly, be the maximal possible power if he controls all that exists to the greatest extent possible, that is, to the extent which is compatible with the measure of independence, if any, constitutive of the things controlled. Finally, a being may have maximal duration by being ungenerated and immortal, by enduring throughout all time. So far, our dimensions seem to admit of maxima as at least conceivable.

But there are other dimensions of value. What could be meant by maximal happiness, or beauty, or " intensity " of joy, or variety, " the spice of life "? A being may enjoy all that exists, but perhaps he longs for what does not exist; or perhaps some of what exists is not altogether enjoyable (such as the sufferings of other sentient beings). Oh, well, you say, but if the being has maximal power, he can produce such beings as he wishes to enjoy. But there is social enjoyment, and this by definition depends partly on the self-determinations of the beings enjoyed. This cannot possibly be wholly coerced by any one term of the social relation, hence not even by the maximal " possible " power. The only escape at this point is to take shelter in the doctrine of the Trinity, which offers to furnish a social relation between persons all of whom are perfect. But still, we may ask, what in this relation is enjoyed? Is it " unity in variety," as seems to be the case with us? Supposing that variety in God is really compatible with his alleged simplicity, we still have to ask, What is meant by maximal variety? Is it that all possibilities are actualized in one actual state? But there are mutually incompatible alternatives (or there is no such thing as logic, or aesthetics). Besides, if all potentiality is also actuality in God, then the distinction between potential and actual must really be an anthropomorphic illusion, invisible from his point of view. At any rate, enjoyment varies as to intensity, and what can be meant by "all possible intensity," or "absolute intensity"?

Of course one could argue that an open dimension involves an infinite regress, and is therefore impossible. But this is a highly technical point, not to be taken for granted at this stage, where we are stating positions to be considered, not positions to be accepted once for all. My own view is that the infinite regress in question is an example of the "non-vicious" type of regress, since it concerns possibilities, and these not (on one view of potentiality) as a definite multitude, whose number is infinite, but as a continuum, which in the words of Peirce is "beyond all multitude," as God was formerly described as being; and indeed, as we shall see, the continuum of possibilities is one aspect of God which may be truly so described. It has also been argued that the maximal case is required as the standard or measure for all cases (Plato). But it may be that the maximal case on the closed dimensions would suffice to furnish the standard for the open ones, that, e.g., perfection of knowledge and goodness is in some sense the "measure" of degrees of happiness, even though the latter cannot be absolutely but only relatively perfect (R but not A).

Let us return to our conceivably closed dimensions and ask if they are not really ambiguous, not really in one sense necessarily open as well as, in another sense, capable of upper limits. To " know all that exists " is, in one sense, to have perfect knowledge, it is literal omniscience (provided possibilities are also known as such, as a special class of existences or, at least, of realities). But perhaps some of what exists is not as well worth knowing as some other things would have been had they existed. This implies no error or ignorance on the part of the knower, but it does imply the possibility of an increase in the aesthetic satisfaction derived from his knowledge, should a more varied or more harmonious world come into existence and be known. Again, one might deal justly and mercifully with *all* of one's world, and still be glad should this world itself improve in some way. The justice or mercy will not be improved from the ethical standpoint, but the just and merciful one will rejoice and gain in total satisfaction should the individuals being dealt with increase in goodness or happiness. Similarly, maximal power over a good world would not be so good as maximal power over a better one, though in both cases it would be as much power as is compatible with the world to be controlled; that is, in both cases it would be maximal simply as power, though not as total value realized by the one having the power.

True, if (as we shall later see reason to question) maximal power means power to create a beginning of finite existence in time, then it would seem that God could have started with as good a world as he chose. But a " best world " may be meaningless. And besides, the very next moment he would begin to confront the results of the choices, the exercises of power, granted to the creatures, and from then on his actual state, as constituting his knowledge, goodness, and power relations, would be as we have described it.

Nor does it help to argue that since God is timeless he knows and enjoys in advance all that the world ever will become. For he cannot enjoy all that the world ever *could* become as much as he would if it actually became it; for example, he cannot enjoy all the good deeds men might have performed as much as he would have, had the good deeds been performed. At least, this must be so if any vestige is to remain of religious ethics, and even perhaps of good sense. No more does it help to suggest that God's value is wholly independent of his relations to the world, whether of knowledge or of will, for this only means that the particular characters of the objects of his knowledge, or the results of his willing, are to him totally insignificant, which is psychologically monstrous and is religiously appalling as well. (It seems against every word concerning God in the entire Bible, for example, so far as any very direct interpretation is concerned.)

Thus we have every reason to take seriously, as the tradition has plainly not done, the hypothesis (at present merely that) of open dimensions of value, even for the perfect one. Let us remember that number is incapable of a maximum, that in whatever sense God may be "beyond number," still number can hardly be in every sense without value to him — or at any rate, variety can hardly be, and there is no more reason to speak of maximal variety than of maximal number. If, however, variety is said not to be a value for God, then one asks, Why a creation at all? Why should he add to his own perfection the contrast of the purely inferior creatures, unless contrast as such is valuable? And then, how can there be a maximum of contrast? It is no use to say that God creates the creatures out of generosity or love; for if he loves the valueless, so much the worse for his love, and what but the value of contrast can the creatures add to existence? Admittedly, they do not add "unity"!

Here then is a theology that either means nothing certainly identifiable (without supernatural grace or high genius in the art of reconnecting with experience concepts carefully divested of relation to it) or else means that the world might exactly as well not have existed, or as well have existed with far more evil or less good in it than it actually presents. In short, we have the view that the world, including the theologian, is strictly valueless to God, an absolute nullity from the standpoint of ultimate truth. I submit that this is a theology to be accepted, if at all, only after all other possibilities have been carefully considered and found hopelessly untenable. If a man denies this, I only say that I scarcely believe he is thinking about what he is saying. And the writings of those who apparently do deny it show little enough evidence of thought on this aspect of the question. The very question seems, by a near-miracle of persistent looking the other way, to be passed over. Is this merely the " method of tenacity " or is there a more generous explanation?

The theological views of Philo, Plotinus, Augustine, St. Thomas, Spinoza, Leibniz, Kant, Schleiermacher, Royce, the Hindu Śankara, present differences that are striking enough, but all of them agree, or fail clearly to deny, that God is a being " absolutely infinite " (Spinoza's phrase) or every way complete and perfect, and there seems little rational place for significant variations of opinion in a doctrine so completely determined as the doctrine of complete perfection. If, nevertheless, historically endless disputes and radical disagreements over the interpretation of the doctrine have in fact arisen, this is one piece of evidence that there is probably something wrong, perhaps self-contradictory, in the basic idea. On the other hand, the proposition that God is *both* perfect and perfectible, or both statically and dynamically perfect, unsurpassable, tells us prima facie nothing as to the respects in which he is the one and those in which he is the other. Here the necessity for exploring various interpretations is obvious. The exploration, however, was left largely to the present century. The opportunity this represents will not be brushed aside too hastily by anyone trying to be scientific in philosophy, whatever his religious or philosophical tenets.

Consider the dispute between Thomistic and Spinozistic theism. The latter is " pantheistic," the former not. But there are at least two if not three radically different formulations of pantheism, one corresponding to each of the three basic propositions. Spinoza's corresponds to the first proposition. It is not merely that he says God is the one reality, or the universe in its essence, but that he says God is the one reality as absolutely infinite (and unitary). But similarly, what Aquinas says is not merely that God is the transcendent cause of the world, but that he is this cause construed through such categories as lead to the conclusion that he is absolutely infinite and perfect and unitary. This technical agreement as to the nature of God is a far more unambiguous feature of the comparison than most of the alleged differences, which concern more the working out of a basic conception than the conception itself. (It could, perhaps, be fairly argued that Spinoza's deductions from the common assumptions are more rigorous, though Aquinas, to my mind, takes more account of some at least of the intuitive bases from which all philosophy at last derives.)

Or again, people have tried to distinguish between absolutism, which denies " personality " to the perfect being, and theism, which asserts it. But if personality is all-ways perfect or absolute, then this requirement, which is rigid, will inevitably bend the more or less vague term " personal " into conformity with itself; and the upshot will be either inconsistency or at best uncertainty, or else the mere addition of a decorative word to what is just absolutism. If the absolute " loves," it does so in an absolute manner, and the question is, What then remains of the meaning of the term? The answer is to be evaluated by comparing it with the meaning which the idea of divine love can have if Proposition Two is assumed. It is for love to determine the legitimate scope of the concept of absoluteness, if the hypothesis, God is love, is ever to be tried out at all. In testing a hypothesis, the first essential is to deduce the consequences of that hypothesis alone, regardless of any beliefs logically separable from it. Only after this has been done is it time to consult such beliefs, to raise the question of a possible harmony of beliefs. Deductive reasoning is a form of absolute recklessness or it slips into fallacy.

It is indeed quite correct, in testing the hypothesis of perfect love, to utilize, as we propose to do, the division of formal possibilities into the " every-way, some-way, and no-way perfect," for this division is not a belief but a logical certainty, like the multiplication table. Quite true, it may turn out that there are no " ways " or " respects " of perfection; but we are speaking of formal, not ultimate or metaphysical possibilities. The latter are the things to be found out, the former the non-controversial tools for discovering them. Moreover, the denial of any real distinction between respects of value (in relation to perfection) is only a special interpretation of the notion of an all-ways or complete perfection, since it equally excludes the admission of a being at once perfect and perfectible, and the admission that all beings are without qualification perfectible; that is, it is the joint contradictory of second- and third-type doctrines. A being perfect beyond even any distinction between respects of value is a being unqualifiedly perfect, unqualifiedly such that nothing better, or with more value, is conceivable; and in regard to any being it must be true that it is unqualifiedly perfect, or it is unqualifiedly non-perfect, or it is qualifiedly both perfect and non-perfect — if perfection is a word that has any meaning. In addition to all this, if real or metaphysical possibilities are at this stage to be brought in, the reality of the distinction between respects of value, such as goodness and happiness, has far more solid prima facie basis in experience than any notion of absoluteness, or causal action without reaction, or changeless mind, or wholly impassive love! We cannot start with the idea that all dimensions of value will blend into sheer simplicity in the supreme case, the divine.

It will no doubt be said that theologians have had no need to consider our trichotomy of views, since they have offered definite proofs which determine not only that God is but also what he is (or at least, it is said, what he is not), and since two of the three formal possibilities are excluded by this definite (though primarily negative) conclusion. But of course the demonstration presupposes certain axioms concerning "causality," "matter," "form," "privation," whose meaningfulness, or fidelity to the relevant experiences, is as widely and sincerely controverted as is the theistic conclusion derived from them. Except among those who are quite satisfied with these axioms (and it has even been made a merit in Aquinas that he scarcely thought it necessary to justify them) we find the most radical disagreements and uncertainties as to the validity of theistic proofs, and as to the "what" which, if anything, they support. Since Descartes, almost every great thinker has rejected the proofs, at least as ground for the conception of God which Roman Catholic and some earlier Protestant theologians supposed them to imply. For instance, Spinoza and Leibniz both deduced, from such arguments as they admitted, the irreligious doctrine of determinism as valid for God as well as man (the doctrine being sugar-coated with decorative words, or inconsistently retracted, by Leibniz) ; Spinoza also deduced pantheism; Hume and Kant denied all theoretical arguments for God, particularly for a perfect God; Schleiermacher was determinist and pantheist; Bradley inferred, from the simple perfection of the absolute, the superficiality of time, choice, love, personality. Recently Dewey, Santayana, Russell, James, Bergson, Whitehead, Scheler, Croce, almost all non-Romanist thinkers of high quality, have agreed on nothing so well as on the invalidity of any and all proofs for the timeless absolute (unless taken as merely one aspect of a being which also really changes), though many of them would accept the validity of certain *disproofs* for such a conception, and many of them would deny that the concept which has been thus deprived of foundation (if not downright refuted) is necessary to or even compatible with the idea of God which really functions in religion. If modern thought has been simply in error in this rejection of the old theological scheme, then it must be really true that only Roman Catholics can philosophize. In that case, there is little left to the idea of rational philosophy or theology as distinguishable from revealed theology. If, on the other hand, philosophy does exist, there is no short cut around careful consideration of the basic theistic trichotomy.

Controversies between theism and atheism have generally leaped over one of the three basic possibilities. People have rejected theism because they held untenable the idea of a mind not subject to change or to interaction with other beings, or a mind omnipotent in the sense that its power was all the power in existence, or a mind having precise knowledge of details of the future (or of all times from the standpoint of eternity), or a mind creating a first state of the cosmos at a finite time in the past, or knowing all suffering although it did not itself suffer, or an all-embracing mind which in no sense could be identified with the universe, or one which could in every sense be identified with it. These and other difficulties, which may be called the absolutistic paradoxes, have force against Proposition One, but are not pertinent objections to Proposition Two. But, on the other hand, it is quite unjustified for theists to hold that we must tolerate or swallow the paradoxes or explain them away (by feats of ingenuity so subtle, and verbal methods so remote from intuitive insight or definite logical structures, that only deity could know with any assurance what was taking place), giving as justification the claim that the alternative position of atheism is even more paradoxical (lacking, it may be urged, any principle of cosmic explanation at all). The fallacy of such reasoning is clear once we see that atheism is not the only alternative to the assumptions which generate the absolutistic paradoxes. Nor, as we have seen, is the remaining alternative pantheism in any traditionally considered sense.

It might be objected to our trichotomy that there are many degrees of " some " between none and all, and that consequently nothing very definite is described by Proposition Two. However, the " some " refers to dimensions of value as significant in describing God's perfection or perfectibility, and these dimensions are so interrelated that if we could come to a decision in regard to a very few of them the decision as to the others would probably follow. Also we could agree to classify under the third proposition all views which ascribe no more perfection to the gods than did the Greeks to their Olympians, whose only point of absoluteness seems to have been their immortality. (Any finite god held to be ungenerated as well as deathless ought perhaps to be held a minimal case of the finite-infinite God of second-type theism.)

It is of some interest to note that atheism and primitive

polytheism are of the same basic type. This does not prove that if polytheism is false, atheism must be; for they are subalternatives within their type. But it does suggest that the radical falsity of primitive religious ideas as they stand is not an argument for atheism, as it is rather commonly held to be. Also the fact that atheism is at least as old (as a philosophy) as theism of the second type (it was much more familiar to Plato, for instance) suggests that there is nothing philosophically very advanced or sophisticated about atheistic doctrine as such. A really clear expression even of first-type theism is apparently indefinitely later than atheism. All of which of course proves nothing except the irrelevance of certain supposed arguments for atheism, arguments more subconscious and informal than explicit and official, but still influential.

The philosophical importance of admitting *some* nonabsolute aspects of God is in the resulting applicability of such categories as change, passivity, complexity, and the like, to him, and for this purpose surpassability of God, *as he actually is,* even if only by God himself as he could or can be, is entirely sufficient. Now though the actuality of deity is, according to second-type theism, in some respects surpassable, his *individuality* as potentially inclusive of other than his actual predicates may be in no respect whatever surpassable, in all dimensions though not in all senses perfect. To say this is not to commit second-type theism to the view that God is an " individual." We are speaking of subalternatives which the second basic proposition admits, not of corollaries which it necessarily implies. All the proposition demands is that there be a God in some respect unsurpassable, in some other surpassable — whether self-surpassable and how, or surpassable by other entities not states of himself, or whether he has " states," being left perfectly open by the proposition. Exploration of the subalternatives may well lead to the conclusion that only one of them is really "conceivable" in the full sense (in the light of the experiential content of the ideas involved). But this again is a matter to be held in suspension until we have established some control of the relations between the basic propositions.

God, for both old and much new theology, is the being whose uniqueness consists in his unrivaled excellence, or whose amount of value defines a necessarily one-membered class (and so in a sense not a class). In some respects he is absolutely unexcelled, even by himself in another conceivable state; in *all other* respects he is (to state the view reached in this book) the only individual whose states or predicates are not to be excelled unless he excel them with other states or predicates of his own. To take an imperfect analogy, no one will ever be or can ever be so Wordsworthian as Wordsworth; but Wordsworth himself, if he (or someone about him) had made a different use of his free will, might perhaps have been somewhat "more himself," might have developed his individuality more than he did. And certainly, at any stage in his life, one could have said that he was the most Wordsworthian being that would ever exist, except as he himself might later become more so. God, however, is not simply more himself than any other can ever be; he and he alone is in all respects superior to any state that will ever characterize any individual unless it characterize him. He is the greatest conceivable actuality, except perhaps as he himself can be conceived as greater (in another, perhaps subsequent, state, or in a state he might have had in the past, had men, say, served him more faithfully).

There is a slight ambiguity in the expression "excelled by himself only." We may ourselves in the future enjoy values which God now lacks (because they are not in being). But according to AR he will not lack them when we enjoy them, so that our self-excelling will be also (infinitely magnified) his self-excelling. Thus R means that " in no possible state of affairs can there be anything in any fashion superior to God as he is in that same state of affairs."

It will be seen that the new doctrine requires careful and somewhat elaborate distinctions, and yet, if some of its supporters are right, the doctrine is nothing at all but the analysis of the simple idea that God is " the perfectly loving individual," in all respects possessed of the properties which this idea requires, even if non-perfection in some respects be among the requirements.

That God is less than he might be (though more than anything else might be) agrees with the religious conception of the free service of God. For if we had no choice but to serve God in the fullest measure, or if we could not serve him at all, then it might be held with some plausibility that he is all that he might be. But the possibility of being freely served seems clearly to imply the possibility of lacking something that better service than may actually be given would furnish. Philosophical orthodoxy has had to finesse this point, and indeed, as I believe, has fallen into sophistry of a rather revolting kind. Really there was to be no service of God, but only a service of men through the — to them — beneficial practices of religion. Sin did no real harm whatever in the universe, since the absolute perfection which the universe involves in its cause could never be more or less than absolute. To say that sin at least harmed *men* is beside the point; for what harm did it do to harm men, parts of a system of reality that as a whole or in its ultimate reality was incapable of loss or gain? The world plus the absolutely infinite is no more than the latter by itself. Only from a purely race-egoistic (and illusory) point of view could the harm appear as such. Thus the motivation which is the (attempted) attitude of pure atheistic humanism was the only one philosophers could approve in religion. The idea of cosmic concern, concern for the divine values, must now at last be considered on its merits.

A very simple way to settle the theistic question is the positivistic analysis, which results in the rejection of theism of the first type as meaningless, theism of the third type (finite God, such as Zeus) as meaningful but devoid of empirical evidence and so not worth discussing, and — yes, what of theism of the second type? Is it meaningless or is it merely not in accord with the evidence? Against the first of these possibilities is to be set the fact that the very arguments by which positivists endeavor to show the meaninglessness of theism of the first type have for some decades been employed by defenders of theism, type two. Hence if the latter is also meaningless it is not likely to be for the same or very similar reasons. The doctrine has been formulated with the requirements of meaning carefully in view. Against the supposition that second-type theism is without experiential support is to be set the fact that its defenders also employ that very argument against theism of the first type, and that the emergence of the second-type theory has been the result of a deliberate and cooperative effort, undertaken by some men of genius and many men of excellent scientific and logical training, to discover the experiential referent, if any, of theism. If these men believe they have succeeded in finding such a referent, then it is not philosophy but debate to assert, without investigation, that they cannot have found it.

It will be seen that the God of second-type theism is not without qualification finite, or growing, or emergent; nor, without qualification, is he the contradictory of these. The traditional distrust of simple statement, and of language as applied to the religious vision, in the new theology ceases to be an inoperative or inconsistently employed formal concession, and becomes a systematic tracing of the relativity of concepts to each other and to experience as a whole. The concepts which still function as absolute are the strictly religious and experiential ones of love and goodness. God is the Holy One, the ethical Absolute, the literally all-loving Father. In these affirmations second-type theism sees no exaggeration. It holds that the distinction between God's ethical perfection (and hence ethical immutability) and his " aesthetic " perfectibility (and hence growth) fits the later Hebrew and other high religions (most of all what some of us would mean by Christianity) far more naturally and unambiguously than does the confusion of every perfection in the unchanging *actus purus* of the Scholastics (and even of Schleiermacher). Furthermore, Whitehead and others have shown that it is precisely love which must be perfect in God — and only love and what is implied by it as perfect — if either love or perfection is to serve as an explanatory concept in cosmology. (The idea that the religious content of Whitehead's system is dragged in, and that what his system requires is some " impersonal " force or function having no essential connection with love, is in my opinion a thorough misunderstanding.)

What has been discovered — to anticipate the argument of later chapters — is that, on one main point at least (the choice between the three propositions), religion at its best was literally and philosophically right, and theology was but a first approximation, vitiated by ambiguities or inconsistencies. In Whitehead's cosmology — which is, in the main, simply the most fully elaborated expression of tendencies widespread in recent philosophy — all existence is " social," is " feeling of feeling," forming " societies " of interlocked experiences, and societies of societies, from electronic, almost inconceivably simple and rudimentary, societies, to the universe. In this completely social philosophy (conflict, which is not denied, being also a social relation) God is that in the cosmos whereby it is a cosmos; he is the individual case on the cosmic scale of all the ultimate categories (including those of social feeling, " subjective aim," etc.) thanks to which these categories describe a community of things, and not merely things each enclosed in unutterable privacy, irrelevant to and unordered with respect to anything else. To impute purpose to God is no dishonesty in Whitehead; for he finds no real or possible thing that is not in its degree of simplicity or complexity endowed with subjective aim. And equally, he finds nothing whose feeling and aim are without sensitivity to other feelings and aims, that is, social. Hence the cosmic individual, the cosmos as the inclusive Society of societies " with personal order " is inclusively, universally sensitive, loving, and hence decidedly not purely impassive or once for all and in all ways perfect. The sense in which conflict, as well as harmony, enters into God is just the sense to which religion refers in speaking of the grief or anger of God over our suffering or sins, the grief being symbolized by the cross. Love is not identical with harmony, though it includes a measure of it. God conflicts, however, only with what he also participates in through his sensitivity or " tenderness." If Whitehead said less than this, it is the logic of his system that would collapse, and not merely its religious applicability.

Similar remarks could (with some qualification) be made about the philosophy of James Ward and others. We have passed the stage of trying to fit our scientific cosmology to an implicitly irreligious theology; for we are finding that it is precisely in its departure from the insight of the most nobly religious men (in their religious moments) that theology also departs from what is useful in secular explanation. The conflict between religion and science turns out to be (in part) a conflict between a pseudo-religious (and philosophically untenable) theology and a science not fully clarified in its philosophical principles and in the main lines of its results.

NOTES

[1] One of the earliest expressions of this attitude is to be found in Otto Pfleiderer's *Grundriss der christlichen Glaubens- und Sittenlehre* (Berlin: Georg Reimer, 1888), Sections 61, 67–69, 84.

[2] The "new" theology can also be called Platonic if one interprets Plato somewhat otherwise than the Neo-Platonists and most scholars have done. See Raphael Demos, *The Philosophy of Plato* (Charles Scribner's Sons, 1939), pp. 120–25.

[3] That possibilities are real, and that the future involves open alternatives, or is indeterminate in essence, I have attempted to demonstrate in my book, *Beyond Humanism,* chaps. 9 and 10, and in an article, "Contingency and the New Era in Metaphysics," *Journal of Philosophy,* XXIX, 421 ff., 457 ff. Cf. Charles S. Peirce, *Collected Papers* (Harvard University Press, 1931–35), Vol. VI, Book I A. For an elaborate defense of the opposite or deterministic view, see Brand Blanshard, *The Nature of Thought* (London: Allen & Unwin, 1939), especially Vol. II. (Blanshard virtually ignores most of what seem to me the chief arguments against determinism, but gives a fine account of the arguments which have often been thought to support it.)

[4] See Alfred North Whitehead, *Modes of Thought* (The Macmillan Co., 1938), pp. 92–95; also my essay, "Whitehead's Idea of God," in *The Philosophy of Alfred North Whitehead,* edited by P. A. Schilpp.

[5] The positivistic objections to metaphysics as such I have attempted to meet in chap. 16 of *Beyond Humanism,* and in "Metaphysics for Positivists," *Philosophy of Science,* II, 287 ff. See Whitehead, *Adventures of Ideas* (The Macmillan Co., 1933), pp. 147 f., 159–65; Peirce, *Papers,* VI, 368. Besides Whitehead, two other leading logicians of our time seem to accept metaphysics in principle: see C. I. Lewis, *Mind and the World Order* (Charles Scribner's Sons, 1929), pp. 10, 16–17; and Bertrand Russell, "The Limits of Empiricism," *Proceedings of the Aristotelian Society,* 1935–36. Lewis says: "The problem of a correctly conceived metaphysics, like the problem of ethics and of logic, is one to be resolved by attaining

to clear and cogent self-consciousness" (p. 10). The object sought is the definition of reality as such. However, "a successful definition of the real in general would not carry us far in any cosmological attempt to plumb the deeps of the universe since it would delimit reality in intension only, and would leave quite undetermined the particular content of reality *in extenso.*" It would not attempt "the total picture of reality," or "describe the course of the universe" (pp. 16 f.). But suppose there is a being whose nature implies existence, that is, suppose intension and extension are not at all points independent. In other words, that reality should be reality it may be necessary that a certain individual should be real, for this individual may be the ground of all reality. True, the *particular* content of reality cannot exist necessarily, but there may be one individual whose identifying or individuating character is not as such particular, but rather the universally immanent ground of actuality and possibility. Again, the universe, as actually and at present, is contingent not metaphysical, but the universe as such, in that which makes it the universe, at all times and whatever happens within it, may be involved in the very meaning of reality, and this essential character of the universe may be the primordial or necessary aspect of the God of religion. In short, Lewis' attempt to reduce to the trivial the results of the metaphysics which he admits as legitimate, stands or falls with the solution of the theistic problem, including the status of second-type theism and of the ontological argument in connection with that type. It is absolute idealistic (first-type) monism, not theism, that *could* not be established by metaphysics.

Russell's point in the article mentioned is that the causal principle, upon which empirical science rests, must have an experiential basis which is logically prior to empirical science. This basis Russell finds in the experience of being constrained to a judgment by perceptual evidence for its truth. Clearly this is a psychological relation, and it seems that if Russell had generalized his result he would have agreed with Peirce, James, Whitehead, and Bergson that the intelligibility of the world is its spiritual character. Only panpsychism and theism can avoid the fallacy of pure empiricism, not that they must desert experience but that they recognize those elements in experience that have metaphysical generality, that are valid of all experience and all objects.

[6] In the writings of neo-Thomists such as Étienne Gilson or Jacques Maritain one finds scarcely a suggestion of the distinction between a perfect-perfectible and an imperfect-perfectible God, between second- and third-type theism. Thus when Maritain (in his *Réflexions sur l'intelligence,* Paris: Nouvelle Librairie Nationale, 1924) discusses the theological views of James and others, he makes the most of the glaring contrast between the indefinitely imperfect God he finds in their writings and the perfection which he of course believes God to possess, with scarcely a hint that there are here two questions, not one. That James was also not clearly aware of the duality of the problem does not alter the fact that

today the neglected distinction is becoming central to the controversy, as it logically should have been all along. On the other side of the theism-atheism dispute, Santayana, Dewey, Russell, and Carnap are no less silent on the intermediate or balanced view of God. All the while, numerous theologians are quietly developing such a view. Thus we are living through a transition between the sheer neglect and the adequate consideration of the real theological question, that of deciding among the three types.

APPENDIX TO CHAPTER I

In the classification of theistic and atheistic doctrines explained in this chapter, the number of cases of perfection was limited to six (plus the purely negative case) by the supposition that the joint denial of "surpassability by nothing at all," A, and of "surpassability by self only," R, is an idea which needs no further subdivision, I. But on purely formal

GROUP	CASE		
I (A)	1 A		
II (AX)	2 AR	3 ARO	
	4 ARB	5 ARBO	
	6 AB	7 ABO	8 AO
III (X)	9 R	10 RO	
	11 RB	12 RBO	
	13 B	14 BO	15 O

grounds there are two possibilities: complete surpassability, by both self and others, and surpassability by others only (and not by self). The distinction between the two has been neglected hitherto, because we have followed the common assumption that by "God" is meant a concrete being, not a mere abstraction. Only an abstraction, it seems, could be unsurpassable by itself and yet surpassable by others. Thus one might say that politeness is inferior to honesty or to justice, but that politeness could not improve upon itself, but must always be just—politeness. If the assumption that God is not an abstraction be set aside, then we have fifteen possible combinations of the four modes of surpassability and its negation together with the threefold logical division of respects of greatness into all, some, and none. The four modes of surpassability are: surpassability (1) by *both* self and others, B; (2) by *self* only (unsurpassability " relative " to others), R; (3) by *others* only, O; (4) by *neither* self nor others (" absolute " unsurpassability), A. Hitherto we have considered B and O only in terms of their common property as given by the definition of I as " neither A nor R."

Combining the foregoing we derive a strictly exhaustive set, so far as the notions of self, others, surpassable, and respect or dimension are concerned.

This differs from the earlier classification only through the substitution of the combinations of the subclasses B and O for I, that is, of " surpassability *both* by self and by others," and " surpassability by *others only,*" for " surpassability *either* by others *or* by others and self as well." The new distinction leaves group one or (A) unchanged, and it cannot enable group three to meet any objections which are due to the absence of the A factor, as were the objections we suggested. As for group two, it is perhaps evident that items in the second and third columns could not constitute significant conceptions of God. For a being which, in certain respects, could not itself improve and yet could be surpassed by others, would seem hardly to be the supreme being, the lord of all, the legitimate object of highest veneration, or the philosophical first cause or all-pervasive reality, which the word God almost universally connotes. Even if God be not an individual, or be not concrete, still he is at any rate, it seems, thought of as supreme over both individuals and abstractions, surpassable by nothing, unless he be in some respects self-surpassable. It is to be noted, too, that while self-surpassability cannot be taken as necessarily implying a defect (without begging the question as to value's being possible at all outside of time and the possibility of growth), to be surpassed by others seems a defect pure and simple. It is to lack some positive property which yet exists, whereas self-transcendence or growth may only mean that one does not actually enjoy all that is possible — perhaps for the very good reason that this would be non-sense because possibility is inexhaustible in actuality. Thus the O factor (as well as the B factor) is essentially negative or a deficiency, whereas A and R contain between them what is positive in the idea of perfection or surpassing. To be at an absolute maximum, even in relation to oneself, in all respects admitting of such a maximum, and to be at a maximum in relation to others and endlessly enriching in relation to self in respects not admitting of absolute maxima (if such respects there be) — these seem to exhaust the forms of highest excellence. It hardly seems reasonable to expect a being which enjoys one or both of the two forms of positive perfection to possess aspects so inferior as to conform to the definitions of O and B. To be R rather than A in some respects may express the very nature of these respects. But if there were respects of value, by which all beings must be qualified, and which would compel a being possessing A and R in other respects to be inferior to other beings in certain respects — this would suggest only that A and R have no meaning. For instance, unsurpassable knowledge would bring all the riches of actuality to the being possessing it. How then could this being in any respect show inferiority to any other? Thus it seems unlikely that the combinations of A and R with B and O represent real (other than purely formal) possibilities. The essential problem is thus, in all probability, to determine the significance of the A and R conceptions, and of their joint denial, as displayed in our previous tables (pp. 8, 9). The essential questions are: (1) Is there such a thing as absolute or static perfection? (2) Is there such a thing as relative or dynamic perfection? (3) Is there a being possessing either or both of them and in what respects?

II

A PROGRAM FOR PHILOSOPHICAL THEOLOGY

. . . In metaphysics, as . . . in ethics and in logic, . . . valid principles must be supposed somehow implicit in ordinary intercourse of mind with reality. . . . The truth which is sought is already implicit in the mind which seeks it, and needs only to be elicited and brought to clear expression. . . . [If the method employed in philosophy] be deductive, then the initial assumptions cannot coerce the mind. There are no propositions which are self-evident in isolation. [If it be] inductive by example, then the principles to be proved are implicit in the assumption that cited examples are veridical and typical. . . . A philosopher can offer proof only in the sense of so connecting his theses as to exhibit their mutual support, and only through appeal to other minds to reflect on their experience and their own attitudes and perceive that he correctly portrays them.

C. I. LEWIS, in *Mind and the World Order*

THE THEISTIC question is now before us. How are we to set about answering it? We might immediately attempt to devise arguments for the existence of God, in the hope that these arguments, if successful, would tell us not only *that,* but *what,* God is, and would thus decide among the three types of doctrines, or, if unsuccessful, would justify us in giving up the idea of God — that is, in accepting the atheistic interpretation of third-type doctrine — or would justify us in declaring the question unanswerable and in adopting an agnostic view concerning the three doctrines.

We might not unreasonably begin with an examination of the traditional proofs for God. These proofs of course lead, if anywhere, to theism of the first type. They have been examined many times by leading philosophers and, with increasing frequency and emphasis, judged unsatisfactory. Ought I to add my mite to this judgment or attempt to correct modern philosophy on a matter which it has so carefully considered? It may be said, however, that the proofs have not been really met on their own ground. There is some justice in this claim. Modern thought has often drifted so far from medieval metaphysics as scarcely to see what that metaphysics was about. But the force of this consideration is weakened, for me at least, by another. Modern thought has not been content to pass judgment on the traditional proofs; it has also proposed disproofs of God as conceived in traditional or first-type theology. These disproofs have, if anything, been even less adequately met by traditionalists than traditional proofs by their critics. To me the disproofs (see chapter 3) are as conclusive as philosophical arguments could well be, and when I see how almost completely they are overlooked by first-type theists I am unable to feel much concerned because the basis of the alleged proofs is not any too clearly understood by modern skeptics.

We might also begin with an attempt to find proofs for second-type theism (and such proofs are now available), with an eye for possible disproofs. But it is impossible to look for evidence without knowing what idea is to be tested. Now it is true that we do have before us a definition of second-type theism. Yet it is to be feared that the definition will be misunderstood, or viewed by some readers with such strong prejudice as to make accurate reasoning difficult. They will think that what the new proofs have to offer is not what anybody has meant and sought in asking about God. They will think that a partially perfectible God cannot be everlasting, safe from corruption, or perfect in benevolence. They will think that the doctrine proposed is " pantheistic," which is a sort of theological synonym for what you don't like. Or they will suspect that the doctrine is not really self-consistent or meaningful.

In view of these difficulties I have chosen to postpone to chapters 8 and 9 the presentation of the revised forms of the cosmological and ontological arguments which I believe to be valid proofs for second-type theism. In the five intervening chapters I attempt to show: (in chapter 3) that the support which tradition appears to give to first-type theism is nullified by a basic contradiction in this tradition itself, a contradiction which second-type theism can best remove; (in chapters 4 and 6) that ethical and aesthetic aspects of experience conflict with first-type and support second-type theory (affording, if you will, an ethico-aesthetic " proof " for the latter) ; (in chapter 5) that only theism of the second type can really do anything with the traditional " way of analogy " with which the emptiness of purely negative theology has been allegedly atoned for; and (in chapter 7) that finally the religious idea of " creation," so far from supporting the purely absolutistic and non-temporal conception of the creator, is much better expressed by the absolute-relative conception, AR. In this way I hope to weaken the prejudices built up by centuries of repetition of certain misunderstandings of the theistic problem (misunderstandings which are less and less frequently found among religious historians), so that the two proofs mentioned will have some chance of receiving careful attention.

In any case, proofs must rest on insights, and it has been found that no axioms are altogether perspicuous to persons sufficiently desirous of avoiding propositions derivable from them. Then too, in the ontological argument the axiom is the idea of God itself, taken as at least meaningful, as neither non-sense nor self-contradictory. The way to establish this axiom is to deduce the consequences of various ideas of God with a view to their consistency and power to express basic aspects of experience.

That philosophy should make elaborate use of deduction, and not merely subsequent but also prior to the search for evidence as to the truth of its premises, may be inferred from the fact that even in physics, which is certainly an empirical science, elaborate mathematical deductive systems have been as much the forerunners as the results of observation. It is very true indeed that it is the mathematical character of the ideas involved that makes definite deduction possible and fruitful. But there are certain simple, formal, mathematico-logical ideas applicable even to philosophical problems. Our formulation of the theistic issues employed one such formal idea, the set of all, some, and none. But there are other such ideas, and other philosophical applications. Mathematics is a way of defining exact alternatives. Thus if we have two ideas, A and B, and their negatives, —A and —B, then mathematics tells us there are four possible cases: AB, A—B, —AB, —A—B. This is nearly the simplest mathematics conceivable, but that is no proof that it must be unimportant. In fact, simple as such notions are, it can be shown that great philosophers have sometimes reasoned at variance with their logical structure while implicitly employing them.

In spite of my evident dislike for first-type doctrine, I have this sympathy for it, this reason for taking it seriously: In defending the idea of perfection, which in some form is the common element of the first two types, traditional theology is able to do justice to the a priori or metaphysical element in theology and philosophy, the necessary aspect of God, which plainly no mere induction could reach. Third-type theism, on the contrary, implies that there is no necessary or absolute factor knowledge of which could be attained a priori. If God is in all ways less than perfect, less than is possible, then how *much* less could not be anything but a contingent fact. Thus third-type theism is logically, and in its actual representatives, a pure empiricism, while first-type theism is equally logically a pure rationalism.

We confront a strange dilemma here: the initial task of philosophical theology is to decide among three doctrines, but if we ask by what method the decision is to be made, it turns out that decision as to method apparently amounts to decision as to result. If we exclude contingent knowledge from theology, we thereby deny contingent aspects to God; if we exclude a priori knowledge, we exclude noncontingent or necessary aspects. The dogmatic insistence in theology upon the exclusive validity of induction, or of deduction from self-evident axioms, is thus purely question begging. Surely a method for answering a question must not, in its mere formulation, imply one among the formally possible answers to the question. To tell a physicist that he must generalize from perceived particulars does not tell him which of the conceivable physical systems will turn out to be true. But to tell a theologian that he must follow this method, not merely as the way of determining accidental aspects of God, should there be such, but as the way of determining the entire nature of God including his essence, is really to say God has no strict or necessary essence but is wholly a contingent being, and therefore that both first- and second-type theisms are false! It is easy to show that the question, Can we have a priori insight into the necessary features of existence? is one with the question, Are there such features? (Positivists please note.) For if there are such features, they must be universally present in existence and experience and therefore not wholly unknowable, and if there are none such, then of course there is no appropriate object for an a priori method to know. To set up as axiomatic in all knowledge, including philosophy and theology, the exclusive use of what is generally meant by the " empirical " method — whose logical principle is that the choice among alternative, that is, contingent, hypotheses is to be made by observation of particular facts — is to commit the methodological fallacy of begging the answer to one of the chief questions for philosophy and theology to solve, which is, Is there a necessary factor, along with the contingent factors, in existence? This question cannot be answered by a method which is meaningless if one of the formally possible (*verbally* conceivable) answers to it is true. The question whether the answer is really conceivable and meaningful is the same (and this can be proved deductively) as the question whether the answer is true. (Necessary truths are those whose contradictory is nonsense, hence those which avoid nonsense only by being true.)

Thus the question of method is in philosophy in part inseparable from the problems to be solved by the method. Is there then no method for determining method which itself is beyond controversy and begs no questions? I believe that there is. All argument, even about method, assumes something, but it need not, for all that, assume something genuinely controversial. There are at least two types of non-controversial assumptions in philosophy: First, self-evident formal structures of pure logic and mathematics, which no one sincerely questions. Second, data of experience so vivid that, however one interprets them, they are universally admitted to occur, such as " pain," " memory," " purpose," " hate." Third, it is self-evident and indeed one of the formal principles mentioned, that the way to deal with controversial matters is to start from the least controversial experiences and, by the application of formal, deductively powerful structures, which are also neutral to the controversies, test the relation of the more controverted ideas to those experiences. This is the general rational method, and it includes more than what is usually meant by empirical, for the experiences which are important in philosophy are observations not of particulars but of the dimensions of experience as such, its temporal character, its character as "purposive," "emotional," more or less "harmonious," "discordant," and the like. Philosophy is concerned with experiences which at least claim to be universal and fundamental — just as religious experience involves at least the *feeling* that "God" is relevant to and involved in all experience and all existence. The problem is not to generalize from such experiences and their claims, but to see whether the complete generality already in them, as a semblance at least, is or is not genuine, to see whether one can successfully, and with all implications in mind, deny their claim to generality.

It seems self-evident, for instance, that all existence has value, for at every moment one values all of it that he thinks of and hence is interested in — that is, he values whatever he can mean by — "all of it." The problem is to clear this apparent insight of irrelevant details, to see what it could conceivably imply, and to relate it to other insights of the kind. To assume that this must not be the philosophical method is to assume definite answers to certain philosophical questions. To assume that this method should be given a trial is merely to allow such answers and their negatives to be adequately considered.

The way to deal with the issue between empiricists and rationalists is to use the elements of reason and experience which neither can deny, in order to state exhaustively what the different conceivable methods might be. Contemporary positivists try to do this when they divide all judgments into analytic and synthetic; but, as I have tried elsewhere to show,[1] though they give a formally exhaustive division, in actual procedure they introduce without adequate discussion certain restrictions on the varieties of the two types of judgment which partly nullify their initial care.

To assert the validity of the metaphysical method is to assert that there is some sort of necessary being. But experimenting with a method is not the same as asserting its validity, but amounts only to admitting that we cannot safely assume its invalidity. On the contrary, to rule out a method amounts to denying that its possible validity needs even to be considered. Now the only type of theism which is compatible with the validity (in theology) of both methods, empirical and metaphysical, is second-type theism; for it alone admits contingent features in the necessary being; and of course contingent features are utterly incapable of being known except by particular observations, that is, experiences whose data are contingent. Thus the possibility that both methods have validity, that neither is merely wrong or superfluous, seems to coincide with the possibility that some form of second-type doctrine is true. Since, therefore, the a priori method could be ruled out a priori only by presupposing it, and since it cannot be assumed in advance that the a priori method will return a verdict against the validity of the empirical method (as appropriate to one aspect of the philosophical problem), there can be no methodological justification for neglecting the possibility that second-type theism is true, and that, accordingly, both methods are valid.

It also seems fairly clear that it is the a priori method, not the empirical, which is capable of adjudicating the claims of the two methods, of generously or justly granting a place to its apparent rival. The only way the empirical method could throw any light on the a priori element in knowledge would be by a reflection upon its own presuppositions. But such reflection is not really empirical. The point is that a priori it *could not* be that mere generalization from particulars could be valid if there were no generalities knowable directly; for mere generalization from particulars is simply the formal fallacy, some *s* is *p*, therefore all, or most, *s* is *p*. Generalization has meaning only when we have accepted, as valid independently of generalization from particulars, the generic (not merely general) idea of the actual world as such, as distinguished from mere possibilities, implying that observed particulars belong to " realities," that is, are not just isolated disembodied qualities, but samples of a universe with some principle distinguishing it from all-possibility, some principle of " limited variety," such as distinguishes a work of art from simply a jumble of all the possible ways of making an artistic pattern with choice of none. True, the principle has no real alternative, we *could not* be experiencing a merely possible world.[2] But this " could not " is a priori and metaphysical, not a generalization from particular experiences. It follows simply from the generic idea of experience, as do all the metaphysical truths.

The more our empirical theologians insist that nothing a priori should be considered, the more sure traditional theologians will become that " modernism " is wandering in hopeless error. Between two such extremes there can be no rational decision, only endless debate, misunderstanding, and a certain amount of contempt. What is the objection to a fair trial for the position that can see sense in both sides of the controversy?

It is not to the point that the empirical method has alone proved successful in science, for it is apparent a priori that contingent or non-generic truths about existence cannot be known a priori. This was admitted in the Middle Ages.

If, nevertheless, the empirical method then languished, this was due not to the fact that the a priori method was admitted as valid of non-contingent truths, but (among a complex of reasons) to the circumstance that the a priori method was held to arrive at a supreme reality which was in *all* aspects necessary, therefore in no aspects approachable by the empirical method, from which it would follow that anything knowable empirically, that is, anything accidental, would not be a part of the supreme reality, and would be of no importance whatever, since the supreme reality equally with or without accidental things would contain all possible perfection. Thus the exclusion of the empirical method from theology implies, if taken strictly, the total unimportance of the objects of empirical knowledge, and thus tends to discredit the method, even in the spheres in which it is supposed to be legitimate, by virtually denying that its objects in any significant sense exist.

The success of the empirical method in modern times, in the spheres in which its legitimacy was, nominally at least, conceded even when the metaphysical method was most popular, proves, not that the a priori method must be given up in philosophy and theology, but that we must investigate the possibility of justifying a priori the legitimacy of empirical generalization even with reference to one aspect of that necessary being which is the only conceivable object of a priori knowledge of existence (more than merely formal a priori knowledge). That is, the hypothesis which on methodological grounds deserves consideration prior to all others in philosophy is that second-type theism is true, and the empirical method therefore, and for a priori reasons, valid and important in its sphere. This result would satisfy all interests involved, except only pride of opinion, anti-religious bias, and other non-intellectual, essentially personal motives. The way to vindicate the method of the special sciences is to show that they furnish the only way there is or can be of knowing in any detail the contingent contents of the divine life, without which that life would be empty of all value, a mere scheme of existence, not an existent.

(As one way to know the " contingent contents of the divine " one might have to admit a rationally purified revelation. For there may be relations of God to man — contingent relations since man is a contingent being — which only the " pure in heart," or the recipients of special " grace," will be adequately aware of. The accidents of God may include immensely important and to secular reason obscure matters, such as man's " original sin," or his " salvation " from this sin by divine " forgiveness." A theology which in principle accepts revelation as affording knowledge to those able to assimilate it *may* have light to throw upon truths otherwise likely or perhaps certain to be missed or seen less clearly. This is here left undecided, since this book deals with the mere essence of God, including the generic property of " having accidents," but not the accidents themselves. These belong to the special sciences, including the science of revelation, if there be such. On the view that God is not subject to contingent relations see chapter 7.)

There are, as we might expect, two opposite errors in regard to method in philosophy. One is to deny that experience can yield strictly universal truths. The other is to exaggerate the type of absoluteness possessed by such truths as we can know them, to misconceive the role of " axioms." The former extreme is positivism, the latter is dogmatism in the proper technical sense. Here I wish to consider the dogmatic extreme.

Dogmatism is of two kinds. One may exaggerate the import of the axiomatic or a priori by trying to derive particular consequences from it, forgetting that it is purely general, and that from the more to the less general there is no valid inference. To yield a particular or a specific conclusion, one premise must be no less particular or specific. This means that the entirety of generalizations less than absolute in their generality must be known otherwise than by deduction from first principles. The entire field of the special sciences is thus liberated from the pretensions of metaphysicians, such as those of Hegelians, who appear to have thought that, if not particulars, at least more or less specific generalities are deducible from philosophical generalities. When scientists respond to such misuses of metaphysics by attacking metaphysics as such, they are merely falling into the opposite form of the same failure to distinguish things really different which was the cause of the abuses they dislike. Of course it may not be a simple matter to determine when a proposition is of complete generality, but many difficult things are yet possible.

The other form of dogmatism consists in the fallacious notion that insights into the absolute must be absolute insights. By deduction (it was thought) we learn the consequences of initial propositions whose truth is arrived at altogether independently of deduction, either by intuitive self-evidence or by induction. Since the latter is inapplicable to necessary truths, these must be known by sheer self-evidence. Deduction could exploit truth already discovered, but could not itself help in the discovery. This is of course a fallacy. By expanding propositions deductively, we find out much more adequately what they really assert, and the more we know what they assert the better we know how well they fit experience or the immediately intuited or self-evident. Even if it be a question of necessary truths, first principles, the value of deduction as part of the machinery for testing and clarifying such truth is as great as in the induction of contingent generalizations. Logicians have come to realize that since the deducible consequences of logic's laws are themselves just as necessary, just as truly laws, as the initial statements or "axioms," it is as reasonable to test the truth of the axioms by looking to the self-evidence of their consequences as vice versa. Indeed, all logical ideas are axioms, the only difference among them being in simplicity or convenience of explication. The same is true in metaphysics. Theists of the first type, however, thought differently. They set up certain axioms, such as that "actuality is prior to possibility," quickly proceeded to deduce the theological consequences, and refused vigorously to consider any apparent clash of these consequences, either with each other or with experience, as indications of imperfection in the assumptions. On the contrary, the inference was rather, "since the axioms are correct, the only problem is as to the best way of resolving the apparent difficulties of their consequences." The prize goes to him who most completely explains, or explains away, the difficulties. The prize goes, in fact, to a beautiful spirit, St. Thomas of Aquin, whose principal technical defect, among magnificent technical virtues, was that he did not realize that ultimately it would be as necessary to justify the axioms as to justify the existence and nature of God derived from them.

Deduction is a way of *magnifying the testability* of assumptions, rather than simply a way of magnifying their importance and meaning, once tested. We should never put all the burden of the evidence upon axioms, but distribute it over the whole chain of consequences. This is well recognized in regard to scientific reasoning. But in philosophy its recognition has been impeded by the contention, in itself true, that philosophy deals with assumptions whose relation to observable facts is not the same as in science. Philosophical principles, being first principles, apply to all conceivable as well as to all actual facts, and what is to be tested is not the frequency with which they obtain, their probability in the usual sense, but their necessity. Truths can be necessary only if their denial is absurd, and this can only mean if insight into the *meaning* of the denial suffices to exhibit it as self-contradictory. In short, the assumptions of philosophy are self-evident upon careful inspection of the terms involved. These terms, like all terms, refer to experience, for there is nothing else for them to refer to. But since self-evidence gives necessity, certainty, there seems no need to consult experience further, once the assumptions have been validated.

The conclusion is a *non sequitur*. There is no point beyond which we can afford to lose interest in the applicability of philosophical propositions to direct experience. If we have deduced that God is love, and at the same time that he is impassive, it is fully in order to ask if it is within the meaning of love to admit impassivity. If not, then so much the worse for our previous assumptions, as well as for our present apparent insight into the essential passivity of love. Both must be held questionable until the self-evidence of the earlier assumptions has been reconsidered, in the light of a full and candid hearing afforded to the contradictory of these assumptions, one by one. Axioms must be defended against a vigorous devil's advocate. In Aquinas there is a devil's advocate for the denial of theorems, but scarcely for the denial of axioms. Experience, especially in recent times, has shown that false axioms can present a striking semblance of self-evidence, a fact that enhances the significance of the difficulties which some of the Thomistic theorems involve. These difficulties were naturally not fully apparent to Thomas, but he did deal ingeniously with some of them, and since it is all in a cause known as good the disciple is more disposed to admire the ingenuity than to push the quest for credentials.

The trouble, then, is by no means merely that the reasoning is toward a predestined conclusion, the existence of God, but just as much that it starts from a preordained premise, the substantial correctness of the Aristotelian conception of matter and form. True it is, also, that the definition of God arrived at (first-type theism) is believed by Aquinas to be true in advance of all his reasoning, since it is the definition made venerable by practically unanimous testimony (on the points here in question) of the Fathers, as well as being in agreement with the Scriptures as then interpreted. Thus when the Scriptures say God is perfect or unchanging, this was taken to mean, in every respect and sense perfect and unchanging, as though the Bible had been written for the express purpose of guiding philosophers as such. How could we expect that a mere human being, even though a saintly one, should have refused to be satisfied with a result which conformed so beautifully both to the assumptions and to the conclusions of his tradition, with such magnificent architectural logic between?

For that Aquinas' logic on its deductive side is magnificent I both grant and insist. The only criticism to be made is that — as I shall argue in the next chapter — equally rigorous logic can be used to derive contradictory theorems; for the premises contain inconsistent elements which equally validly point in opposite directions. Still, in a sense Aquinas is correct even here, in that his procedure is one which makes the maximal use of the experientially sound implications of the premises with a minimum of warping of the deductive chain. Most of those who have tried to patch up the traditional system have permitted more of the erroneous implications (those involving a misinterpretation of generic experiential insights) to figure in the deduction, without doing equally well by the sound ones, and usually without so much systematic skill in setting out the relationships. The only way to beat

Aquinas is to take as doubtful what he took as most certain in philosophy, and to experiment with other axioms. Until this is done, Thomists are entirely right in holding that Spinoza or Kant or Hegel or Bradley or Royce is, taking his system as a whole, at least no more rigorous than the gentle master — while at the same time as true to experience; although I for one am convinced that each of these men is more defensible on isolated points. Their value was that of explorers, who found new truths at the cost of forgetting some of the truths already known. Only three evaluations of their work are plausible: (1) it marks genuine but one-sided advances, whose full value must be found in a systematic revision of the tradition in the light of their discoveries; or (2) it marks for the most part mere decay, and had best be dismissed in favor of the medieval synthesis; or (3) it represents the lingering self-annihilation of the superstition that metaphysics is a legitimate study, and we had best start over again with a purely positivistic program. These are also the three reactions most in evidence today. The time has gone by for patchwork. A radical but systematic revision of Thomism from top to bottom, a radical rejection of the metaphysical enterprise — these are the two ways of finding positive value in the work of modern philosophy. On any other view it is a failure, as Roman Catholics accuse it of being.

If the ultimate object of philosophy and theology — God as the integrated sum of existence — is both necessary and contingent, both perfect and perfectible, then metaphysics, which studies the necessary aspect, is not the whole of philosophy or theology, which must consist rather of a synthesis of metaphysics and all special sciences whatever, including any " revelation " of contingent aspects of God there may be. People often think exclusively of this synthesis when they speak of philosophy, and they sometimes even infer that philosophy is primarily a dream for the future, when the task of the sciences is completed — if it ever is. But philosophy in its totality is rather the contemplation of what has an everlasting, necessary, and at all times knowable essence, together with the contemplation of as many of the contingent features of the contemplated object as may be accessible to us. Thus philosophy (and theology is only philosophy as developed from the standpoint of the faith or religious experience of a person or group, rather than from the standpoint of the minimal common faith or experience of men in general) is all of knowledge, though there is an aspect of philosophy which is independent of all other knowledge, as there is an aspect of the object of philosophy which is independent of all other things.

The conflict now going on between second-type theism, as necessarily dual in method, and third-type or purely empirical theology, may seem to refute the suggestion made in the previous chapter that present-day theology is tending toward convergent results. This is true except to the extent that empirical theologians may not be wholly free from metaphysical arguments, and in a number of cases (for instance, the outstanding one of F. R. Tennant) they seem to me in fact not thus free, and in this way they attain to some form of second-type doctrine. For example, Professor Brightman says God's will is perfect, though his ability to carry it out is not.[3] But on empirical grounds (unless religious experience be made the decisive datum) how can we decide between this view and the notion that God's ability is perfect, although his intentions are not wholly benevolent? Either way we explain the facts of evil which Professor Brightman has in mind. Further, his notion of the Given as an intrinsic limitation of God's power, a passive element in his activity, analogous to sensation and emotion in us, can be defined and defended only in the context of an adequate analysis of what is or can be meant by " passivity," " sensation," etc.; and the exploration of such concepts taken in their most fundamental or general senses, as they here must be, can only amount to a metaphysical system whose defense is not merely empirical, since the very meaning of " experience," " facts," etc., will have to be grounded by this system. (In such a system it might, I suggest, appear that " passive " only means " acted upon by another," so that the Given can only be a relation to some activity other than the divine, and therefore cannot be explained merely by a limitation, or anything else, in God alone.)

However this may be, I do not see how one can survey theological writings of recent decades and not feel that a new reformation is in progress. Protestantism, having lived on the crumbs of medieval theology for centuries, is now really facing the issues for itself.

The severity of some of my strictures against first-type theism must be weighed in the light of my contention that this doctrine serves to " block the path of inquiry " (Peirce) , thus committing the greatest of logical sins. Defenders of the doctrine in effect hold that the maximal verbally possible formulation of God's superiority makes such perfect and undeniable sense that no careful examination of more qualified formulations need or should be made.[4] They urge that the verbally maximal is also the minimal conception of God worth considering, without inquiry into the possibility that absolute maximization results in nonsense rather than in a positive maximal concept, or into the possibility that both maximality and a protean character of infinite expansiveness, rather than mere expandedness, are required for a consistent view of the supreme being. The two concepts may be polar contrasts each of which is essential to the other. Thus the attitude of first-type theism has in common with that of atheism the tendency to bar the path of inquiry into the formal possibilities.

On the other hand, " empirical " theologians or philosophers also (because of their consciousness of the abuses to which deduction is subject) frequently fail to examine adequately the formal character of their " hypothesis," its consistency, simplicity (or hyper-simplicity), deductive structure, and logically possible alternatives. Empiricists, like metaphysicians, are often too impatient to arrive at proof, even though in their case it is an empirical proof that is sought.

That there is no unambiguous priority of the " proofs " for God over his definition (material for the definition being furnished, say, by religious tradition) can be seen in another way. One of the alleged proofs, which, according to Kant at least, is presupposed by all the others, is the ontological, and this proof is based on the definition of God. The proof has been rejected by many illustrious theologians; but also it has been accepted by many illustrious theologians. Rejection has generally been on the ground that we cannot know the nature of God (as at least not impossible — and so much the ontological argument must presuppose) except by the same proofs as serve, without the ontological argument, to establish the existence of God. (This is not quite the Kantian treatment of the matter, which will be considered in chapter 9.) This reasoning is based on the old principle that we do not positively and literally know what God is, we do not know him in himself, but in the creatures, in his effects, as infinitely less than and other than himself. However, this principle is so equivocal, so subject in most theologians (with a few honorable exceptions — or seeming exceptions — as in the candid Maimonides, or the perhaps less candid, certainly less systematic, Philo) to dilution through the doctrine of "analogy," taken positively, that it is a dubious foundation for the rejection of the ontological argument. This much I believe can be maintained with safety, that if the description by analogy is not purely dishonest, a bluff, it does give us some dim notion of what positively God is, and furthermore, even such a dim notion should teach us something about whether or not a being so described is conceivable (which, as we shall see, is the only form of possibility here required). To have absolutely no notion of the consistency or inconsistency of an idea, or no notion of whether or not one really has an idea and not rather a set of words without meaning, is to have no idea whatever, even analogical. Therefore there ought to be some significance to the ontological argument, some of the usual objections to which are demonstrably untenable.

It is, for instance, demonstrably illogical to object that properties cannot imply existence on the ground that in the case of beings other than God they do not do so; for it is plain that the properties of contingent beings must be contingently related to existence, and equally plain, as based on the converse of the same reason, that the properties, at least the essential properties (whether or not these are the only ones) of a necessary being, one whose existence is not accidental or derivative, *cannot* be contingently related to existence. Now to all theologians (of type one or two) God is a necessary, and the only necessary, being. Hence to object to the ontological argument on the basis of a supposed principle that essence cannot imply existence is to argue from a premise that is equally fatal to any argument for God (first or second type) and to the mere possibility of there being a God — in short, is to argue from an atheistic (or at least finitistic) assumption.

Since necessity of existence is essential to God (as he is almost universally conceived), one of two things must be true: the conception, universal as it is, is sheer nonsense, contradicting the basic law connecting properties and individuals; or this law is not absolute, because of the metaphysical uniqueness of the supreme being. In the latter case the ontological argument is in so far valid; in the former, we must admit a negative ontological argument, in disproof of God, and such an argument is likely to be accepted by atheists. It is quite conceivable that some definitions of God, at least, contain discoverable self-contradictions, and hence suffice to disprove the God so defined. Indeed, it is a common accusation against traditional theology that its basic definition is in truth inconsistent with itself (a mind without a body, a will without change, etc.). This might be apparent quite apart from an estimate of the proofs supposed to establish the existence of an object of the definition. For, once more, if we have no content for our conclusion from the theistic arguments, no content conceivable in abstraction from the arguments, then it is hard to see in what sense they are arguments or the conclusion is a conclusion. If we have a content, its consistency must be open to inquiry. If it proves inconsistent, then we have a valuable clue to the interpretation of the alleged proofs. We know that they are unsatisfactory (certainly many great minds have thought them so) and, more than that, we have an indication of the locus of the fallacy. We know that it need not necessarily lie in the proofs, in so far as they are proofs for God, since it may lie rather in them in so far as they are taken as proofs for the *kind* of God covered by the self-contradictory definition. If there is an alternative definition available, with enough in common with the traditional definition to apply reasonably to "God," perhaps with even more exact appropriateness to the real nature of religion from which the idea of God seems to have sprung, and on the other hand differing from the older definition on just the points which involved this definition in contradictions, then it may turn out that the proofs as revised to fit the new definition are not fallacious at all.

Any fair-minded person must admit that it would be rationally satisfying to learn that the trust placed in these venerable proofs by so many of the most acute minds of all times has not been purely unfounded, and yet that on the other hand the confidence with which the proofs as they stand have been rejected by minds as great as Hume, Russell, Kant, Dewey, was also well founded. Any other eventuation to the ancient controversy is so deep an insult to human reason itself that one who thinks candidly must feel that he himself can hardly escape the implications of this insult. If theology has been sheer folly — and many of the wisest men, even down to the present, have been theologians — then who can have confidence of being wise? And if theology has been practically pure wisdom, while at least a respectable minority of wise men have seen little in it but folly, then again the human mind is a feeble instrument indeed. Perhaps it is that, and certainly it has its feebleness, but any less despairing hypothesis that seems capable of explaining the conflict deserves a hearing. Such a hypothesis, as we have suggested, is available. It cannot have been adequately refuted; for those who do not accept it are those largely unacquainted with it. To end this situation is a major philosophical task of our generation.

The question, Is there a God? methodologically considered means, Is there an inherent harmony, capable of logical expression, between the religious and the secular functions of the human mind, and of the world as portrayed in these functions? It is the possibility of " secular functions " (Whitehead) for God which makes the bridge, if there is one, between faith and reason. Or, the bridge may be expressed as the possibility of implicit religious functions for secular concepts (concepts like that of time or space or the cosmos). If there be such an ultimate identity in the implications of religion and everyday life, it follows that the non-believer is mistaken in thinking he does not believe, since merely to live a secular life is, on this hypothesis, to affirm God in the same sense, whatever it be, in which the religious person affirms him, although in the latter case there is fuller consciousness of the content of the affirmation. I am totally unable to conceive any argument for the religious conception (first or second type) which does not imply that the difference between believers and unbelievers is nothing but a difference in self-consciousness and consistency in regard to what all believe " at heart," or in so far as action is the ultimate expression of what a man believes. For if God exists, then, according to nearly all theologies, he is ubiquitous, hence present in the experience of the most hardened skeptic or sinner, and only by some sort of self-contradiction denied by any mind. To deny God cannot mean to shut him out of one's experience, if so be that he exists; and since we are always talking about experience if we talk significantly at all, and since God is in every fragment and aspect of experience or nowhere, hence either we must always be contradicting everything we say when we deny God, or else there is no God in anyone's experience, and consequently it is the believer who means nothing when he says, " There is a God " (for God could mean something only through experience). The theological question, like all genuinely philosophical questions, is infinitely radical, and this being so the difference between the theological yes and the theological no cannot possibly be measured by the variations in wholly genuine human belief, but only by the gap between what must, in some underlying stratum of affirmation, be intended by all men, and what cannot really and wholeheartedly be intended by any man. Philosophers might be divided into those who see this radical nature of their problems and those who do not; and this division seems to me almost to coincide with that between philosophers and (at most) students of philosophy. By this test, logical positivists are philosophers; for they see that if, for instance, there is no (absolute) God, it can only be because nobody really thinks there is, and the question is meaningless, except when we are feeling rather than thinking.

Though it is annoying to some persons to be told that they may really believe what they think they doubt or deny, yet, on the other hand, the invidiousness of theological dispute is really, it seems to me, greatly mitigated if we recognize that what we are engaged upon is an effort, through cooperation, to discover what the bottom layer of our common human thought really is. And those who are irritated or scornful concerning the alleged ability of their fellows to tell them what they themselves "really" believe should remember that the reverse claim is equally in order: religious people, for example, must admit, as a hypothesis for discussion, the view that whoever says of himself that he believes in God is quite mistaken as to the reality of this belief of his.

In short, we not only believe, we believe that we believe. There are strands and levels of belief, by no means necessarily wholly consistent with each other. The task of philosophy is entirely that of finding, by the two methods of logical analysis and recollection of key phases of experience, those truths which in terms of feeling and living we never can be wholly separated from, and therefore must also consciously believe if belief is to achieve consistency and sincerity.

The theist who says he believes in Providence, but shows that he has little but anxiety for the future, contradicts his words by his deeds and attitudes. But so, one might argue, does the atheist who says there is no Providence, and yet relies upon a long-run future such as will never destroy the significance of his present choices and efforts. The difference between the two cases is that (1) it is possible to face the future with an indefinite approximation to the serenity implied by faith in Providence (so interpreted, however, as not to imply that there is no kind of risk in the time process), and (2) it is desirable to set up this approximation as an ideal; whereas an indefinite approximation to a complete lack of trust in the future is simply an indefinite approximation to the destruction of the will to live and is the reverse of an ideal, being denied by the mere continued living, even though halfhearted, of pessimists. (It would be denied even by suicide; for that too is an act, a choice. Only the man who dies by sheer force of despair — nay, not even he, unless the despair be wholly involuntary, and can it be so? — could really be said to believe nothing as to the reliability of the cosmos.)

Faith in God means trust in the value of choice not merely in practical affairs; there is also a phase of the problem in the theoretical life. The very " ground of induction " (the reality of natural laws or reliable uniformities) is some sort of faith, even though it is one to which there is no conceivable alternative — as there never is to a philosophical tenet, if we see clearly into our own minds. The alternative to faith is merely confusion or unconsciousness, not a doctrine credible in the same sense. I do not believe atheists have yet succeeded in drawing the theoretical boundary between their obviously real faith and that which they say they deny. The difference seems to be one of explicitness, except in so far as atheists rightly reject certain explicit formulations of traditional theology which there is good reason to think do not represent the actual content of theism as a working faith.

In the last few sentences, I have slipped into a statement of my own religious beliefs. But, whatever one's beliefs, it is a corollary of the incomplete credibility of the philosophically false that alternative "hypotheses" are not, as in science, equally meaningful as possibilities, though differing in truth value, but rather a class of quasi-possible views, only one of which is genuinely conceivable and possible. It is for this reason that we must strive for formally exhaustive divisions, since to reject at the outset as patently absurd, or to overlook altogether, a formally possible view is to forget that *all* the views *but one* will prove patently absurd when their pretended meaning is adequately scrutinized, and that it is more or less accidental and personal which views exhibit their absurdity most easily, immediately, and reliably (for the true view, if subtly misunderstood, will also appear as absurd).

Formal classifications, being neutral, preserve us from overemphasis upon accidental and subjective factors, force us to give careful consideration to all of a set of views among which the true must, by formal necessity, be included, and hence enable us to judge the absurdity of the others by the only safe criterion, which is the "light of the true idea itself" (Spinoza). If any view is omitted from consideration, and this happens to be the true one, then we will only be comparing absurdities; and the one which appears to us least absurd will be the one which is most protected from our adequate scrutiny, for some reason personal to us, such as the force of tradition or the charm of novelty, or at least it will be the one whose inadequacy is less readily seen in a given state of culture, or even one harder to detect owing to the very generic character of the human mind (Bacon's " idol of the tribe ").

Since, of the three principal logical possibilities in theology, two (One and Three) have long ago been widely and carefully explored, and since now at long last the third (Two) is receiving widespread attention, the most general question which theology involves must be not very far from such possibility of a rational answer as human powers permit. The rest depends probably upon non-rational factors chiefly, such as the varying strength of clerical and anti-clerical politics and emotions, or the degree of concentration of attention upon narrowly limited problems of science and life. Man's various interests must compete as well as cooperate; for his attention span is small. And one cannot remain wholly rational about an idea which is the final integrating principle of thought about emotions and values in general, as well as about truth values or facts. He can only do the best he can, by striving to sympathize with the positions of other thinkers, by cultivating interest in the logical aspects of the problem as fascinating intellectual patterns like any others, by meditating upon the ethics of inquiry, and by recalling that men of fine minds seem to live not badly, some of whom do and some of whom do not accept any given idea concerning God. Anyone who knows how many concealed as well as overt forms prejudice and stubborn pride or other forms of intellectual incompetence in these matters can take will not be too anxious to condemn my book utterly because of the signs of such failings which he may all too probably discover in it.

NOTES

[1] See *Beyond Humanism,* chap. 16.

[2] See Lewis, *Mind and the World Order,* pp. 367 ff.

[3] See E. S. Brightman, *The Problem of God* (Abingdon Press, 1930). Professor Brightman's position is perhaps not intended to be empirical in the narrow sense which I am criticizing. Professor D. C. Macintosh calls his own method empirical, but expressly provides for a metaphysical element.

[4] This is how Jacques Maritain characterizes Scholastic metaphysics: "It knew with perfect certainty that it had followed without the least interruption the thread of the logical necessities" (*Réflexions sur l'intelligence,* p. 281). Previously Maritain has informed his readers that William James and other pragmatists have reached "humiliating absurdities" in their theological speculations because they followed a method which renounces interest in the truth. It should, I think, be clear that Maritain's own rhetorical method, as here displayed, is well enough adapted to defend such truth as Scholasticism may have in its possession but less likely to be helpful if perchance there are important truths with which Scholastic doctrines are incompatible.

III

THE TWO STRANDS IN HISTORICAL THEOLOGY

Now if we look at the definitions of God made by dogmatic theology, we see immediately that some stand and some fall when treated by this [the pragmatic] test. God . . . as any orthodox textbook will tell us, is a being existing . . . *a se,* or from himself; and out of this " aseity " flow most of his perfections. He is for example, . . . simple, not compounded of . . . substance and accident, actuality and potentiality. . . . He is inwardly and outwardly unalterable; he knows and wills all things . . . in one indivisible eternal act. And he is absolutely self-sufficing, and infinitely happy. Now in which of us practical Americans here assembled does this conglomeration of attributes awaken any sense of reality? And if in no one, then why not? Surely because such attributes awaken no responsive active feelings and call for no particular conduct of our own. How does God's " aseity " come home to *you?* What specific thing can I do to adapt myself to his " simplicity "? Or how determine our behavior henceforward if his " felicity " is anyhow absolutely complete . . . ? The attributes I have quoted have absolutely nothing to do with religion, for religion is a living practical affair. Other parts, indeed, of God's traditional description do have practical connection with life, and have owed all their historic importance to that fact. His omniscience, for example, and his justice. With the one he sees us in the dark, with the other he rewards and punishes what he sees. So do his ubiquity and eternity and unalterability appeal to our confidence, and his goodness banish our fears. . . . And yet even these more real and significant attributes have the trail of the serpent over them, as the books on theology have actually worked them out.

WILLIAM JAMES, in "Philosophical Conceptions and Practical Results," reprinted in *Collected Essays and Reviews*

IF ALL IDEAS are in some sense derived from experience, then one of the first steps in examining the idea of God should be to ask, From what aspects of experience has it been derived? No doubt so fundamental an idea is based in some way or degree upon widely different experiences, but still, if it is a conception distinguishable from others, there must be privileged experiences which particularly serve to give it meaning — whether or not they suffice to prove it true. At any rate, such privileged experiences with respect to the idea of God do seem to exist, and they bear the familiar name of religious experiences. In a philosophical theology one does not wish to make such experiences the chief reason for the conclusion that God exists, since the purpose of philosophical inquiry into theology is to discover what other reasons, if any, there may be for this conclusion. But in view of the large if not decisive part which religion has had in the very origin of the theological idea, and in view of the enormous social importance which this idea enjoys only through religion, it is doubly reasonable to begin the investigation with an attempt to discover what God may be *as the God of religion.* (In this sense, the distinction between natural and revealed theology cannot, by the canons of the former itself, be made absolute.) If the resulting conception proves unsatisfactory philosophically, then we may consider whether philosophy can, from non-religious sources, improve upon the religious view, either by denying any God or by setting up some concept of God sufficiently similar to the religious to perhaps justify the use of the same term. (For religion seems clearly to have first title to the word.) But these possibilities should not chiefly concern us until we have isolated the religious idea, defined it as accurately as possible, and then evaluated the idea, so defined, by whatever philosophical resources we can muster.

Much theological writing is badly confused by the assumption that by " God " is to be meant indifferently what religious people as religious mean by it, and what various philosophers, who may also have been religious men, have meant philosophically by the term. Thus it is hard for some to imagine that the God of the latter portions of the Bible, surely the religious God, needs distinguishing from the God, say, of Anselm, Augustine, or Aquinas, as described by these men speaking as philosophers. Because they were sincerely religious, it is assumed that they could never have departed from the religious idea. I am morally certain, however, that unconsciously they did so; and I have some confidence that readers with reasonable patience will find that this conviction, which is shared today by many thinkers, even some distinguished Roman Catholics, is not without grounds worth taking into serious account.

Santayana has said, apropos of Bacon's famous remark, that, while " much philosophy " may indeed restore the faith which " a little philosophy " tends to destroy, it is not faith *in the same God* that finally results. That this is what has happened to many philosophers, for example to Spinoza, would be widely admitted. That it has happened to *all* the great orthodox theologians of past ages has been less generally admitted; while a clear statement of the points of difference between religious and philosophical conceptions of God, with an evaluation of the possible philosophical uses of the former, is not easy to find anywhere in the vast theological literature.

The charge that philosophers have not taken the religious idea seriously may seem strange. In a sense they have taken it very seriously. Most philosophical theologians — that is to say, probably, most philosophers — have supposed their doctrines to contain the content of religious faith plus only certain logical refinements, or minus certain anthropomorphic crudities. But it is possible that the refinements are of such a nature as to destroy the value of the idea; or it is possible that the idea of God *ought* to be "anthropomorphic," not only for religious but even for philosophical purposes. Anthropomorphism has been shown to be one horn of a not easily evaded dilemma: either we assimilate things to our own human experience and nature, and so perhaps fail to appreciate the extent of their differences from us, or we try to interpret them quite apart from our experience and nature, and then find that this is the same as having no idea of them at all. The only obvious complete alternative to anthropomorphism is the doctrine of an absolutely unknowable, a "thing in itself." What things are for us, what we can get out of them, do with them, enjoy in the experience of them, that we can know. Also, what they may be as analogous to ourselves, like us, knowing, willing, loving beings — though perhaps less or more knowing, willing less or more powerfully, loving less or more comprehensively — all this we can conceive. But how we can even significantly ask, What can things be, neither as values to us nor as beings conceivable by analogy to us? has proved of the utmost difficulty to explain. Hence if God is the "wholly other," he is, philosophically regarded, an unattractive theme, to say the least.

In view of the dilemma mentioned (so brilliantly analyzed in Hume's *Dialogues*) we should be willing to give careful attention to religious anthropomorphism, as well as to philosophical attempts to transcend it, without too much initial confidence that either one, in traditional form, can be entirely accepted. This is all the more true because the contrast between anthropomorphism and its alternative falls within religion as well as between religion and philosophy. Primitive religion and polytheistic religion are indeed " crudely " anthropomorphic, whereas the " higher " theistic religions are precisely those which avoid at least some among the ways of humanizing deity. The difference is in brief this, that while in pretty much all religion the object of worship is the superhuman, in the higher religions the superiority of deity is taken much more strictly and absolutely, so that God becomes as it were the mathematical limit or maximum of certain properties that admit of more and less, and yet without his being regarded as a mere ideal or abstraction. Just here is the problem: can there be a concrete maximum of attributes like goodness, knowledge, or power? For instance, power must be exercised upon something, at least if by power we mean influence, control; but the something controlled cannot be absolutely inert, since the merely passive, that which has no active tendency of its own, is nothing; yet if the something acted upon is itself partly active, then there must be some resistance, however slight, to the " absolute " power, and how can power which is resisted be absolute? If these questions can be satisfactorily answered, we have also to consider the possibility that some dimensions of value, such as happiness, are inherently protean, capable of expansion beyond any concrete case whatever. Yet such protean dimensions may necessarily apply to God, since it may well be that the non-protean dimensions require them, so that God cannot, for instance, be maximally good or powerful unless he is capable of endless growth, say in happiness. I care not how absurd this may seem to some readers; they must none the less face the fact that any other view seems absurd indeed to some of us, and the further fact that to distinguish real absurdity from the merely unfamiliar or misunderstood has been proved a delicate matter in philosophy.

Because of these difficulties, by no means all of which will be found adequately discussed in older theological writings, it is important to avoid hasty answers to the question, In what sense, or senses, precisely do high religions conceive God as the maximal, the " supreme," being? Very likely the answer is, In *every* sense in which the idea of a maximum has a meaning; for it is fairly obvious that piety has centered in the notion that God is exalted beyond all that we can conceive, so that genuine exaggeration in the praise of God is felt to be impossible. But to talk sheer nonsense is not to praise, with or without exaggeration; so that our question still remains, What are the dimensions or attributes of comparison in terms of which God may be the absolutely highest instance, or concrete limit, and how is this limiting case to be conceived? Is the highest degree of anything different from limited degrees by a " difference in degree " or by a " difference in kind "?

Our concern now is with such questions not as for philosophy to answer, but as for *religion* to answer, not so that philosophy may accept, but so that it may weigh and consider these religious answers. It cannot do so till it knows what the answers are. This knowledge philosophy has possessed only to a very imperfect degree during the twenty-five centuries of philosophical theologizing. The reasons are highly complex. A bare hint must suffice here. The problem for medieval thought was to harmonize the technical knowledge of the Greeks with the higher wisdom of the Scriptures, taking an optimistic view of the literal truth and adequacy of both. We today wish to know rather what is the main kernel of religious doctrine, first of all regardless of any philosophy whatever, and without assuming the infallibility of scriptural texts or their complete consistency. We do not necessarily assume that religion has any kernel that makes sense, but we take as methodological principle the advisability of looking for a reasonable religious tenet; since only he who has honestly looked for something can significantly report the failure to find it. And he must have looked without any other absorbing preoccupation, such as ecclesiastical dictates, political ambitions, faith in the near-rightness of Plato or Aristotle, or in previous commentators on the Scriptures. In short, a little of the garden variety of Protestant freedom and recklessness, plus some sense of historical objectivity, is called for.

But how can one hope to hear the testimony of high religion uncontaminated by philosophy, in view of the fact that the high religions came to maturity only after the rise of philosophy? There seem to be two answers. One might go to what is technically classified as revelation, for instance to the Scriptures — perhaps Hindu, Chinese, Mohammedan, etc., as well as Christian — and one might also consult the official creeds of the various churches. Possible objections would be that revelation is itself almost if not quite a philosophical concept, that some of the scriptural authors were philosophically inclined, and that the creeds certainly are not free from philosophical influences. See, for example, the term " substance " in the longer Christian creed. Still, there is little philosophy of the technical sort in the biblical writings, at least, and not much in the more popular creeds, such as the Apostles'. In any case, we can check the results of this method by another. This is to ask ourselves what kind of idea of God, or what aspects of the usual philosophical idea, are actually used in recognized religious functions and attitudes, such as prayer, sense of sin, salvation. Fortunately, this method has already been followed with admirable care and precision by

D. C. Macintosh, in his book *The Reasonableness of Christianity*.[1]

The two methods lead without much appearance of disharmony to a fairly definite idea quite clearly distinguished from the traditional philosophical one, and distinguished not only from the idea that philosophers have generally accepted, but even from any idea that they have until recently conceived sufficiently clearly even to criticize — an oversight that makes ordinary adjectives seem futile! Naturally, the religious idea cannot be unfamiliar to most of us; what is unfamiliar is the sharp definition of this idea so as to make it explicit on philosophical questions without smuggling in assumptions not logically involved in it.

Whatever the gods were taken to be, man's relations to them were conceived as social, or quasi-social. All the gods were either friends or enemies, akin to man; all of them had some power to pass judgment upon human affairs, either moral or selfish, merely personal, judgment. In the process of cultural advance religious friendship with gods was finally conceived as the maximal case of friendship, as on the side of deity at least the one perfect social relationship, involving complete understanding and love. Also the judgment of deity upon human affairs came at last to be thought of exclusively as one of the highest ethical type,[2] a judgment sensitive to the interests of all parties concerned, and hostile only to those who themselves were averse to the recognition of the interests of others (or at least blind to them) and hostile even to such persons only so far as they were limited in this manner. This is of course the same conception as that of the perfect friend, but with emphasis upon the universal scope of the divine friendship.

The concept of maximal friendship or justice did away with the idea of many gods; for the plurality of these was relevant only because of the partialness of their functions as friends and judges.

But the gods were not merely the terms of social relations of understanding, sympathy, and appeal to judgment; they were involved in practical social relations, relations of co-operation. They were powers, agents with effects in the world of nature, as man himself has effects, but here again with the difference that eventually the maximal case emerged, and the gods became the one God whose effects, like his understanding and justice, were universal, cosmic, supreme.

Thus the God of high religion is the all-loving and supremely efficacious friend of men and of all creatures, of the lion seeking his prey, of the birds building their nests. As supremely efficacious, God is the everlasting and ungenerated controlling power of the universe — the only way a maximum of efficacy can be conceived.

Thus it is a short step to the assertion that God is that without which other beings would not exist at all, would be nothing. And it seems only another way of saying this to state that God is in some sense Being itself, while all other things participate in being through God. Or as Ikhnaton, in his superlatively beautiful way, said over three thousand years ago, "Thou of thyself art length of life, men live through thee."

Although for all high religions, with the not unambiguous exception of Buddhism, God is the supreme agent in the universe, yet that he is also "creator," in any further sense than that of being the *maximal productive power* in every stage of reality, however remote in time and space, is not by any means clearly implied by religious feeling. The Hindus seem to have been little concerned with the idea of a beginning of reality in time; the book of Genesis, according to some scholars at least, is not clear on the point;

for Plato the religious view seemingly is that the matter which creation molds is itself uncreated. The New Testament has little to say on the question. And legends which describe how a god made the world which we know, the earth, the heavens, etc., are quite consistent with the view that though God created, in the sense of first producing, the present system of nature, this production consisted in the transformation, as radical as you please, given time enough, of an earlier, to us unimaginable, nature, which itself may have been similarly produced out of a still earlier state of things. (Origen believed in an infinite series of past worlds, though he did hold each world to have been made out of not-being rather than out of its predecessor.) Not only is the unambiguous contradiction of this view not nearly so widespread as is high religion and its idea of God (as we have defined it) but there is in this idea and its implications no obvious necessity for any such contradiction. The perfection and efficacy of a friendship cannot depend upon its having been exercised only upon the present cosmos, rather than also upon an infinity of earlier universes, each produced out of its predecessor, more or less catastrophically or gradually. Does it make God more powerful to say that he has acted creatively, with respect not to infinite but only to finite past time?

However this may be, the God of religion is certainly to be described as the supremely loving *friend,* the perfectly righteous *judge,* and the primordial and everlasting ruler or supremely controlling *power* of the universe. He is that without which all lesser individuals would be nothing, since devoid of definitive measure, ground of relationship with others, etc. So far, this may seem to be the usual philosophical idea of God. But philosophers have generally affirmed these religious tenets subject to the proviso that they should not conflict with certain other assumptions, of quite other than religious origin and justification. Unfortunately, this proviso, carried out logically, nullifies the religious idea completely.

Such non-religious tenets, to which religion has been forced to bow, are: that God is non-temporal in the sense of having no past or future, since he knows all things in one eternal present; that God is purely active, in no respect or relation passive to anything; that he created the world "out of nothing," implying a beginning of creaturely existence in time; that he is "without body, parts, or passions," absolutely "simple" or unitary, a superintellectual being void of emotions, and also of will, if will involves internal distinctions between anticipatory and consummatory experience, or if it involves the prior lack of any value which is subsequently to be realized.

There are several remarkable features of these ideas. First, they all belong logically together, so that there is little use in judging any of them in isolation. Either we accept them one and all, or we reject them one and all, or we merely bungle the matter. Here is the explanation of the failure of many attempts at reconstruction in theology: they sought to pick and choose among ideas which are really inseparable aspects of one idea. Here also is seen the genius of the great theologians of the past, that they really saw the logical interrelations between a large number of affirmations (they are really and admittedly denials, negations) about God. But the second point is that the logical relations between what I have called the religious and the non-religious tenets are less satisfactory. They are indeed satisfying enough from one standpoint, and in justice to the older theologians this is the one from which the matter was considered. I refer to the fact that from the non-religious tenets the religious can after a fashion be derived. (We shall see later wherein consists the qualification " after a fashion.") But the crucial point is that the reverse derivation, of the non-religious from the religious tenets, cannot be exhibited; worse still, the religious tenets can be shown to imply the falsity of the non-religious. Since, on the other hand, the non-religious do imply the religious tenets, what we have is a contradictory system of premises whose own conclusions imply their falsity. If this is the situation, as I am about to try to show, then any logician can see the consequence. The non-religious tenets are implicitly self-contradictory, and hence not true, while the truth or falsity of the religious tenets remains, so far, an open question. (If p implies q, and q implies not-p, but q does not imply p, then p is self-contradictory, but q need not be so.)

From the assumption, God is a purely actual, impassive being, the absolutely independent cause upon which all other things depend, it follows that he contains actually all possible value, or is perfect. Being perfect, he cannot change; possessing all " perfections," he must know all things by an immutable act above time; he must have power, will, love, all the truly " positive " attributes in maximal degree. He has everything except what connotes negation or deficiency, such as ignorance, wickedness, conflict of purposes, sense organs, etc. Thus from the mere notion of self-sufficiency or " aseity " Scholastics deduce all the other attributes of God, including those I have termed religious. This is the seeming logical power of their system, extremely crudely sketched here. But the system has three weaknesses.

First, the derivation of religious tenets works only, as I have said, " after a fashion." If you raise the question, Is God righteous, or all-knowing, or all-loving? then the Scholastic tenets do require the affirmative answer. But from the tenets themselves one would scarcely know that such questions could even be asked. That is, from the mere idea of self-dependent causation, or the uncaused cause, or pure actuality, one would never know, it seems, even that there were such attributes as love or goodness. Knowing otherwise of the attributes, and knowing, if we do know it, that they are not deficiencies, then we also know that God has them in highest degree; for he has everything in the highest degree which is capable of a highest degree. It is almost as if one were to say that God knows President Roosevelt, since President Roosevelt exists, and God knows all existence. But surely the truth, if it is true, that God loves is not a contingent fact like the existence of a man. Yet the Scholastic way of deriving this love seems almost to imply that it is a mere contingency. I say almost, because the bare way I have stated the matter is undoubtedly more or less of a caricature. Taking the whole of the Scholastic system into account, the externality of the derivation of religious tenets can be considerably mitigated. What I am very confident of is that it can be far more radically overcome in a different type of philosophy. But I do not wish to put the primary stress upon this objection.

The second weakness in the traditional system, with all its logical power, is that it is quite impossible to deduce the non-religious tenets upon which the system is founded from the religious tenets which the system also accepts. That is, all logical support is one-way only, from the philosophical or secular tenets to the religious, but not vice versa. Since all the tenets concern ultimate or necessary truths, they should mutually sustain and require each other. But only halfhearted attempts have been made to show that the religious require the secular (although colossal efforts have been expended to show the reverse relationship), and all such attempts seem to have failed. God could be all that religion believes he is, and yet the whole system of pure actuality, aseity, impassivity, immutability, immateriality, simplicity, be false. (The only difficulty would then be that we should have to seek some other secular assumptions from which the existence and nature of God could be determined if religion is to receive support from philosophy; but the discovery that certain proofs for a proposition rest upon false premises affords no certainty that sound proofs cannot be found.) It is, for instance, perfectly possible to conceive an omniscient being who changes. True, a being who changes will know more at one moment than at the preceding moment; but this implies that he was previously " ignorant " *only* if it be assumed that events are there to be known prior to their happening. For knowledge is true if, and only if, it corresponds to reality, and things that have not happened are, in so far, perhaps, not real. To know them would then be to know falsely, for there is nothing of the sort to know. If the future is indeterminate, if there is real freedom between alternatives, any one of which *can* happen, then the true way to know the future is as undetermined, unsettled. To know just what " is to happen " is to know falsely if there is in fact no definite thing which is to happen.[3]

Of course, it is held that God knows the future not as future to him but as belonging to all times in a single eternal present. But this doctrine is not deducible from the mere idea of omniscience, or the knowing of all reality as it is, until or unless it has been demonstrated that that which to us is future possesses objectively the same reality as that which to us is present or past; and this is a quite special and by no means self-evident doctrine about time, not in the least implied by any essential religious idea. Certainly the future as we experience it seems to be the partially unsettled, indeterminate, the somewhat nebulous. We may suppose this to be due to our ignorance, but how do we know that it is not rather, in part at least, the real character of the future? To be sure, much about the future that is unsettled for our knowledge we can indirectly see is not really in itself unsettled. When a new causal law is discovered, we can apply the law retrospectively and see that characters of once future events could have been foretold more definitely than we were in a position to do when the events were future (and before the discovery of the law). Also we know that we do not make anything like complete application even of all the well established laws, because of lack of time or inclination or ability to assemble the data or make the calculations. Still, none of this offers the least proof that, taking all the laws together, the future is wholly determined. This is precisely the question of determinism, over which the affirmative side has been fighting a rather losing battle during the past sixty-five years. Moreover, theologians have generally not been determinists. They have admitted that, since man is free, not all of the future could be known determinately through laws; but they have held that God knows events not through laws but in their individuality, and supertemporally. But *they did not validly derive this conclusion from the mere idea of omniscience.* For if the future is in fact unsettled, indeterminate, it would not be ignorance to see it as such, but, rather, true knowledge. Now, since the only way we have of knowing that the future is less indeterminate than our ignorance makes it appear is through the discovery of laws, in the manner just explained, we cannot use the admitted fact that some of the apparent indefiniteness of the future is only apparent as proof that all of it is so, since the real and the apparent are here distinguishable only so far as laws are known to extend, and it is an open question how far they do extend. We cannot inspect the contents of omniscience to discover if the future is determinately there.

To know that omniscience knows all individual events in their individuality, and not merely through general laws, does not help us here unless we also know that future events, as individual, exist; whereas, of course, some indeterminist philosophies conceive the contents of the future as, so long as they are future, partially general, unindividual, in essence.

It is sometimes argued, however, that we do know that future events are determinate. The law of excluded middle may be invoked. Either I will write the letter tomorrow or I will not write it tomorrow — only one of these can be true. The indeterminist may reply, Yes, only one of them can be true, but perhaps both of them are false; for the truth may be that it is unsettled that I will write the letter, and equally unsettled that I will not. The proposition, " I will write the letter," is either true or false, but to say it is false is not to say that the proposition, " I will not write the letter," is true. For " I will do it " means that the present state of affairs (perhaps my resolution of will, in part) determinately excludes my *not* doing it, while " I will not do it " means that the present state of affairs excludes my doing it; but between these is the situation expressed by " I may or may not do it," which means that the present situation of myself and indeed of the world in its totality is indeterminate with respect to my doing it. Or, in other words, it " will " occur means that *all* the possibilities for tomorrow which are still left open involve the occurrence in question; while it " may " occur means that *some* of the open possibilities involve the occurrence; and it " will not " occur means that *none* of the possibilities involve it. Thus we meet once more the fundamental triad, the almost childishly simple but generally neglected mathematical key to philosophical problems, of all, some, and none. And no violation of the law of excluded middle as applied to propositions is in question. For surely to deny "all" is not to decide between "some" and "none." Hence if "it will occur" is the proposition *p*, then the corresponding negative or not-*p* is, not the proposition "it will not occur," but rather the following: "Either it will not occur or, at least, it *may not* occur." Hence, granting that, given any proposition *p*, either *p* or not-*p* is true (the law of excluded middle), it does not follow that the future is determinate. The only "middle" which indeterminism refuses to exclude is that between all (possibilities) and none, and this middle is universally admitted in logic.

The only escape for our opponent must be in denying that there are such entities as possibilities, distinguishable from necessities or actualities, inherent in the constitution of the future as such. And for this denial logic has, to put it mildly, no legitimate support. Logic requires the idea of alternate possibilities (as the referents of conceivable, though mutually incompatible, hypotheses), since mathematics and the theory of induction alike require the idea. The only question is, Shall we locate such alternatives in time or not? If not in time, then not in the real world so far as we know it; for what do we know but the world of process? Thus logic must at the least refrain from denying the indeterminist theory of time, if it is not almost driven to assert it.

But still, you say, the future, when it comes, *will be* determinate. Yes, it will tomorrow be definitely true that (it rains or it does not rain). For when tomorrow comes, the possibilities for tomorrow that still remain "open" possibilities will have dwindled to zero, since the choice will have been made; hence it will no longer be true that some of the open possibilities involve the occurrence under discussion and some do not; for there will be no open possibilities. Thus, I may-or-may-not-do-it is only true in advance, and is in common sense only intended to be true in advance, of the time spoken of. The three cases of all, some, and none, dwindle, when the time spoken of arrives, to one case, which *must* be either the all or the none (say of the possibilities involving the letter-writing), although it may be false that there was any " must " making it the one or making it the other, since the must spoken of above only compels it to pass from the indeterminate to the determinate relation to the alternative.

It is of course true that may-or-may-not is ambiguous, having either a weak, subjective meaning, "*so far as we know,* either the expected event, or its non-occurrence, is compatible with the present state of the universe, with the totality of what exists," or a strong, objective meaning, such as "*even for perfect knowledge,* either of the two cases would at present be incompatible with actuality." In the case of " rain tomorrow," the weaker or subjective interpretation would usually be intended. But in the case of future personal decisions, or even the future behavior of an amoeba, it is more or less natural to common sense to intend the objective interpretation, namely, that existence includes both members of a pair of alternative possibilities as such, as real alternatives between which the course of events is to decide but which way it is to decide being definitely *not* decided. To reject the distinction between the subjective and the objective interpretation is merely to deny the relevance of the idea of possibility to actuality, and since Spinoza the difficulties of so doing have become increasingly clear.

It is to be admitted that the view I am defending is not so simple as the usual philosophic view. (Philosophic error can perhaps be more compendiously described as oversimplification than in any other way.) Thus, suppose I say, " It is unsettled whether I write or do not write the letter tomorrow." " Very well," says the determinist, " let us wait and see." Tomorrow comes, and I do not write the letter. " There, you see, it was true that you were not going to write it. Anyone who had so prophesied would have been vindicated, his prophecy would have been verified." " No," says the indeterminist, " all that has been shown is that when tomorrow had ceased to be tomorrow and had become today, it was definitely what it was; this is no proof that it was definitely 'going to be' what it in fact became." The prophecy in question was fulfilled, it " came true," but it is not necessarily to be regarded as vindicated, verified. If the prophet had seen that my character was such that I was likely to do as he foretold, then indeed he would have had knowledge of the future (as probable, not certain), but this kind of determinateness of the future we are admitting — namely, determination through law. For a man's character is a sort of law of his being — whether or not it can be reduced to a mere special case of the general laws of nature. But the question is, How far do such determining tendencies go?

A solitary case of successful prophecy may be mere coincidence. Unless the prophet makes many successful predictions, we cannot assume that he has knowledge even of mild probabilities, not to mention certainties, absolute predeterminations. A successful prediction is quite distinguishable from a verified one, inasmuch as the determinateness of the future as future can be verified only so long as the future is the future, that is, so long as it is not the present — *except so far as the future consists of laws* which, being general, can have been observed in the past and yet have application to the future. The future as strictly individual could be verified only by direct anticipatory intuition, such as many clairvoyants claim to enjoy. (Or do they, for the most part, content themselves in effect with claiming simply an unusual insight into relatively specific determining tendencies?) It is too late to verify such intuition in an isolated case when the future has become present. We verify only a more or less exact correspondence between expectation and result which is perfectly conceivable as a coincidence in a world in which the outcome were not determined to come out as it did.

I conclude that omniscience does not imply a knowledge "above time." There could be a future even to an all-knowing being. When a future event comes to happen, such a mind will know more than it did before, but at both times it will know all that there is, though at the later time there will be a new event to know. No ignorance will be involved, if ignorance is accurately defined, namely as the failure to know some existent thing as existent, or some possible thing as possible, or some partly determinate, partly indeterminate thing as both determinate and indeterminate to just the extent that it really is so. Ignorance is a lack of correspondence of knowledge to what is known, a lack of adequacy to the object. Indeterminism justly denies any such lack in a mind's not knowing details of a future which as future has no details to be known.

It is astonishing that the impossibility of inferring divine foresight of details from omniscience has escaped so many great minds. It is, however, evident what a relief to religion it will be to realize that "predestination" is a religiously groundless conception. It might, of course, seem that this conception has religious value; but I hold it to be too evident almost for argument that it has, rather, irreligious value, that it has often nearly ruined religion, caused it to fall into hopeless conflict with itself and to make nonsense of the relations of God and man. In the whole of the world's Scriptures, Mohammedanism apart, it is hard to find the idea.

But, you will ask, what becomes of the idea of Providence? The religious conception of God as friend certainly implies that God has prearranged the course of events so far as it would be friendly to do so. Is it evident that it would express friendship to prearrange things to the last detail? To me the opposite is evident. Friends respect the independence of their friends. Why should God insist upon deciding all things for us? If he does, he is an absolute tyrant, not the God of religion. Theologians themselves have generally admitted that God gives us real freedom and responsibility. In that case why need Providence, as predestination, be anything more than a plan setting wholesome limits to our eccentricities, and guiding the world as a whole in a desirable general direction, in spite of the fact that each member of it has within limits its own determining initiative?

But we must consider "omnipotence." That to be capable of change is to be weak rather than omnipotent is, I suggest, a weak argument. Theologians usually grant that men, not God, are responsible for human choices, at least the evil ones, and that God's creative action is prevented in this way from producing a perfect world. How change could limit omnipotence any more than this admission does I fail to see. If "omnipotence" is defined reasonably, both "limitations" will appear as implied by the term rather than as limitative of it. This we shall see more fully later. Omnipotence or "perfect power" is by no means the same as pure impassivity, and does not imply it. It is surely not simply because of their weakness that men are influenced by each other. A strong man is open to many an influence that leaves a cat beautifully "impassive." Weakness is in being influenced in the wrong directions, or disproportionately, as by a friend more than by a stranger in a dispute in which both have equal right to be heard. Love is exalted as much through its passive as through its active side. Insensitiveness is power only to the extent that it may compensate for the lack of sensitiveness in some other direction, producing in a negative, that is, inferior, form the value of balance which the strongly sensitive have in positive form.

But is not the religious sense one of " complete dependence " upon God, implying his complete independence of us? No, it is not so simple as that. Complete or absolute dependence (Schleiermacher) in every respect would make God, not us, the sinner as well as the saint. *Division of responsibility* is as necessary to religion as anything can be. Now if, in any sense whatever, we are other than purely passive in relation to God — that is, if in any sense we have responsibility for sinning or not sinning against his will — then in some sense he is not purely active in relation to us, but (what else can it be?) genuinely passive. If we determine the sin, then we determine that he shall know the sin; for had we not sinned he had not known us as sinning. If determining what an individual shall know is not acting upon that individual, what would be? Thomists deny that it is so, but there is nothing in *religion* to compel us to agree with them; and it is the religious strand in theology that we are now discussing. (It may be urged that had we not sinned, God would still have known us as potential sinners, but the knowledge of the potential as such is still not the knowledge of the actual as such. God could know it to be a *fact* that we sin only if it be a fact, and that it is or is not a fact is supposed to express *our* choice, *our* activity, in some degree or fashion. Thus either we determine something of what there is for God to know and hence of what he knows, or else there is no human freedom whatsoever, and God is alone the sinner.)

The absolute dependence upon God which religion involves is dependence for existence. Without God we should be nothing, and existence itself would be the same as non-existence. The great " I am " is for religion the essential factor of existence as such. It does indeed follow that no matter what we may do with our freedom, our responsibility, God will not fail to exist. We are not to think that by sinning we can jeopardize his being, or that by good acts we can make the universe safer for him. But it is one thing to contribute to the safety of a being, its freedom from the danger of annihilation, and another to contribute to the color and richness of its existence. Granted that God will continue to exist, with his essential characteristics of power, goodness, and wisdom, no matter what we may do, it does not in the least follow that he will also have the same concrete experience no matter what we may do. For his essence may be independent of us but his accidents may not be. To say he has no accidents is to beg the question just now under discussion. What is there in religion to imply that God has no accidents? From the premise, " God exists necessarily," the inference, " therefore his whole nature is necessary and he has no accidents," is a fallacy of ambiguity. God's " essence " is not accidental — that is indeed required by the premise, which implies that in any possible state of affairs God will be included, and this means that there will always be something by which he may be identified as God, and no other. This something is his essence. But from all this we learn nothing against the possibility of accidents, details, in God, any one of which will or will not be present in him according to circumstances.

The ambiguity spoken of appears in many related forms.

It is one thing to say God could exist without us, or without *any* creature or group of creatures you wish to specify; it is logically quite another to say he could exist were there *no* creature at all. For God's necessity of existing, while our existence is contingent, may simply mean that had we not existed, still *some* creatures or other would necessarily have existed, sufficient for God's needs. Any particular contingent thing might not have existed; but it does not follow that there might have been *no* contingent things. It would be a contradiction to say that a certain accidental thing happens by necessity; but there is no contradiction in saying that it is necessary that some accidents or other should happen, that there should be accidents. It is, to use Charles Peirce's example, as if a cook should say, " I *must* have apples for an apple pie, but there is no one apple or group of apples I must have, provided I have some group or other." If the cook possessed unlimited power to guarantee herself sufficient apples, then her operations would be independent of any given apples, since the assumption is that should these fail she would only have to wave a wand and others would appear.

Thus God may depend, even for his essence, upon there being creatures, but he may have power to guarantee absolutely that there should be such; while beyond his essential characters he may necessarily have accidental ones, just *which* ones being contingent and depending upon which creatures exist — and since the creatures are partly self-determining this means, depending partly upon what the creatures may choose to do. To have failed to discuss these distinctions systematically is a technical defect of procedure in the tradition, altogether regardless of what the truth of the matter may be. For the purpose of philosophical theology is to analyze the logical interrelations of the ideas implied in religion, and to prevent the answering of religious questions without regard to the conceivable, or not obviously inconceivable, alternatives.

That God is the cause, the " creator," of all things, again, does not imply that he is in no sense the effect of anything. For his essence may be the cause, the necessary condition, of all other essences, and the effect of none in particular nor of any totality of them; and yet his accidents may be both cause and effect in relation to other things. In terms of accidents man may be part-creator of God. When he sins, he *causes* God to grieve; when he does well, he causes God to rejoice, as a child similarly does a parent. When Beethoven, by his devotion and partly free action, made new forms of beauty not hitherto contained in all of creation, he created a new detail of value in the experience of God, he contributed to the divine reality, without thereby in the least deciding that there should be this divine reality to which contribution could be made.

It is true, and important, that religion can hardly admit that such contributions should make any difference in the degree of righteousness in God, his holiness. This, for religion, is not an accident. But, as we have seen, all this is perfectly compatible with there being accidents, and even implies that there must be such, in the one who is necessarily holy.

Just as the notion of the necessity of God's being may be both true and false, according as the essence or the accidents of God are intended, so may he be both mutable and immutable.

Any changing enduring thing, indeed, has two aspects: the aspect of identity, or what is common to the thing in its earlier and later stages, and the aspect of novelty. A man is a new, different person every moment; but equally he is the same person every moment. There is no paradox in this. By change is meant exactly this combination of identity and difference. A being which changes through a finite time has an identical aspect which changes only at the beginning and end of the stretch of time during which the thing endures. (We shall see that even this is to understate the aspect of immutability involved precisely in the changing.) A being which changes through all time has an identical aspect which changes at no time whatever, that is, it is in this aspect immutable. Thus there is a character in God which is exempt from change. The ancient Hebrews discovered what this character is, namely, God is unchangeable in the sense that at all times he is equally, because wholly, righteous and wise. It by no means follows, and the Scriptures do not assert it as true, that he is at all times equally and absolutely happy, completely good aesthetically as well as ethically and cognitively. On the contrary, the Scriptures depict God as in different states of joy or grief at different times because of the different states of righteousness or sin of mankind. His state of righteousness does not vary with these changes of pleasure and displeasure; on the contrary, it is just because he remains equally righteous in attitude that he must change in total value-experience in appropriate accordance with changes in the objects of his righteousness. The wicked or stupid man may be unmoved by deterioration or progress in other men, the perfectly righteous and wise individual cannot be thus insensitive. Changes which really make a difference to the value of reality must make a difference to God because he is not selfish or stupid, and in respect to this unselfishness and wisdom is indeed beyond all possibility of falling into a different state, is indeed beyond all shadow of turning. Thus it would be false to say that the new theology makes simply no use of the traditional concept of immutability and its corollaries. Rather it assigns that concept its place, tells both how it is true and how it could be interpreted and for ages almost universally was interpreted (in technical theology) so as to be partly false.

Of course, the distinction between the immutable and the mutable aspects of God cannot be defended without renouncing the doctrine of "simplicity," which was precisely intended to cut off such distinctions. And yet even here, the issue is rather one of level of discrimination than of mere contradiction. The immutable aspect of God is also simple, just as it is impassive, immaterial, etc. The unchanging righteousness as such has no parts, and it cannot be acted upon or made different. Yet it may require that the concrete reality in which it exists have passivity and complexity; perhaps as a universal, though not itself particular, yet may imply that there are particulars of which it is the universal or common property. The goodness which has no parts may belong as an abstract aspect to a being of which all things whatever are constituents.

All this is a way of saying that the righteousness or wisdom of God is not the whole of his nature. We say, God is holy, not that he is holiness. Only "love" is an abstraction which implies the final concrete truth. God "is" love, he is not merely loving, as he is merely righteous or wise (though in the supreme or definitive way). This is because in love the ethico-cognitive and the aesthetic aspects of value are both expressed. The lover is not merely the one who unwaveringly understands and tries to help; the lover is just as emphatically the one who takes unto himself the varying joys and sorrows of others, and whose own happiness is capable of alteration thereby. Of course, one could distinguish between the abstract invariable lovingness of the perfect lover, and the concrete varying love-experiences he has of his objects in different stages. But love is the one abstraction which makes it almost entirely obvious that there *must be* such a distinction between the generic unchangeable factor and the total value enjoyed. It is not an accident that love was the abstraction least often appealed to in technical theology, though frequently suggested in the high points of Scripture and other genuinely religious writing.

True, there are two scriptural texts which seem to assert the changelessness of God. But the context makes clear enough that the writer was concerned in each case with the fixity of God's ethical character, with his lack of fickleness, his fidelity or constancy of benevolent purpose. In so far as God has *resolved* what the future shall be, he never relents or changes his resolution. We can rely completely upon his righteousness, today as in the past. But when we say of someone that he adheres strictly to his ethical principles, we do not thereby assert that he changes in no way whatever. A mother may be equally devoted to each of her successive children, just as true to her obligations to each in turn; but the detailed content of her devoted awareness and action will be different with each one, and *ought* to be. To treat every event, as it occurs, in just the same way, and yet with equal wisdom and goodness, is nonsense. If the religious idea of the divine constancy is ethical and cognitive, meaning that God is always adequate to every state of the world, then this does not conflict with, but even seems to imply, a different state of God for every state of the world.

Change of purpose is clearly not the only kind of change. A man may have an undeviating purpose to be kind to his friends, but just what action this will imply will properly be different with each occasion. We can distinguish well enough between change which is disloyalty to principle, and that which, unchangeably if you like, conforms to it. Without such a distinction all ethical judgment would be at an end. An authoritarian church may declare that the implication of context or that of common experience is not to be used to limit the meaning of biblical texts, but not being a member of such a church I shall not discuss this further.

But is not God the everlasting, incorruptible being, and can he be this if he is changeable? Why not? That a being subject to change is *therefore* subject to decay or generation is a mere dogma, a *non sequitur*. It depends upon what kind of change is involved, or upon *how* the being is subject to change. You can as well argue that a being who wills must will in all conceivable ways, and therefore in wicked ways. Birth and death are changes, but in their absence change would still be possible.

Perhaps enough has been said in support of our thesis that the religious tenets of traditional theology do not imply the secular ones. What is the significance of this fact? It seems to me the definite refutation of this type of theology. For religious ideas claim absolute ultimacy. They must involve all ultimate truths, which must be deducible from them. Otherwise, secular truth would be more final than religious. Traditional theology makes religion a corollary from universal truths knowable without it; but the reverse derivation does not hold. Of course contingent truths, mere matters of fact, should not be deducible from religious ultimates; but the secular tenets of traditional theology are not proposed as contingent.

The fact is that traditional theology makes the abstract the basis of the concrete, whereas the reverse relation is logically correct. The abstract is reached by abstracting from some aspects of the more concrete. Religious ideas claim to be the concrete form of ultimate truths; it follows that the more abstract ultimate truths should be derivable from them. But the secular tenets follow in no way from the religious. Hence at least one of the two must be wrong.

But there is a third objection to the traditional technique. This is that (as partly worked out above), though it seemed possible to derive the religious God from the technical definition, it could also be argued, and by great minds was argued, that the very opposite of the religious idea was implied in that definition. For instance, knowledge seems to imply an internal distinction between subject and object — but God is said to be simple. Volition seems to imply change — but God is changeless. Purpose seems to imply a present lack of something — but God is perfect; and for him there is no contrast between present intent and future realization. Love involves sensitivity to the joys and sorrows of others, participation in them — but we cannot infect God with our sufferings (since he is cause of everything and effect of nothing), and our joys can add nothing to the immutable perfection of God's happiness. Though in religion one speaks of "serving" God, in reality, according to technical theology, one can do nothing for God, and our worst sins harm God as little as the finest acts of sainthood can advance him. Religious motivation is not altruistic desire to benefit God but solely individual or collective egoism of the creatures, who serve themselves through God, but never God through their own achievements. And God's altruism toward the creatures is the exact opposite of man's "love" for him, since it is just as free from self-interest as the latter is exclusively constituted by it. What then becomes of the religious motivation of living in imitation of God? ("Ye therefore shall be perfect, as your heavenly Father is perfect." Matt. 5:48.)

Thus, although religious doctrines do follow, "after a fashion," from secular ones, they are at the same time incompatible with the latter. From the same premise that God is immutable and wholly the cause of his own states, a purely impassive being, Spinoza deduces that God does not love men, while orthodox theologians deduce that he does. Both consequences do follow. Being all positive value, unenrichable perfection (" absolutely infinite," as Spinoza expresses it), God must involve the value of love. But on the other hand, since love involves dependence upon the welfare of the beloved, and in so far is a passion, God, being passionless, wholly active, is necessarily exempt from it. One may go through all the religious attributes and show that all of them must, and all of them must not, belong to the immutable deity. An immutable purpose is meaningless, yet the possessor of all perfections, of all positive predicates, must not be without purpose. But since he has once for all everything that he could purpose to have, there is no sense in his purposing anything. It may be said that the purpose could be altruistic, to benefit others. But for what purpose does God benefit others? In the overflowing expression of his own glory or superabundance, said theologians. But he would have been just as glorious had no creation existed; for God eternally is all value, world or no world. Pure altruism is all we can say, from the side of God. This solution involves two grand difficulties.

1. Altruism is identifiable in experience as a process of participation in the good of others, so that some sort of value accrues to the self through the very fact that value accrues to another self. This does not mean that all motivation is merely selfish. One may plan the welfare of others in the distant future, and expect no benefit oneself in that future from this welfare (as in making a will, without the belief that one will be aware of the lives of the beneficiaries after one's death). But at least one does gain

some present value, some advance satisfaction from the planning. Love *is* joy in the joy (actual or expected) of another, and sorrow in the sorrow of another. Theologians went through many contortions to show that God's love both was love and was nothing of the kind. Just as the Stoics said the ideal was to have good will toward all but not in such fashion as to depend in any degree for happiness upon their fortunes or misfortunes, so Christian theologians, who scarcely accepted this idea in their ethics, nevertheless adhered to it in characterizing God. They sought to maintain a distinction between love as desire, with an element of possible gain or loss to the self, and love as purely altruistic benevolence; or again between sensuous and spiritual love, *eros* and *agape*. But the distinction between lower and higher forms of love which is alone given meaning by experience — that is, which alone has meaning — is not of this character. Benevolence *is* desire for the welfare of others, and this desire is worthy to be called spiritual just to the extent of its freedom from partiality, fickleness, and other limitations inherent in the lack of inclusiveness of human other-regarding desire. Of course it must be a superrationally enlightened, an all-comprehending, never wearying desire for others' good, that is attributed to God. But still desire, so far as that means partial dependence for extent of happiness upon the happiness of others. In this is nothing unspiritual, if that means irreligious. Lincoln's desire that the slaves might be free was not less desire because it was spiritual, or less spiritual because it was desire — that is, a wish, *capable of being painfully disappointed or happily fulfilled.* It was all the more godlike in that it was no mere one-sided partiality, but was given due perspective and restraint by the presence of other desires, such as those for the preservation of the union, and, so far as possible, of peace. Such perspective and restraint of desire due to its inclusiveness, both of the totality of what is actual and of the potentialities inherent in actuality, is what is meant by spiritual, where anything positive is meant.

2. But there is an even more patent impossibility in the older view. If God is purely altruistic in relation to men, then men must be purely race-egoistic in relation to him. You cannot be motivated by consideration of the value you contribute to another, if that other is so constituted that he can receive no value from any source. The greatest joy is in giving joy, but we can give none to God. Of course religion says just the contrary, but the agreement of this with the secular tenets is not apparent, and so far as I know no decent effort will be found in the literature of first-type theism to mitigate the difficulty. Is not the noblest aspect of religious aspiration the wish to have a cause to serve, some value to enrich by our contributions, which is more satisfying as an object of service than mere men? Men die, the race seems destined to die, taking all our contributions back into the nothingness of blind matter again. Besides, we often try to help men and fail, with none perhaps even to know of our attempt, and never any to fully understand and appreciate it — none except mayhap God. But now we are told, directly or in effect, that we can do nothing for God, that he certainly will gain nothing from our actions. At this I for one cannot do other than say no! Give me some other God, or none. The whole point of religion is destroyed. I cannot do other than scorn this proposal.

Lest I be thought to battle a straw man, let me quote.

> All action . . . even whether good or bad, contributes to the glory of God, for our acts may be deprived of their good, but nothing can deprive God of his glory. . . . The act of a good which has no good to acquire remains a mystery. . . .

The Christian universe is entirely good as regards what it is, but incomplete. . . .
— ÉTIENNE GILSON.[4]

" For since the soul in the mystic union has been made one thing with God, it is after a certain manner God by participation." . . . Thus it gives God to God; its act of love, which measured in itself is finite and limited, gives to God, by the infinite Love of God, the infinite itself, a gift without measure. A donation which evidently must not be understood as being in any degree in the entitative order, as though the soul were able to exercise any influence on God or add to his perfections, to enrich the being of God with that being itself, which would be absurd. A most real donation, but . . . .
— JACQUES MARITAIN.[5]

What does it come to? That, be we saint or sinner, no matter what we choose to do, it is all just the same to God, for his glory has the identical absolute perfection in either case. The universe is incomplete, but it matters no whit what is done or not done to complete it, for the universe contributes nothing to the value of existence, since in abstraction from the universe there exists absolute perfection. A " most real donation " leaves God exactly the same as he would have been without the donation — perfect, no more and no less.

I submit that writers who do not even see the appearance of sophistry in such reasonings may have something to say to their devoted disciples, but not to the critical reader. To many it seems clear, though not because they have not considered both sides of the question, that if God has no good to acquire and hence cannot permit us the privilege of contributing value to himself, the sole worthy cosmic recipient of values, the only one able to receive *all* we can give, all the good that we are (some of which escapes all human friends) , then he is incapable of responding to our noblest need, which is that there should be a cause to which nothing of ourselves is merely indifferent, and nothing good is without positive value. If this need, which is rational not " emotional," since no other means is available to relate human values to the cosmos as a whole, must be renounced, then atheism seems the simpler and perhaps the more honest way to make the renunciation.

I call the reader's attention also to the undiscriminating use of the term " glory." If by this were meant the " beauty of holiness," the abstract ethical goodness of God, then this is for religion indeed that glory which God is bound to have, no matter what happens. But it would not follow that our good and bad acts contribute by equal necessity to God's glory; for it is precisely his holiness to which we *cannot contribute.* Where we can make a contribution (to God's happiness), good and bad acts are by no means equivalent. Note, too, the unconscious sophistry — is it anything else? — of inferring " contributes to " from " cannot deprive of." What Gilson means, it seems, is merely that good and bad acts contribute in the same sense to the glory of God, that is, both totally and therefore equally fail to make *any* contribution; for the sum of God's glory is fixed independently of our acts.

Here is no trick to deceive us, but rather, unless I am blind indeed, an innocent and tragic inability, in two otherwise magnificent minds, to think carefully and accurately about a subject whose treatment authority has prescribed — unfortunately, authority as largely crystallized before the logical structure of the problem had been adequately traced, that is, studied with a view to the formal possibilities involved, and with all the main aspects of experience consulted in the light of these possibilities in turn. The results of this inadequacy are now sacrosanct, and efforts toward adequacy sabotaged. The issue, at any rate, seems clear.

Maritain's argument about the impossibility of enriching God with his own being cannot be fully answered here (see chapter 8). But we may say that the being which God is to gain from us is to be a certain particular case of mutual being, and that the only way to enjoy mutuality is to depend for it in part upon others, since such dependence *is* mutuality, is love. We, through our voluntary acts by virtue of which in part we are whatever, at any moment, we actually are, make it possible for God to love us in each new state of our existence and to gain the increment that a new object of love brings, not to the lovingness, but to the total resulting aesthetic value. And that it does depend upon us in part whether the contribution shall be made is not a paradox, but a deduction from the definition of love.

Thus we stand before the fact, or what seems to numbers of devoted, learned, and distinguished minds to be the fact, that the theological tradition is not one doctrine but an inconsistent compound of two, a religious doctrine and a secular one. These are so related that the secular implies both the religious conception and its opposite, while the religious doctrine implies only the contradictory of the secular doctrine. The secular concept is thus shown to be self-contradictory, while the religious one may, so far as these relations of ideas are concerned, be true.

Since, in the realm of necessary truths, such as we are dealing with, a false proposition is an impossible one and an impossible proposition implies (as C. I. Lewis has pointed out) all other impossible as well as all necessarily true propositions (at least, all of the same generality, a qualification here fulfilled), it is not surprising that from the axioms of medieval theology both religious ideas and their negations have been arrived at by superior minds, which sort of consequence being elicited depending naturally upon temperament and circumstances. Equally naturally, orthodox inferences for long ages predominated, and the unsoundness of the axioms therefore escaped notice.

The logical relationships discussed in this chapter may be diagrammed as follows:

FACTORS IN TRADITIONAL THEOLOGY

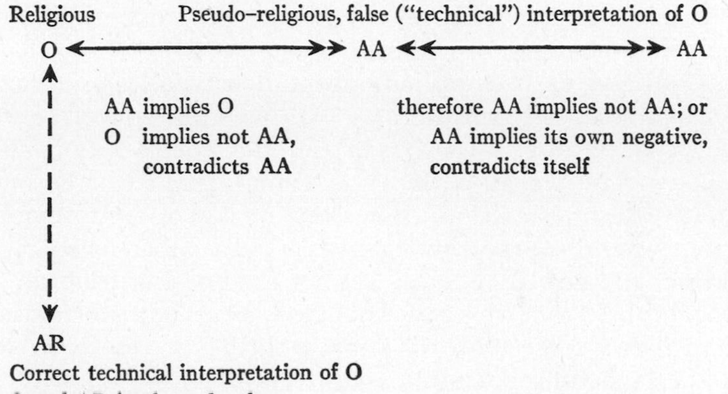

EXPLANATIONS:
O, the religious attributes, omniscience, etc.
AA, the notion of God as absolutely perfect (unsurpassable even by self) in all respects
AR, God as absolutely perfect in some respects, relatively perfect (surpassable by self only) in all other respects
⟶ implies
⟶⟶ contradicts, implies the falsity of
Broken line indicates relationships which have been largely overlooked, implicit rather than explicit in the tradition.

That the secular tenets imply contradictory conclusions will seem less surprising when we note that they are self-contradictory in themselves. The idea of " pure actuality " is the idea of the absolute realization of potency where there is no potency to realize. The very meaning of actuality involves the contrast of possible and existential; to suppose that the highest actuality destroys this contrast is to suppose nonsense. Again, we have the idea of pure unity with no inner complexity to unify, the idea of an activity not related to any other activity, or if so related devoid of passivity in this relation. It is a tissue of incompatible thoughts, not less so because verbal distinctions are introduced to create the appearance of consistency; for the distinctions themselves conflict with the only experientially possible meanings of the primary concepts.

To be sure, the simplicity of the first type seems almost to guarantee its consistency. Against this, however, we must set certain indications of a hidden complexity in the doctrine of the all-perfect — a complexity strongly suggestive of contradiction. The doctrine is at once supremely positive and supremely negative. God is all-actuality, all-value, all-knowledge, etc. Yet not for nothing have theologians held that we know what God is not, in a more strict and literal sense than we know what he is. He is in all respects the *un*surpassable, *in*finite, *im*material, *un*measurable (" immense "), *im*mutable, *without* body, parts, or passions, *in*dependent, *im*passive. Now perhaps these unqualified negations are incompatible with any positive attributes whatever, therefore with such attributes as will, knowledge, goodness, even though in their perfect form. Of course every affirmation implies negation, as omniscience implies the negation of ignorance. But ignorance is itself a negation, the negation of omniscience, and this suggests the principle that only essentially negative predicates need or should be absolutely negated of the perfect. Change, passivity, having parts, these are not unmistakably the negation of any positive predicates whatever. There is no positive predicate given in experience which is negated by change. The " permanent " may very well change, since destruction is not the only species of alteration. Nor is the " passive " that which lacks activity, for the wholly inactive cannot be influenced, and to obey is also an act. That which " has parts " is not at all the same as that which lacks unity, unless one takes parts in some absolute sense in which no experience can exhibit them. If we know anything about aesthetic experience, for instance, we know that unity and variety are not contradictory of each other. Perhaps God has not the least but the most change, passivity, complexity, etc.? This would imply, however, that he is, in certain respects, only a *de facto* maximum or supreme being, since there is, as we shall have occasion to argue, no definite upper limit to complexity.

There is, then, reason to question the consistency of simple perfectionism. Of course subtle attempts have been made to justify the extraordinary role of negation in this doctrine. It is said that since we know God not directly but through the creatures, and since he is not a creature but the creator, we must know him through negation essentially. But if God is known wholly indirectly, then he cannot be immanent in experience, and this conflicts with his ubiquity and immensity. Even Aquinas will be found admitting that we are not wholly without direct awareness of God, quite apart from special revelation or mystic states.[6] And besides, Aquinas and almost everyone else asserted positive as well as negative knowledge of God, such as that he is good and loving. And it is precisely these positive predicates which are not readily, if at all, reconcilable with the sweeping negations, as many great theologians have more or less completely admitted (Maimonides, Philo, Spinoza).

Second-type theism avoids absolute negatives, except of predicates themselves clearly negative, such as ignorance, lack of interest in others, cessation of existence. To the contention that the creator cannot share predicates with the created, it replies that even the idea of causality is not so sacred that it can be applied without qualification, that in a very real sense the First Cause is also effect (not in his essence), the creator is also (in some aspects) created, and the creatures are also creative. To the contention that our human concepts are not adequate to, and must be denied of, the divine it replies that this must also be true of "causality" and "creator." Probably no simple affirmation or denial is fool-proof here. To the contention that God is "not in a genus" and hence cannot be defined positively through differences, the answer is that this argument is based on some of the negations in question, such as that there is no matter or potency or complexity in God. Undoubtedly God's relation to genera is a unique relation. But this uniqueness is not best arrived at by simple denial. God's relation to "goodness" is doubtless unique but does not consist in his being simply non-good; his relation to time is certainly a special case but may not consist in his being timeless; etc. First-type theism seems to waver and adopt opposite solutions to parallel problems here, fortified by arguments which are ingenious but not such as to satisfy other minds equally ingenious and less bound by the past.

Such expressions as the "finite-infinite," or the "perfect-perfectible," suggest that second-type theism is also a self-contradiction. To be sure, it is in different senses that the two contradictory predicates are to be applied, different respects of value. But perhaps it may be thought that perfection on any dimension implies perfection upon all! The perfect, it may be argued, is the complete, and the complete is above all limitations of dimensions. But let us remember that we have defined perfection not as completeness, but as unsurpassability or maximal value in *any* respect in which "better" and "worse" are possible, or as the property of that which, *in a given dimension* of value, could not be better than it is. Is there any reason why the impossibility that anything should be better than x in respect R should imply the impossibility that anything should be better than

x in any respect you choose? Surely only a careful development of a theory of value could justify such an assertion. In the following chapters we shall present reasons for a contrary conclusion.

It is an extraordinary habit of many theologians to consider contradictions in doctrine a positive merit. It is argued that since God is beyond our understanding we *ought* not to be able to conceive him without difficulty. But on the other hand, if we give up the intellectual criterion of consistency, only one is left, namely, adequacy to experience. So let us consider this remaining criterion. Is it not precisely first-type theism, traditional theology, which is one-sided, meager, incomplete in its use of experience to arrive at the nature of God? It simply denies certain all-pervasive, infinitely fundamental aspects of life — change, variety, complexity, receptivity, sympathy, suffering, memory, anticipation — as relevant to the idea of God. It will not do to justify the contradictions of this theology on the ground that it is more important to include all aspects and dimensions of the truth than to see exactly how these aspects are compatible with each other. The contradictions are due too plainly to the opposite cause, to the deliberate poverty, not the unmanageable richness, of the conceptions. Thus both criteria, all that we have, are flouted in traditional procedure. The Absolute is not only an invitation to a moral holiday, as James said; it is likewise, as he also, though less clearly, saw, an invitation to an intellectual holiday, to irresponsibility in regard to every ideal whether of goodness of conduct or of goodness of thought. Only illogicality made it possible to overlook this. And perhaps the popularity of the doctrine is partly due to the dim realization of the implied freedom from ideal demands.

Theologians may have underestimated at least one effect

of " original sin," its influence upon the development of their own doctrines. I believe sincerely that even saintly theologians are not exempt from the effects of subconscious egoism, cowardice, laziness, even cruelty. Consider how they have frequently striven to demonstrate the eternal rightness of slavery, tyranny, and many forms of injustice! In theologizing, too, we must try to obey God — by seeking truth — rather than men and their traditions and will (however sublimated) to power and self-satisfaction, their more or less incurable blend of ignorance and determination to appear to know. I make no pretensions to complete innocence of such defects. I merely suggest that in philosophy there is no man we can trust too absolutely, nor any group of men, short of all mankind, so far as pursuing the truth cooperatively through the centuries, with the current chapter of the story being no less worthy of careful perusal than any past one, and with an eye to the possible surprises of the future. Theologians would be no more justified in denying offhand that they can have misled religious thought for centuries than doctors were in their indignant denial that it was they themselves who consistently infected mothers with puerperal fever. Human nature is like that, even theologian-human nature. Infallibility, individual or class, is lightly assumed.

But is there no way in which contradictions may usefully serve to bring out the essential limitations of human thought? I believe that there is. An idea can always be kept free of apparent contradictions by leaving it sufficiently vague. For the less definite an idea, the less we can know with what it is compatible or incompatible. Now our ideas about God will never be free from vagueness. We cannot simply rest in this vagueness, however, since we can get the most value from our ideas only by making them as definite as we are able. But sooner or later, in the course of introducing sharper definitions, error will creep in, and contradictions will result (for error in regard to first principles, necessary truths, is always absurdity, self-contradiction). What we should then do is not at all to make a merit of this temporary defeat — for that is all it is — but to retreat to the vaguer stage of the idea, and start over again to give it a more definite meaning. The process may well never wholly end, so that ever anew contradictions may be met.

As for the idea that as created beings we can know God only as he is not, or as he is in the creatures not as he is in himself, this idea I believe to be crude. It is vagueness, not blank ignorance, that we have to struggle against. The whole idea of religion, at any rate, is precisely that we can know God as he is in himself (though vaguely), for we know him through love, and love is "taking the standpoint of the other" (Mead). True, we know human beings whom we love somewhat indirectly and externally, but this is just because they are our metaphysical equals and are localized partial entities, who can be external to us, not the indwelling, supreme, and universal being, God. Love of God is the norm of creaturely love; for religion, all other human love is deficient. God as cause is *in* his effects, and God as cause is God himself. We do not know the creatures at all, if theism is sound, just in themselves, and then by negating their limitations infer God. On the contrary (and this is why human friendship is no substitute for religious love), we know ourselves and everything else in relation to our dim but direct sense of God's love, with which we are one by our subconscious but inalienable returning love for him. The arguments by which it is held to be shown that God cannot be positively (even though vaguely) known by us simply beg the question, turning as they do on the characteristic categories of first-type theism, such as the idea of a being wholly without accidents, hence having no essence distinguishable from accidents, etc. These arguments cannot be used to justify the inability of first-type doctrine to give even vague positive (and consistent) character to God, until the claims of second-type theism to do so have been considered on their merits.[7]

The two strands in theology, then, are as follows: There is the popular or operative religious idea of the God of love, perfect in lovingness, and hence all-understanding and everlasting, so that nothing has ever been or ever can be deprived of his love while existent at all. Then there is the set of secular concepts by which this religious idea has usually been interpreted: pure actuality, immutability, impassivity, uncaused causality. This set is mutually implicative, so that it must be right clear through, wrong clear through, or in some qualified way both right and wrong clear through. That it is entirely right clear through is impossible, for as we have seen it has contradictory implications, and is not an accurate rendering of the religious idea it is to interpret. Yet the secular set need not be unqualifiedly wrong, for as we have seen it is possible to distinguish two aspects, an abstract and a concrete, of the religious God, such that in one of these aspects, A, he is indeed immutable or incapable of being acted upon, while in the other, R, he is not merely mutable and passive, but preeminently so, to an extent infinitely beyond the mutability and passivity of all other beings. Thus the secular strand becomes indeed the philosophic rationale of the religious strand, provided it be used twice over, once positively and once negatively. (The secular concepts being themselves negative, their negative use is really positive in meaning, thus: God *does* change, or is not unchanging, he *is* complex, or not without parts.)

The denial of the traditional ideas as they stand has the

curious and fortunate result of enabling us to see a profound truth in these ideas, whereas, if we persist in the tradition, then all opposition and criticism become stupid or sinful error, and nothing else. " That which changes " *of course* has an aspect which does not change; that which is passive of course has an aspect which is impassive, active; and since God is the supreme case of change and passivity, he is also the maximal case of the immutability and impassivity which these ideas imply, just as a very great capacity for joy implies a very great one for sorrow. That which endures all change whatever also enjoys all permanence whatever, in no paradoxical sense, but in the simple plain one of being the abiding substratum of a *maximal range* of temporal differences. To change through *x* states is to be, in one aspect, permanent through those states; to change through infinity-times-*x* states is to be infinitely more permanent.

(This permanence includes the immortality of the past in the divine memory. To say an event is " past " for God does not mean that it is *absent* from his present awareness; it means that it is *not* the " final increment " of determinate detail contained in that awareness, the final increment being that which involves all the others though it is involved by none, the " next to last " being that which involves all the others but one, and is involved solely by that one, etc. To say a past experience is part of present experience is not a contradiction, for the *date* of present experience as a whole is the date of its final increment, not of its non-final increments, this being the meaning of " date." Those who deny this must offer some other account of the unity of time, and of how the past can be *known now*. A non-final increment as non-final, as " past," in or to a certain subsequent date, has yet its *own* date — the " when it was present " — namely, the date in which it was and is the final end of the whole chain exclusive of what the increment fails to involve. Nor is it impossible to give the meaning of "involves" in the above definition of pastness. To remember the execution of a certain antecedently entertained purpose is to see the antecedent entertainment as involved in the experience of the act which was conscious of expressing the purpose; but the prior purpose itself is not remembered as involving just the act which in fact did execute it, for it is not the nature of a purpose, however exalted, to specify just one unique realization, but rather to indicate a region of possibilities any one of which will serve. To make anticipation and purpose individually determining is to destroy the difference between memory, or the past relation, and foresight, or the future relation. The future must not be contained individually in the present; otherwise there would indeed be a contradiction, for all dates would then be in all others in a symmetrical fashion incompatible with any distinction between them. What time requires is *not that the past be lost,* but that the future be *really unattained* so long as it is future, for then this not-having-been-attained-in-its-predecessor can belong to each event even after it is past and establish the temporal order even within an omniscient present — that is, one absolutely conscious of all its contents, as some philosophers have thought human experience to be.

Thus, to attribute change to God, so far from conflicting with permanence or stability in his being, means rather that nothing positive that ever belongs to God can change, but only the negative aspect of *not yet* being this or that. Except in his negative determinations, his not-being, God is utterly immutable. Yet since negative determinations are inherent in positive, God really is mutable. To be this is to be not-that — not because of any weakness of finite being, but because of the meaning of "being." Yet the

" not-that " need not with respect to all that's be permanent, for one may be this and *then* that; and the that will include the this, although the this could not have included the that; for such is *the logical structure of time, that it gives determinations a unique asymmetrical order of involvement.* Of course, the " that " in the not-that is a universal of which the that in the " then that " is one possible instance. To laugh is to not-smile, but any subsequent smile will be unanticipated, even negatively, in its individual flavor. Otherwise, the temporal involvement would be symmetrical. The whole of classical metaphysics is more or less vitiated by the assumption of the symmetry of time. To take such symmetry for granted is to think in a pre-Bergsonian, pre-Whiteheadian, and pre-Peircean manner, and in my judgment is somewhat as though a physicist were to ignore quantum mechanics. Omniscience in the old sense that excludes gain as well as loss, and the naïve view that the past is as literally lost as the future — while future — is unattained, are equally incompatible with the nature of time, as interpreted by some of the greatest recent philosophers. This interpretation seems to be the last chance for a solution of the problem. For of the logically possible views of time, all the others have been long and carefully explored without generally satisfactory results.)

Among the secular concepts was that of simplicity. This, taken absolutely, at once shut off any possibility of reaching a synthesis of positive and negative versions of the concepts; for the only way to avoid contradiction in such a synthesis is to distinguish two aspects of God, and, in so far, to make him complex, not simple. On the other hand, if we start with the negative version (really positive in meaning) that God is not simple but complex, then there is no reason why we should not be able to find an aspect of God which is simple, and simple in supreme or maximal fashion, and thus we may render justice to this time-hallowed conception.

If it is really true that the idea of God is, because of its exalted character, but barely conceivable by human beings, is it not to be expected that in order to reach him we should have to make the most of our ideas, to use them in as many ways as possible, both positive and negative? Which theism, then, has the best title to claim that it faces the limitations of human thought, that which relies upon unqualified assertions (really denials) or that which systematically stretches our categories to the limit by employing them both positively and negatively, though withal consistently, thus admitting that whether we assert or deny we are bound to see God inadequately, and doubly so in proportion as we fail to use our powers both of assertion and denial to the uttermost?

Second-type theism enables us to give a new meaning to the old doctrine that we know that, but not what, God is. If God has accidents, it is clear that our only clue to them is our detailed knowledge of contingent being in space and time, since it is contingent being that forms the accidental content of the divine experience. But our acquaintance (of any appreciable accuracy and clearness) with contingent being is infinitesimal in extent — in comparison to the whole of time and space — and is at all points more or less lacking in clarity and accuracy. Thus we know no accident of God just as it is, and we know with appreciable accuracy only a vanishing proportion of the ever growing totality of events which is given to God. We know *that* an infinity of accidents must belong to God (if we know the truth of AR) but as to what these are we know very little, and that little imperfectly, beyond that they have the common generic properties of contingent being, such as those of being temporal, spatial, and having other such categorical features in their bare universality.

It is only with things which come under a genus that it means anything to say we know the *that* and not the (specific or individual) *what*. For if neither an individual (or specific) nor a generic *what* is known, then the *that* only means bare "something" (or is that too a genus?), and we could not even say a something superior to or better than other things, for that would impute value, a positive what. On the other hand, it is the very nature of the universal that one can know the genus without knowing all the species, or any of them with perfect distinctness, and certainly without knowing the individual natures which the genus makes possible. Not even God sees the individual natures as items in the generic, for it is a contradiction to make the common property imply the differences, past and future alike, thus destroying temporal distinctions (see chapter 7 and also *The Universal Orthodoxy*). Now the accidents of God come under the genus of possible states of God, a genus inexhaustible through any series, even though infinite, of actual states, it being part of the meaning of possibility that it cannot be translated without remainder into actuality. We do know the nature of the genus, but of practically all the instances coming under it we know virtually nothing.

There is another sense in which (according to AR) one might say that we do not know what God is, though we know he exists. Our insight into the meaning of such concepts as define the essence of God, which includes the generic aspect of the accidents, the having-accidents as such, is fluctuating, more or less confused and unclear. Such concepts as better than all others, better than all others except other states of God himself, have only so much meaning as we can put into their constituent terms, such as " better than." The ways in which things can be " better than " are illustrated in our experience with no perfect lucidity, and very likely with radical incompleteness as to the possible dimensions of better and worse. Something like Spinoza's doctrine of infinite attributes, only a few of them (with any clearness) known to us, may be true.

I ask the reader to note these two ways in which second-type theism can equal or even surpass traditional first-type doctrine in its admission of our human ignorance of God. In spite of the seeming definiteness of certain aspects of the new doctrine — for instance in its ascribing the whole of nature, with all its known detail, to the accidental aspect of the nature of God — the indeterminateness and mystery which yet remain are literally infinite. The difference seems to me to be that the new doctrine states once for all wherein the mystery lies, and abides by this statement; it does not play fast and loose with it, as the older doctrine so often appears to do, with its oscillation between positive description and denial that there can be positive description of a being held to have only one perfectly simple nature (which in consistency must be known as a whole or not at all).

In formal terms, the " religious strand " in theology is the view that God is a maximum (compared to all that is actual or possible — even as a possible state of God himself) on *certain* of the dimensions of value; while the " secular strand " is the view that he is maximal on *all* dimensions. The religious view is A but not (A), that is, it is not explicitly committed between A and, for instance, AR; though implicitly we have found it to favor AR. Formally the two views are compatible; but when one considers the more than formal aspects of the religious strand, it appears to negate the secular. The basic religious view is that man's good acts and happiness have a value to the supreme being which his bad acts and misery do not. But, human experiences being particulars, then, since no maximal sum of particulars is possible, the contribution of these experiences to God is either zero, contrary to religion, or it is less than maximal, and hence the resulting divine value is on at least some dimension other than maximal, contrary to the secular tenets. Either they or religion must be given up.

In more religious terms, love means happiness varying somehow with variations in the happiness of others, and hence maximally happy love would mean love all of whose objects were maximally happy, an impossibility if the objects are to include created, imperfect beings. How little some theologians understood this is seen in their willingness to suppose God in the enjoyment of absolute bliss while numbers of his creatures suffered incurable pains (however refined the conception of these) in hell. While ostensibly maximizing value in God, they reduced even below the human level his lovingness, the very dimension with which religion is concerned. So frail are human reason and insight!

To hold that God " wills " or purposes human welfare, but is absolutely untouched by the realization or nonrealization of this or that portion of the purposed goal (due, for instance, to human sin or unfortunate use of free will), seems just non-sense. Making all allowance for subtle doctrines of the non-univocal, " analogical " meaning ascribed to such conceptions, are we entitled to think that *any* law of analogy is being adhered to, rather than being played fast and loose with? It is admitted by Thomists, for example, that God's knowledge is to his objects as the objects of human knowledge are to the knower! (See chapter 7.) Here the analogy is exactly in reverse.

Is this, then, what religion meant by saying God is love — that he is its exact opposite? I believe this is what traditional theology comes to.

Apart from religion it seems clear that some dimensions, which yet are essential to any value at all, cannot be maximized. Thus knowledge seems to imply a known, a not-self enjoying some sort of partial independence from the knowing; hence even omniscience must be related to something not in every sense wholly dependent upon it, and from which therefore it cannot itself be wholly independent (as, for instance, it would not be if it were a changing being and the known were its own past, the past conditioning the present in a sense in which the present does not condition the past). Also knowledge, as maximal, in still another way implies a non-maximal aspect of the knowing experience. To know the actual as actual and the potential as potential is to be wholly free from error and ignorance, and yet it is to be sure of an increase in content should the potential become actual, hence knowable as actual, that is, as somehow more than the merely potential or unactual. That the potential *could* become actual is an analytic judgment, expressing the very meaning of potentiality. Now if something could happen, then whatever this happening implies could also happen, that is, the omniscient *could* have actual content which it lacks. If it be said that to know the actual as such is to know no more than it is to know the potential as potential, is this not to say that we should all think it no better to know that our friends exist, now that they do, than it would be to know that such beings are possible, were they merely possible? Both would be exact, complete, and true knowledge under the posited circumstances. (The denial that the objects of God's knowledge contribute anything to God will be dealt with in detail in chapter 7.)

The conceivable "increase" involved in knowing potentiality is not got rid of by insisting that omniscience must be inclusive of all time in a changeless present; the possible increase then must be translated into a non-temporal form, equally incompatible with the notion of maximality, but by no means equally satisfactory on other grounds. We then have the additional difficulty that a portion of the possible is in effect impossible, since at no point of time could it ever have been, or can it ever be, added to reality (since for all points it is excluded by the single point of omniscience); or else one must deny the category of possibility, and hold that what never occurs is necessarily non-existent, and one must also define necessity otherwise than as the impossibility of the contradictory (for where nothing that does not occur is possible, possibility has no meaning distinguishable from that of actuality). Thus we have all the paradoxes of necessitarianism, according to which my hat is as necessary as God (whatever necessity would mean if possibility meant nothing), the particular is as necessary as the universal, although contingency is the essential logical meaning of particularity (that from which one can abstract as non-essential to existence and thought). Thus timeless omniscience can also be an all-dimensional maximum only if both necessity and possibility, and with them all logic, be emptied of meaning. Temporal omniscience, capable of increase in content and value, though not in accuracy or freedom from ignorance of its objects, is therefore not only not a paradox but the only view of omniscience which is not paradoxical.

Thus the religious strand, freed from entanglement with the all-dimensional maximum, with first-type doctrine, gains rather than loses in consistency, and leads to a more than formal interpretation of second-type theism. A doctrine is reached which is equally advantageous from a religious and a metaphysical point of view. ("Pure actuality," for example, is just as absurd as maximally happy righteousness. Actuality implies potentiality and hence its own impurity. Thought is irreducibly polar.[8])

From the argument of this chapter I conclude personally that first-type theism is false beyond reasonable doubt, while second-type theism conforms to religious experience and is at least not so manifestly absurd as first-type theism. However, I shall not assume so strong a conclusion for the remainder of this book. The man whom I shall regard as beyond the reach of reason is not the man who continues to believe in first-type theism, but only the man who insists that the case for that doctrine is so clear of difficulties that alternatives do not deserve careful consideration, at least as careful as they are given in later chapters of this book. Such a man I cannot think has the concerns of philosophy at heart. For if the difficulties urged against his doctrine are not serious, then no difficulties urged against any philosophy are serious. There is always some possibility of defense in philosophy. But if the defense so far given of absolutism (the all-dimensional, or superdimensional, maximum) is satisfactory as it stands, then by similar standards so is the defense of atheism, and of other philosophical tenets which traditional theists suppose themselves to have refuted. Whatever the conclusion of theistic argument is to be, the argument itself cannot remain where the Thomists, the Spinozists, the Hindu absolutists, or the Hegelians [9] wish to leave it. This I believe I have shown. But to make assurance doubly sure, additional evidence will be adduced throughout most, if not all, of the following chapters.

NOTES

1 See also Macintosh's essay in *My Idea of God,* edited by Joseph Fort Newton (Little, Brown & Co., 1927), pp. 135-58.

2 The ethical view of deity appears with some distinctness in Egyptian documents of over three thousand years ago. See James H. Breasted, *The Dawn of Conscience* (Charles Scribner's Sons, 1933).

[8] That omniscience sees the future as it is, that is, as partially indeterminate, might be called the Principle of Gersonides, for the earliest statement of it, so far as I have been able to find, is set forth in the writings of Levy ben Gerson, Jewish astronomer and theologian of the fourteenth century, whose doctrines furnished a counter-balance to the pure absolutism of Maimonides. See Isaac Husik, *A History of Mediaeval Jewish Philosophy* (The Macmillan Co., 1916), p. 345. The principle was also clearly stated by the Socinians, two centuries later. See Otto Fock, *Der Socinianismus* (Kiel, 1847), pp. 437 ff. For a recent defense of the doctrine see Alfred E. Garvie, *The Christian Faith* (Charles Scribner's Sons, 1937), p. 105.

Apart from the theological application, the view that it might not be definitely true either that *x* will occur or that *x* will not occur is found in several ancient logicians, e.g. Carneades and Aristotle, and in some recent ones, e.g. Lukasiewicz. For the last mentioned see "Philosophische Bemerkungen zu mehrwertigen Systemen des Aussagenkalküls," *Rendus des Séances de la Société des Lettres de Varsovie,* Classe III, Vol. XXIII, 1930, Fascicules 1–3, pp. 51–77. Cited and discussed by C. A. Baylis in "Are Some Propositions neither True nor False?" *Philosophy of Science,* III, 156–66. In conversation Bertrand Russell expressed himself to me as open-minded on the question.

Ockham and some other late Scholastics, who followed Aristotle in his analysis of propositions about future contingents, inclined to the view that this analysis, although philosophically sound, was not, for secular reasons, compatible with divine omniscience, although revelation compels us, they thought, to assume such compatibility. Perhaps it was their brand of revelation, not their philosophy, that was here chiefly at fault. God cannot, they suggested, know truths which are not there to be known, but a few biblical texts, like Christ's prophecy to Peter ("Thou shalt deny me thrice"), as well as the whole theological tradition, seemed to assert that God eternally knows the details of the future, even where free-will acts are in question. The Socinians worried particularly over the prophecy above referred to. It is not smoothly to be fitted in, one must admit. (Perhaps it was a statement of probability, not meant as sheer fact or certainty. Perhaps it meant that in that respect the act was *not* free. It would not follow that there was no sin in it, for that Peter was not free to do better might have resulted from earlier acts that *were* free, so that there might have been a time when even divinity could not have made the prophecy. The Socinians seem to have missed this way out. The feeling of guilt over an act does not prove that we could, at the moment, as we then were, have done otherwise, but it does imply, if valid, that at *some* time or other a course had been open to us that would not have led to the act.)

What seems lacking in most discussions of the matter is the distinction between the *falsity of "x will occur"* and the *truth of "x will not occur,"* the first of which asserts that the possibilities still include the non-occurrence of *x*, while the second asserts that they include only its non-occurrence, that they exclude its occurrence. Only by means of this distinction can one combine the indeterminateness of the future with the law of excluded middle, to sacrifice which, as Lukasiewicz suggests we should, seems to involve serious inconvenience, at the least.

It is to be observed, however, that even if one of the two, " *x* will occur " and " *x* will not occur," is always true, the argument of this chapter could still be maintained, and that in one of several ways. There are logicians, e.g. Baylis (*loc. cit.*), who would say that in " truth " all the details of the future are fully determinate, but that conceivably these details are not wholly knowable because there is nothing in the present to indicate them. We could then say that omniscience is all the knowledge that is possible, which by definition is perfect knowledge, but that since some truths about the future could not be known at present, omniscience does not know them. But even granting that there is definite truth concerning all the details of the future, and granting further that all truth is knowable, one could still hold that omniscience as an idea actually functioning in religion does not mean all possible knowledge, but only all-possible, or perfect, knowledge of the past and present, and sufficient knowledge of the future to constitute a providential plan, but with enough uncertainty in details of execution to allow for human choice. It would be difficult to show that more than this is implied by concrete religious attitudes and sentiments. Thus there are at least three ways of dealing with the religious idea of omniscience which do not imply that God is above change. All of these ways, and perhaps others, must be refuted before it could be regarded as established that religion requires the conception of an immutable Knower.

For the purposes of science, the mode of speaking suggested at the beginning of the last paragraph may be more convenient than the one I have advocated in this chapter. I believe Bergson has shown that what is convenient in physics may be most inconvenient and misleading in philosophy, which cannot accept fictitious simplifications simply because they cover all that we are able to measure and predict. I take Bergson also to have shown that relativity physics does not conflict with the notion of a real cosmic past and a real cosmic future, the latter not yet fully determinate, and the two divided by an objective and cosmic (though for physical measurements useless) simultaneity (see *Durée et simultanéité*, Paris, 1922, p. 122). Physics is merely not interested in such a conception, because human observation is not cosmic but local. Yet Bergson gives reason for holding that relativity physics is more favorable to such a view than Newtonian physics. Those who hold that the new physics supports absolutism, or the notion that time is merely another dimension of space, and that consequently the future is incomplete only for our human ignorance, should undertake to refute the arguments of Bergson (and of many others) on this point.

4 Étienne Gilson, *The Spirit of Mediaeval Philosophy* (Charles Scribner's Sons, 1936), pp. 145, 103, 146.

5 Maritain, *The Degrees of Knowledge* (Charles Scribner's Sons, 1938), pp. 458–60.

6 See G. Picard, "La Saisie immédiate de Dieu dans les états mystiques," *Revue d'Ascétique et de Mystique*, LV, 45–51. Against this view Maritain argues that there can be no direct seizure of the divine nature without grace, for the divine essence, being simple, must be grasped entire, rather than "obscurely or by halves." But does it not follow that the successful *mystique*, the one rewarded with grace, intuits God with complete adequacy, that is, becomes cognitively equal to God? This seems to be M. Picard's reasoning, and it is hard to see why it is not conclusive. (See Maritain, *Degrees of Knowledge*, p. 333.)

7 Maritain's discussion of William James and other recent theologians in his *Réflexions sur l'intelligence* (pp. 262–87) is a good example of the confrontation of first- and third-type theism with no recognition of the possibility of an intermediate position. It is significant that he closes the discussion with the charge that the theologians under consideration "change the glory of the incorruptible God into the likeness of corruptible man." As if it were not perfectly possible to maintain intact the incorruptibility of God while admitting his capacity for increasing richness of content, for creative though not destructive change (not reckoning suffering as destruction, however)!

8 See Morris R. Cohen, *Reason and Nature* (Harcourt, Brace & Co., 1931).

9 If Hegel was a second- rather than first-type theist, he failed to enlighten most of his followers on the point. Hegel is a clear writer only if "clear" be given a very Hegelian meaning. But in so far as he is clear, he is, I think, a first-type theist. If there are also contrary indications, this only illustrates the inherent contradictoriness of this form of theism. Some learned scholars indeed think that Hegel believed both in a changeable God and in real contingency. But then for Hegel the real is the rational, and that for him seems to mean the deducible, the necessary, so that what we come to is that there are contingent entities, but they are unreal! And doubtless there is change, but it is unreal! Schelling, in later life, did affirm a changing God, but he seems to have tried to combine this with a Spinozistic necessitarianism — all the while talking much of "freedom." Recent philosophy shows, I hold, a fundamental advance in such matters.

IV

GOD AND RIGHTEOUSNESS

It is extraordinary how limited is the human conception of God. Men are afraid to ascribe to him inner conflict and tragedy characteristic of all life, the longing for his other, for the birth of man. . . . Self-sufficiency, stony immobility, . . . the demand for continual submission are qualities which the Christian religion considers vicious and sinful, though it calmly ascribes them to God. It becomes impossible to follow the Gospel injunction, " Be ye perfect as your Father in heaven is perfect." That which in God is regarded as a sign of perfection, in man is considered an imperfection. . . . To deny tragedy in the divine life is only possible at the cost of denying Christ. NICOLAS BERDYAEV, in *The Destiny of Man*

THE RELATIONS between goodness and theistic belief have been conceived in ways that are extraordinarily various. The main European tradition is, of course, the supposition that atheism or agnosticism connotes moral disintegration. But not only does experience present what to most of us appear to be more or less flagrant instances to the contrary, it even suggests to certain persons a very real connection between some of the most unethical aspects of modern life and belief in God. Those who profit most by social injustices have only to recall that since God's in his heaven, all must be right with the world. Those who have reasons of their own for opposing social change have only to reflect that the Orderer of all things is above time and change, and that all possible value is realized — despite the seeming evils of the world — in the eternal perfection of the Creator. Those, again, who have power of such a kind and degree as virtually to enslave their fellows point to the absolute righteousness of the Dispenser of all powers. Moreover, those who are on the other side of social inequalities tend to accept these religious apologies for their misfortunes, and to console themselves with the hope of restitution in a future life. Thus the chief use of faith seems to be to disarm criticism of social arrangements — to promote smugness in the fortunate and stoical resignation in those deprived of the means of life on a really human plane.

Another type of ethical objection to theism questions its compatibility with intellectual honesty, in the exacting sense which scientific progress has given to that conception. Can a mind which permits itself to accept a belief so devoid of scientific foundation as theism has been shown by Hume, Kant, and many others to be, really maintain, with respect to its other interests, the critical alertness and integrity which ethics must regard as an important duty, perhaps as the foundation of all other duties? Furthermore, how can the effort to maintain a belief so beset with obstacles fail to drain off much of the best energy of the mind which might otherwise be more profitably expended? Are not those theists who escape ethical nullity in the form of smugness rendered no less its victims in the form of anxious and exhausting absorption in metaphysical preoccupations?

It is further said that so far from being able to illuminate ethics, theology presupposes and merely applies an ethic. For we cannot infer what is good from our concept of God unless we know that God is good, and how can we know what this means unless we know what " good " is independently of our theology? This seems unanswerable, yet it is a fallacy. For to conceive the goodness of God is to make an ethical experiment which cannot otherwise be made, namely, the experiment of trying to extend our concept of goodness to the maximal degree, the infinite case, in order to see whether the concept thus extended can meet the requirements of this most exacting of all applications. These requirements are not merely ethical, their fulfillment is not judged by the ethical sense alone; for they are also cosmological or metaphysical, and their fulfillment is to be certified by the metaphysician as well as the moralist. Thus we have an independent check on our ethical insight — the logic of metaphysical concepts; and we have an independent check on our metaphysical reasoning — our ethical sense. This interplay of inquiries is the chief merit of theological philosophy, and it cannot in equal degree be attained by non-theological systems for the simple reason that such systems do not, at least not so clearly and consistently, represent the supreme reality or cause as ethical in nature. They divorce the questions of cosmic reality and of the measure of goodness in such a fashion that the one question has little pertinence to the other. It is obviously the very essence of atheism, at least in all popular forms, to insist upon this divorce.

In general, the possibility of a theology depends upon the possibility of making our basic conceptions adequate to a supreme instance. Thus, there cannot be a perfect love if love is such that it must necessarily be imperfect. One of the ways in which atheists sometimes put their conclusion into the concepts from which they affect to derive it is by so conceiving love that a divine instance of this conception becomes impossible. The most drastic form of this procedure is the not unfamiliar one of denying that there is any genuine love at all, since in reality — it is suggested — all motivation comes back to self-enjoyment or self-interest. Not atheists alone have held to this doctrine. It has been set forth by revered bishops, who did not know that they were making nonsense of their religion.

Let us examine this view. To act rightly is, we are told,

to act rationally, and this in turn is explained to mean, to act in accordance with enlightened self-interest. In other words, virtue is intelligence in the choice of means to one's ends, all of which, it is held, are included in the supreme end, to promote one's own welfare. If one is also urged to do good to others, it is because it is to one's own interest to earn the good will of others, or because acting socially fulfills one's interest by developing social impulses without which one is not a complete or happy human being.

The whole idea is unsatisfactory. There is no sufficient reason for the assertion that all of a man's ends are included in the end of realizing his *self*-interest, unless self-interest is only a name for the sum of interests a man has. Of course a man can only do what, in some sense, he is interested in doing. But this does not prove that all he is interested in doing is to promote his own welfare, if this means anything more than that what he is interested in doing he is interested in doing. Suppose he takes an interest in sacrificing himself for his child or his loved one. You may say that satisfying this interest adds more to his welfare than the sacrifice subtracts. You may even argue that were this not the case the sacrifice could not be made, for to *will* the sacrifice is to find one's greater good in it. But here there is an ambiguity, a very simple ambiguity which has yet escaped many great minds. It turns upon the time factor; as in general the neglect of temporal distinctions, the failure to "take time seriously," is one of the chief defects of our intellectual tradition.

If a man desires to bring about a *future* state of affairs, then clearly the expectation of this state *already* gives him pleasure. We are bound to be pleased by the prospect of bringing about what we desire to bring about. But it does not follow that what we desire is our own state of *now* being pleased. On the contrary, it can never be that what is desired is the identical pleasure of desiring or expecting that which is desired, any more than when we assert a proposition, the proposition ever asserts simply, " This proposition is true." If the state of affairs which is desired is future (and that is the definition of desire) and if the satisfaction of now contemplating the desired future is not future but present, then clearly the state of affairs desired is not the satisfaction we now take in desiring it. The *present* self always receives a reward from its every attitude and choice and effort; but the *future* goal of the attitude or choice or effort *may or may not be a reward to the future self* of the same human person. I may desire that I shall be comfortable in my old age, and to this end take out an annuity policy. From this action I now derive pleasure. I also may desire that in event of my death my dependents shall be comfortable, and to this end take out a life insurance policy. From this action too I derive pleasure. But if in the former case the goal was the future comfort of myself, in the latter it is, by the same principle, the future comfort of others; and in neither case is the pleasure now derived from the desire (and the effort to fulfill it) the object desired. It can be shown by many lines of reasoning that the future welfare of others can be a motive as direct and genuine as one's own future welfare.

It is true that if a man reflects upon his own future welfare he will see that helping others is likely to contribute to that end; but it is also true that if he reflects upon the welfare of others he sees that it is likely to contribute to that if he helps himself; and if intelligent interest in self encourages one to take an interest in others, it is also profoundly true that one's interest in oneself depends in great measure upon one's interest in others. To believe, or rather half-believe (for no more than that is possible), that one's welfare is of no importance to others is to have little heart for furthering it, is in fact to be tempted to destroy oneself. Thus for every relation to the self in terms of the future there is a parallel relation to others. There is sadism, but also masochism or self-torture. There is excessive concentration upon self-preservation, and excessive neglect of it, even extravagant absorption in the destiny of others — foolish altruism as well as foolish egoism.

It is certainly true that usually one expects to derive future as well as present pleasure from acts calculated to serve others. If a man who does not expect to die for a long time insures his life, it is perhaps partly with the thought that he will live more comfortably, knowing that if he should die his relatives will be cared for. Thus his own future welfare is also involved. But it is because he is interested in and desires the welfare of others that promoting their welfare contributes to his own, not vice versa; just as a man can think about his thought of *x* only if he thinks about *x;* he does not think about *x* because he thinks about his thought of *x*. Similarly, we desire to enjoy the fulfillment of our interests in others because we have those interests; we do not have them because we desire enjoyment. Without an initial interest in others a man would not know that other persons were real at all, or that he was himself a person in any significant sense.

Suppose a man expects to die shortly, perhaps in a few minutes. Often such a man takes the keenest interest in promoting the welfare of others (or hindering it), for instance by making a kindly (or unkindly) will, or by confessing a crime so that an innocent man shall not suffer. Here the time he will have to enjoy the good deed (or the vengeful one) is negligible. The man is thinking not of what is due himself but (even if it be punishment) of what is due others. (There may be no thought of a future life.)

To desire is to " take pleasure " in the thought of something. If the something is a state of future pleasure (or, in morbid cases, of pain) for oneself, the desire is a case of self-interest; if it is a state of pleasure (or pain) for others, the desire is, just as literally, a case of other-interest. In the only sense in which egoism or selfishness has a meaning and is possible, altruism is equally conceivable. The only incorrigible egoist whose self-interest is *always* served in every choice is the self of the present moment as now enjoying its choices. But this unfailing egoism is yet far from absolute, or enlightened self-interest would be as impossible as altruism. For enlightened self-interest means that something beyond present satisfaction becomes the goal of present satisfaction, and this something beyond may, according to all the facts, be *either* future self-satisfaction or future satisfaction to others. In other words, the only incorrigible egoist (the present self) is also an incorrigible altruist. The present self *never* acts merely for itself, but always also for some other self, and this may be either its " own " future self, the self not now existent which will bear its name, though clearly not simply identical with it, or else some " other " future self.

What unites the present self to others, its own future self included, is imagination. Those who cannot imagine what it will be to be old do not sympathize intensely with the old, even the old people they will some day be themselves. Those who can no longer imagine what it is like to be young care little for the emotions and needs of the young, even of themselves when they were young. They may have suffered as children; it matters little to them now. They may have been happy; they derive scant pleasure from that now.

" I guess I won't worry myself much now about what won't happen till I'm forty or fifty," said William. " My teeth'll last *my* time, I guess."

That brought a chuckle from Mr. Genesis. "Jes' listen!" he exclaimed. "Young man think he ain' nev' goin' be ole man. Else he think, 'Dat ole man what I'm goin' to be, dat ain' goin' be me 'tall – dat goin' be somebody else! What I care about dat ole man? I ain't a-goin' take caih of no teef fer him!' Yes, suh, an' den when he git to be ole man, he say, 'What become o' dat young man I yoosta be? Where is dat young man agone to? He 'uz a fool, dat's what – an' *I* ain't no fool, so he mus' been somebody else, not me; but I do jes' wish I had him hyuh 'bout two minutes – long enough to lam him fer not takin' caih of my teef fer me!'" [1]

The very characters in a book and their joys and sorrows can easily mean more to us than our own remote past or future. Of course there are some who will argue that this is because we identify ourselves with the characters. Exactly! That is the point; that is altruism — participating in the life of another so that his needs become yours. Those who think to save egoism in this way are persons more interested in words than in ideas. They have given up everything in their doctrine except its label. Even to speak of "self-love" is to imply a difference between the self loving and the self loved, and that difference makes room for everything from one's own future state to other persons, animals, God, as the self which may be loved.

The mechanism of all interest in any self, even one's own self, is this: In representing to our present selves any emotion or desire, no matter what individual we suppose this emotion or desire to belong to (it may be a dog), we inevitably participate, to some extent, in the emotion or desire represented, and sympathize with it. This is true even in cruelty. To realize that we are making someone suffer we must in imagination suffer somewhat with him, even if in addition to this suffering — which may be slight, if the realization is not vivid — we *also* derive pleasure from the realization. As Spinoza said (and what psychologist would dispute it?), hatred and cruelty involve both pain and pleasure in the sufferings of others. The sympathetic character of imaginative realization is the very basis of there being any self at all. If in imagining what is coming in our lives we felt no sympathy for ourselves as destined to experience in such and such ways, we would have no self-interest, and no long-run-self as the goal of endeavor; and if in imagining the experiences of others we felt entirely unmoved by them, we would be social monsters, unrecognizable as human personalities. In fact "imagining" as so used is meaningless.

To take another example of the innumerable ways in which self and other self are scrambled together in motivation, why are we so pleased by flattery? After all, why should I feel benefited because another admires me? True, his admiration may lead him to help me in some useful way; but no one will argue that this is the essential charm of flattery. Even though I may need no help, I always like admiration. Why? Because in realizing the feeling of another toward me I tend to experience that feeling myself, I tend to enjoy myself with his enjoyment of me. It is not merely that this helps me to a pleasant belief in myself; it is also that I like to feel the happiness others enjoy in relation to me. Even if it be true that I like to have others admire me chiefly because this confirms my admiration of myself, it must be remembered that this is only because I have faith in the wisdom of the admirer, regard him as of some importance, a fellow human being with the same essential capacities as myself. And in so regarding him, I am implicitly accepting the legitimacy of his interests along with mine. Thus the seemingly highly egoistic desire to be admired is really shot through with altruistic elements; just as the purest altruism is not without some concern, however subordinate or slight, for the self.

It is said that we always take some satisfaction in the misfortunes even of our best friends. But is it less true that we always feel some dissatisfaction, however slight, in the sorrows even of our worst enemies? Again, it is said that he who despises himself also esteems himself — as a despiser. Yes, but he who overesteems himself also despises himself in his heart — as a conceited person! Thus there is an equally valid altruistic counterpart for every piece of cynical egoism.

The ultimate motive is love, which has two equally fundamental aspects, self-love and love for others. Neither is ever in human affairs totally unmixed with the other; but either may predominate in a given case. Nor is this a mere empirical truth about man; *any conceivable* mind will be both egoistic and altruistic, for selfhood is social or nothing.

In one case there does seem to be such a thing as sheer self-interest. That is in the desire for one's own physical enjoyment. In itself, bodily pleasure seems to have no reference beyond one's own personality. Always, indeed, there is reference beyond the self-of-the-instant to the self that is to be, the self that will enjoy, as well as the self that does enjoy. But otherwise the social nature of the self seems, in physical pleasure, to be in abeyance. Yet this appearance is not necessarily final. It is perfectly possible to interpret physical pleasure as social with respect to individuals other than oneself. For in all human enjoyment a multitude of individuals of a non-human kind participate. These of course are the bodily cells, which in a sense are human, but equally are not "human beings." In all our physical pleasures the cells are somehow involved; this is certain enough. How are they involved? The simplest, and I believe the only intelligible, answer is that the cells are involved because they also feel the pleasures in question, though of course feel them after their own fashion. The alternative is merely to say that the cells " cause " the pleasures; but, since Hume, causality is a concept seeking its datum, whereas the concept " feeling of feeling " has its datum in, for instance, the experience of remembering a pleasure and, in remembering it, enjoying it. We can well enough understand how feeling a feeling should partly determine the character of the feeling first mentioned, in a sense in which we do not understand what is meant by calling something the cause of feeling, unless cause really means the relation of feeling to feeling in " feeling of feeling."

The notion that physical pleasure is enjoyed by the bodily cells, and participated in by us, is not a mere hypothesis, to be indirectly verified, but, like all philosophical ideas, is a hypothetical description of the immediately given. It claims to make explicit what we all, without definitely saying so to ourselves, already believe and know.

Now consider physical pleasures or pains as they are given. They have a certain localization in phenomenal space. They are given as " there," as " objects," to a certain extent, of our awareness of them. They have by virtue of this fact a certain detachment from the self. The self contemplates as well as endures them. With certain of the less definitely physical, the more subjective joys and sorrows, this detachment is more difficult or partially impossible. The subject is, rather than beholds, such affections. Here the effort to contemplate tends to destroy vividness. Physical pleasure and pain are by contrast partially objectified. But, since the being of a feeling is its integration into a self, if certain feelings possess " distance " or objectivity with respect to a given self, must they not have at least a semblance of functioning in more than one such integration? Distance from one self can only mean *rapprochement* toward another.

Plato seems to have divined the situation, characteristically without exploiting it in dogmatic or unambiguous fashion. According to him, fellowship is that which binds together gods and men and the entire universe. And there is the passage in the fifth book of the *Republic:*

> That city is best which comes nearest to the condition of an individual man. Thus, when one of our fingers is hurt, the whole fellowship that spreads through the body up to the soul, and there forms an organized unity under the governing principle, is sensible of the hurt, and there is a universal and simultaneous feeling of pain in sympathy with the wounded part; and therefore we say that the *man* has a pain in his finger: and in speaking of any part of our frame whatsoever, the same account may be given of the pain felt when it suffers, and the pleasure felt when it is easy.

Plato of course need not have meant this description at all literally; but its vividness suggests to me that he had some intuition of the truth of what I am contending for. It could even be held that what Plato says here is much more literally true of the body than it could be of any possible city. Immediate sympathy such as reigns in the organism is not even possible in a society of human beings, whose social relations are largely mediated by highly indirect means of communication. The mechanisms of signaling from person to person involve transformations of what is to be communicated, so that, instead of concrete feeling, what actually "gets across" is some generalization, some abstract schema of feeling and sensation. Thus the "group mind" is more metaphorical than literal.[2] But between a man and at least a part of his body, such as his nervous system, there is no mechanism. He communicates with these parts by a direct transaction which nothing further can explain, but which may well be the type of transaction which, adequately generalized, explains everything else.

On such a view, the ethically supreme standpoint, that of love, would be proved relevant even to the most private enjoyments, and the superiority of the " higher " satisfactions could be rendered in quantitative terms without violation of its essential meaning. For if the lowest human pleasure is social, inasmuch as it is a participation in the positive affective tone of bodily cells, the degree of realization of this social relationship, as such, is incomparably less than in the more explicit, imaginative, and rational participations. The old dilemma: *either* enjoyment is divided into two perfectly heterogeneous kinds, in which case there can be no rational basis for an integration of the two into a whole, the ethical life; *or* there is but one kind of pleasure, and then the sole basis of comparison is according to intensity and extensity — this dilemma dissolves as one grants that pleasures can be all of one kind and yet differ in a way that comes closer to the real meaning of " higher " and " lower " than does mere intensity, or mere repetition later or in other subjects. As feeling *of* feeling, enjoyment varies not simply according to the intensity of the feelings so related, but according to the vividness with which the duality implied in the " of " relation is itself felt, and according to the level of the social " other " involved. The higher feelings are participations wherein that in which we participate is adequately distinguished from the participation, and reciprocally distinguishes itself — in short, explicit, mutually conscious, communion, " social " in the narrower or pregnant sense. Once this point of view is adequately grasped, the partial truth of the notion that intense feelings are superior to feebler ones can be recognized, in so far as one can agree that the right act is the one promising the more vivid as well as the more social enjoyment, not, however, necessarily to the agent, but to the ultimate referent of all really social motivation, the totality of members of the social community.

Self-love is not the key to the love of others. The key to all relationships is social integration, by which, more or less impartially, one recognizes in the present the significance of one's own weal and woe in the future, or the appeal of the same values in one's neighbor. Self-love is merely a particularly prominent — perhaps usually, but by no means invariably, *the* prominent — aspect among others of the absolute of absolutes, the bond of social rapport, by the conscious representation of which all conduct ought to be inspired. But this bond cannot intelligibly be thus regarded as the absolute motive unless it can be seen as the immanent principle of all values, however humble. The possibility of seeing it as such a principle appears to depend, we have seen, upon remembering that the constituent parts of the body are living individuals, that the union of mind and body is therefore the integration of life with life, and that this integration — since the essence of life is most plausibly identified as feeling, irritability which is a fact for itself as well as for external spectators — is best interpreted as affectivity in immediate social rapport, or love in an embryonic stage. In agreement with a number of philosophers and scientists, I regard this social-panpsychic principle as capable of general application to reality as such (see *Beyond Humanism,* Part II, and *The Universal Orthodoxy,* chapters on " The Formula of Immanence and Transcendence," " The Synthesis of Extremes," and " The Conflict and Convergence of Science and Theology ").

We have now to consider the ethical significance of the

idea of the perfect or divine love. Ethics today generally accepts the assumption that among alternative modes of action some are " better " than others in the sense that anyone vividly aware of the circumstances and probable consequences involved would prefer such better alternatives to their worse correlates. Now traditional theism posits among the circumstances of all acts the existence of an absolutely perfect being. It appears to follow inexorably that no act can, in its consequences, be better than any other, for in either case the outcome can be neither better nor worse than the hypothecated continued or eternal reality of a value from which real subtraction and to which real addition are meaningless. Love of such a God and ethical choice are mutually irrelevant. This is a paradox at the heart of medieval theism.

On the other hand, if we give up the idea of an existing perfection, we are confronted with an opposite difficulty. The probable consequences of an act which determine its ethical value are those which hold in the long run. But where shall we draw the line in this projection of an act into the future? What — to plunge to the heart of the matter — is the use of serving tomorrow's good if, for all we know, the final state of things, however far off in the future, may be the complete destruction of all the values which our efforts have created? Those who object that in the meantime these values will have been really enjoyed seem to me unconsciously to smuggle in an assumption contrary to the hypothesis. For if, after the hypothetical final catastrophe, it would indeed be true that values would " have been " realized, and that this would be better than if they " had not been " realized, then surely some value would have escaped the allegedly complete catastrophe, namely, a sort of anonymous reminiscent savoring of past enjoyments. This assumption may be as inevitable as (is it not identical with?) the assumption that what occurs will always have occurred, or that the past is " immortal " in some sense. It is none the less true that, apart from the theistic idea of a cosmic memory, it is an assumption which we do not in the least understand. Moreover, I cannot for a moment take seriously those who say that they regard the future reduction of all values to the status of mere reminiscences, in a universe which will have ceased to create values, as an intelligible and credible conception. To believe is to stand ready to act in a certain way. Now no action, not even suicide, could express the belief in the possible eventual nullity of all action. I must politely decline to entertain the supposition that anyone, except in words, doubts the existence in nature of some factor which is incompatible with eventual unrelieved catastrophe, and in relation to which our acts have their long-run fundamental meaning. Some reliable tendency in nature toward the average production, *even in the infinite long run,* of greater value from acts which embody our best judgment than from those which do not is, so far as I can see, an inescapable implication of ethical concepts. To ignore the question of the ultimate long run, as do for instance many pragmatists, seems to be to evade an important issue. (The two earliest pragmatists, Peirce and James, did not evade it.[3])

Admitting for the moment that nature contains such a tendency, how is this to be understood? The simplest, perhaps the only, answer is the theistic one. If there is in nature a purposive intelligence, benevolently inclined toward other purposive beings, and so powerful that its destruction or utter defeat is impossible, then we have the required condition. At once, however, we face the dilemma: if the cosmic intelligence is perfect, then there can be no unrealized values, and action is once more nullified;

and if the intelligence is imperfect, there seems no guarantee against its ultimate defeat or destruction. Only infinite power seems safe from the development of superior power or combination of powers. Thus, both a finite and an infinite God seem to elude ethical requirements. (The latter seems to have the additional disadvantage of suggesting callousness to the evils in the world, which omnipotence implies to be preventable evils.)

There is need for perfection, that we may have a cause infinitely worthy of our devotion. For though we may make reservations about all ordinary causes, there must be a deeper cause that we wholly accept (even though we cannot sharply formulate it), or we are in so far not wholly ourselves in any act. Moreover, as ethics should note, this deficiency, though an ethical one, would not be our fault if no wholly acceptable cause exists. On the other hand, there is need for imperfection that we may remake the world to some purpose. The traditional theistic course has been to accept the paradox, with more or less indirection and glossing over, as insoluble. Traditional antitheism has denied, or as I should say, simply not noticed the (undeniable) need for perfection. But there is a third possibility. Perhaps "perfection" (or infinity) is ambiguous. Perhaps a being may be conceived as perfect in one sense and capable of increase in value in another.

Now in fact we have only to go, where theologians have too seldom betaken themselves, to experience, to find operating there an ideal of perfection which does not mean the possession once for all of all possible values. We do not say that a man's love for his friend is, as love, defective because he must admit the presence in his friend of unrealized capacities. Yet we should never deny that the actualization of some of these capacities would provide new content for the love of which the friend is the object, nor that this new content would enrich *aesthetically* the value of the love — without for all that rendering it necessarily more complete or perfect in the *moral* sense. Adequacy, loyalty, to the given content, not the scope of the latter, constitutes perfection in the only sense in which love can, without self-contradiction, be conceived as perfect. Owing largely to Greek influences, the medieval theists overlooked the essentially ethical meaning of the divine constancy as posited by Hebrew writers. Clearly it is unalterableness of character, not of value in the full sense of aesthetic enjoyment (with which indeed the Hebrews were all too little concerned), that is meant by " in whom is no shadow of turning."

The entire notion of deity as out of time is unethical, responds to no demand of ethical aspiration, centrally contradicts that aspiration. Granted an eternal moral fixity in the divine love, there remain as the sting of time precisely those genuine dangers and opportunities which give ethical choice its meaning, without the possibility of eventual complete nullification of efforts which would conflict with such meaning from an opposite angle. As for the melancholy destruction of values which has been lamented as the very essence of passage, it cannot occur except as memory is defective, and need not, therefore, occur at all for the divine memory. For such memory, as we have seen, there is ethical need. On the other hand, for complete prevision of the future in all its details there is no ethical need. General foreknowledge, corresponding to whatever degree of predeterminism exists in nature, is enough for any practically usable notion of providence; while foresight of absolute details would entirely eliminate temporal passage, and with it choice, activity, or purpose, in any intelligible senses. The ethical dimension would thus be banished altogether.

The idea of providence, conceived as issuing from a

timelessly perfect being, has sometimes encouraged extreme conservatism — " whatever is, is right " — and sometimes doctrinaire progressivism, the distorted influence of which can still be seen in the views of Comte and Marx. The truth is that, given timeless perfection, the process of temporal values is an irrelevant and superfluous addition, whether it be a process uphill, downhill, or on the level. There is need for a view of the cosmic reason which will have more definite implications for human purposes, so that the dangerous sense of aimlessness which haunts the social sciences can be kept within bounds by a growing consciousness of a world goal into which human goals can be integrated. Here the conception of panpsychism again becomes relevant. This conception means that physics is only the behavioristic aspect of the lowest branch of comparative psychology. But it is more and more being realized that all psychology is in some sense social psychology, so that the final empirical science will be a generalized comparative sociology. The lowest known organisms have aspects that deserve to be called social. Whitehead has shown that the human individual himself is a society of occasions on his mental side, and a society of such societies on his bodily side, and a society of societies of societies altogether. This analysis brings abstract questions of motivation, of " self-interest " and " altruism," down to a concrete level of definite relationships in terms of which the problems of human cooperation can be understood. Self-interest as the absolute of behavior drops out, and the real limitations of social interest can be traced to their genuine relative causes, knowledge of which will tell us how far improvement is possible. And in any case the vision of a world social to its least units should prove an inspiration to cooperative behavior; whereas the notions of absolute atomic individuals together with the non-social interpretation of the "survival of the fittest" have obviously tended to promote egotism. So also have conceptions of God as purely absolute and self-sufficient — and hence even less capable of social relations than the most savage and competitive of beasts!

There is, however, a reason why theologians might easily be led — as Bishop Paley was — to suppose a perfect coincidence of love and self-interest. In God there is indeed a perfect agreement of altruism and egoism. For whatever good God may do to any being anywhere he himself, through his omniscient sympathy, will inevitably enjoy. The future welfare of all beings will be entirely included in the future satisfactions of God. Hence God can make no sacrifices, except in the sense that he does take upon himself the sufferings as well as the joys of his creatures. Theologians apparently sometimes overlooked the fact that such an agreement between love and self-interest depends upon the complete transparency or omniscience of the love. They held that omnipotence would be appropriately employed in producing in man a similarly perfect harmony of self-interest and good will. But, even granting an immortal personal life for human beings, it still does not appear how a finite mind could be precisely rewarded for its virtue; for what is "precisely" to mean here? The precise reward I can conceive would be the enjoyment of the very happiness one contributes to another; but this presupposes perfect knowledge of the other's inner life, and hence is possible only to God.

Why should not a finite member of the world society make some genuine sacrifices for the society? The greater good thus predominates over the lesser. And if you ask, What motive can inspire the sacrifice? the answer is clear: The will to the general good, the good of persons as such, oneself included, in short — love, the only motive that is self-justifying, since it expresses the attitude essential to the self's being a self at all. God has no other motive; but in his case the total good of all persons is no more comprehensive than his own present and future welfare, this comprehensiveness of his personal good being his unique superiority rather than the general property of selves. The " interest in interests " (I take this phrase from C. W. Morris) is the final motive; but only *one* self includes all interests in its " own " interest, though all rational selves admit that it is interests as such, and not as one's own, that one should have as end (wherever it is in one's power to serve them), even though one does not know how far one will ever oneself enjoy the achievement of the end when it has been attained.

The feeling that good men should not go unrewarded has a legitimate, though relative, meaning in the consideration that there can be no greater good without particular personal goods, and that if in the very act of serving the good of others one normally and to an equal extent sacrificed one's own, such service would interfere with one part of the general good while promoting another, so that the process would be futile. But, as an exceptional case, sacrifice, like other forms of evil, seems compatible with the idea of a world fundamentally good and appropriate to rational endeavor. Perhaps the demand for absolute rewards is only a subtle manifestation of the desire to be God, omniscient and beyond the possibility of sacrifice or beyond the temptation to choose a lesser good for oneself as against a greater for another.

It follows from the above that if " ethical " means resistant to temptation, or willing to sacrifice joy (not just to suffer pain) for others, then in so far God is not ethical. But if it means being motivated by concern for the interests of others, then God alone is absolutely ethical; for to know interests, fully and concretely, and to share them are indistinguishable. The " simplicity " of God has here its true meaning, that there can be no duality of understanding and motivation in a being in which either understanding or motivation is perfect. Both come down to love pure and simple and indivisible. To fully sympathize with and to fully know the feelings of others are the same relationship, separable in our human case only because there the " fully " never applies, and we never know the feelings of others but only have knowledge about them, abstract diagrams of how in rough, more or less general ways they feel. If we saw the individuality and vividness of the feeling, we would have the feeling. As Hume said, without perhaps knowing what a contribution to theology he was here making, the vivid idea of a feeling is in principle coincident with its " impression," that is, with such a feeling as one's own.

It is often maintained that the only really pure — or, at least, the highest — love is that which springs from no " need " of the beloved, that which " overflows " from a purely self-sufficient being who derives nothing from any other. This is one of those apparently refined and superior thoughts of theologians which analysis shows to be really crude. Need and self-sufficiency have several senses and everything depends upon discriminating them. The need of the child for its mother is a need not for the beloved as such but for nourishment and other things to which the mother tends to be merely a means. God has no external environment which has the option of either serving him or destroying him. Self-preservation is not a problem for the necessary being. God " needs " only one thing from the creatures: the intrinsic beauty of their lives, that is, their own true happiness, which is also his happiness through his perfect appreciation of theirs. This appreciation *is* love, not something extra as a motive to love. God "needs" happiness in which to share, not because the alternative is for him to cease to be, for this is not a possible alternative, but because the exact beauty of his own life varies with the amount of beauty in lives generally. *Some* other lives he must have, but his perfect power consists in this, that no matter what the creatures do with their free will they cannot bring about the destruction of the cosmos as such, they cannot reduce God to solitariness. All they can do is to determine *how much each new event adds* to the sum of event-values already stored in the memory of God. God has need for the maximum possible addition, not in the sense that he must have it " or else," but in the sense that it is to his interest to have it. His interest is the universal interest in interests, that is, love in the highest conceivable sense. It is not the interest in nothing, or the bare absence of interest, or interest in his own bare self-sufficiency or glory, whatever that (in the theological not the biblical version) may be.

The Trinity is supposed to meet the requirements of giving God an object of love which yet agrees with his absolute self-sufficiency, and also an object of love "worthy" to be loved with so perfect a love as the divine. This is done by making the lover and the beloved identical — yet not identical. But whatever be the truth of this idea — whose meaning seems to me just as problematic as its truth, for, once more, nonsense is only nonsense, however you put a halo around it — it leaves the essential problem of the divine love unsolved. For either God loves the creatures or he does not. If he does, then their interests contribute to his interests, for love means nothing more than this. If he does not, then the essence of the religious belief in God is sacrificed, and one still has the question, How then is God related to the creatures' interests?

The incarnation is supposed to solve the problem also. I can only say that if it is Jesus as literally divine who loves men, really loves them, then my point, so far as I can see, is granted. If not, then the problem is unsolved. Instead of simply *adding Jesus to an unreconstructed idea of a non-loving God,* should we not take him as proof that God really *is love* — just that, without equivocation?

The idea that the highest love will love only an object equally exalted with itself seems contrary to all analogy. It is the highest terrestrial animal that takes an interest in the interests of the lower animals, sometimes even the lowest. " Worthy of love " is a rather silly phrase, if love means adequate awareness of the value of others, whatever that happens to be. Everything is completely worthy of love, that is, of having its interests fully appreciated. If its interests are not on a high level (e.g., if they are ultra-simple, or chaotic) , then complete love will not assign it to such a level but precisely to its proper level. Absolute *adequacy to the object* is the definition of perfect love, in the basic sense assumed in this book.

To speak of the religious ideal of love at the present juncture may seem dangerously irrelevant. Sentimental humanitarianism might, it seems, succeed only in smoothing the path of the oppressor, who will obliterate the humanitarian along with his sentiment. Now if religious love means sentimentalism, then I agree with those who regard it as an obstacle to the only type of advance now possible. But " love " as religion intends it is not a mere emotional glow toward others, nor is it a self-defeating program of attempting to deal with quarrels by offering appeasement to those who will not be appeased. Love is the effort to act upon adequate awareness of others, awareness at least as adequate ideally as one has of oneself. Love thy neighbor as thyself means, even better than one without religion can love himself, since we are first of all to love God and to make the relation of all men, including ourselves, to the divine love the key to their significance. So far from being fanciful or wishful dreaming, an unrealistic appraisal of things, religious love is action from social awareness, with the will to endless growth in such awareness toward the perfect social appreciations of God. It means pure and literal realism, provided the virtues of men and their potentialities for improvement and happiness as well as their liability to degeneration, their vices and misery, are included in what is real.

Which has caused the fearful catastrophes of the past decade — excess of social awareness and of the striving for it, or deficiency of these attitudes? Let us see. The German republic collapsed, students agree, partly because of its adherence to a theory of freedom which says, in effect, grant civil rights even to those who will use them to deprive others of these same rights. Is adherence to this theory an expression of social awareness or is it not rather just bad thinking? Of course one should appreciate, be socially aware of, the desire of some to deny to others the rights they claim for themselves, but since this desire conflicts with other desires of men with which one should also sympathize, one has to make an adjustment in which in some sense there results the least sacrifice of the desires sympathized with. Any other course shows a net deficiency, not a net excess, of social awareness. It shows a failure in so far to imitate the divine awareness, which feels all desires for what they are, and seeks the lesser sacrifice, the most valuable adjustment. *To veto a desire is not necessarily to fail literally to sympathize with it;* for sympathy only makes the desire in a manner one's own, and even one's own desire one may veto, because of other more valuable desires. Love makes all control of others also self-control, all denial self-denial, it does not abolish control or denial.

Again, the German republic fell partly because of a theory of proportional representation which says, in effect, that the minority is to be ruled by the majority, but in such a way that any minority is always to be free to put such obstacles in the way of the will of the majority that that will is bound to come to nought, although the will of the minority will not come to anything either. This theory may seem to careless inspection like a corollary from the principle of social awareness, but really it contradicts it.

Why were the Germans first hindered by other peoples from succeeding in their democratic venture and then ineffectually opposed after they had given it up and made themselves into a self-announced threat to mankind? Clearly the reparation and guilt-admission sections of the Versailles treaty showed a lack not an excess of social awareness or even-handed sympathy. So did American tariff policy combined with a lending program that made unpayable debts inevitable. As to the ineffectual opposition to the subsequent tyranny, it does indeed seem clear that those pacifists who deduced absolute renunciation of military means from their conception of love were in effect staunch allies of Hitler rather than of his victims. But is this doctrinaire pacifism the expression of too much will to or achievement of social awareness? The saintly English pacifist who held that Hitler was not beyond the reach of kindly impulses because Hitler had been courteous to him personally seems to have shown in this argument the dominance of blind sentiment or of fanatical doctrinaire bias, rather than the reality of social appreciation. It is not love to deny what men are, rather it is love to get out of oneself sufficiently to see what they are. To try to keep life on a pleasant level by suggesting that tyrants are not so very bad, nor so very powerful or dangerous, may be preferring one's own sentiment or theory to the achievement of social realization.

But there is the argument that love is not only a motive and goal, it is also a method, the only valid method, of influencing others. Yet to try to base one's own action solely upon social awareness, and to wish that others might do so also, seems not necessarily to imply the exclusive use of the direct appeal to this attitude in others as *means* of expressing it in oneself and of promoting its growth in the world. Social realism — and unless that is what love is it is pernicious, and is besides unworthy to be used as the defining trait of deity — may enable us to see that to hand over the use of force to those inferior in love is to guarantee that there will be less and less social awareness in the end. To oppose by force is not necessarily to fail in social appreciation; one may be sorrowfully aware of what the force means to its victims, innocent or guilty. To deny this is merely to bear false witness against many noble soldiers, whose departures from love can be matched by those of other classes of men. There is evidence enough that dogmatic pacifism is often the expression of a preference for a certain enjoyable sentiment as against facing the tragedy of existence, which even God does not escape, and which we must all share together. To decide to shorten a man's life (we all die) is not *ipso facto* to lack sympathy with his life as it really is, that is, to lack love for him. It may be to love not him less but someone else more, in comparison with the pacifist. Where lives come into fundamental conflict, sacrifice of life there will be, even if only by slow starvation. To fight without hate or indifference may be hard, but so is it hard to do business or compete for honors in art, or to live at all, without envy, callousness, willful blindness to others. Love, being in its literalness the unique privilege of deity, is infinitely difficult. Many a pacifist is clearly no model of love. The few really noble ones can be easily matched by the nobler warriors, so far as my observations go at least. And theoretically I do not see why we should expect otherwise.

From all this it does not follow that war is not a tremendous evil, but only that there are even worse ones, just as liberty for others is sometimes better than life for oneself. Nor does it follow that most of those who take to the sword have a justification in love for doing so. Nothing is more horrible than the lightness with which men have been slaughtered, even on the merest whim. Indeed a just objection to sheer pacifism is that by making war as such the greatest possible evil it puts discrimination as to wars and their causes to sleep even more effectively than does extreme militarism. If to fight is *ipso facto* to give up love, then it is vain to ask, Does this *particular* cause rightfully demand military support from the loving or does it not? All such discrimination between causes is left to others by pacifists, who naturally enough like to point out the virtues of the bad causes and the vices of the good ones until all comparative judgments, the only ones by which men can live, are discouraged and action ceases to have meaning. The field is then open to those who know too well what they prefer and also know how to get it — which the pacifists alas do not, whatever services they may perform in counteracting irresponsible militarism or in other ways. Undoubtedly, pacifists can remain more aware of *some* of the social realities than can those engaged in the military struggle. They can specialize in their sympathies. The soldier cannot dwell too much on the sufferings of the enemy, any more than a lawyer can be as aware of the interests of his client's opponent as of those of his client.

Only God can entirely avoid specialization of sympathy without falling into utter superficiality. What we have all to do is to try to see in abstract principle what the interests we have not concretely attended to require of us. As to this the pacifist has no monopoly.

As to the argument that the greatest exponents of love have been pacifists, that one cannot imagine Jesus leading men into battle, etc., I wish to venture a word or two. Can one imagine Jesus as a corporation lawyer or a policeman? After all, founding a religion is one thing, winning battles or law cases or arresting criminals another, but it does not follow that the principles of that religion condemn the other mentioned activities. Also it is not clear that the Jewish nation, had it fought the Romans, had a very valid cause of battle, including a reasonable chance of gaining the victory. The Roman Empire was probably the best organization of affairs available at the time. (Should anyone say this of the nazi empire today, he would, I think, be radically mistaken. Germany is strong enough to organize Europe by brute force and to enslave the whole to twenty million ruling-class Germans, and for this reason alone it would be better for Britain, which *cannot* control Europe except by getting it to control itself more or less cooperatively, to have the leading part in the beginning. The advantages would be not for a decade; they might be for a thousand years. Those who speak of the rebelling of the conquered do not tell us, even vaguely, how it is to be done.) Had Jesus a definite stand on military ethics it is strange that his only references to military affairs state nothing any militarist need deny, except as incontrovertible facts compel denial of one statement in its literal unqualified meaning. (Not all who take up the sword do perish by the sword.) And if the injunctions to love enemies and turn the other cheek have absolute scope and the meaning strict pacifism requires, then the pacifist must be ready to cooperate with anyone who sets out to take advantage of him. Who supposes that he will be ready actually to do this, to rely exclusively upon " heaping coals of fire " upon all men who are ready to infringe upon his rights? There is plenty of meaning left to these words, indeed all the real consistent meaning they ever can have, without any such literal absolutism being involved. The tendency to think revenge its own justification, resentment its own excuse for being, to meet injury with injury whether or not there is another, superior method for achieving important adjustments, is one of the greatest evils in life. No man ever threw such a bright light upon the possibilities for avoiding this evil as did Jesus. It is quite another matter to exclude the use of force even where no superior method can be found. And there are such occasions, as can be seen perfectly well today, when those who are not in favor of stopping aggression by force offer no alternative likely to stop it at all until the world is in the hands of the aggressors and pacifists will not even be allowed to argue any longer.

The career of Gandhi is another possible case from which to argue for pacifism. It is to be noted that Gandhi is admittedly a partisan, not just a lover of humanity. His cause is first of all India's. Now there may be a method superior to military resistance to wring freedom from the British. The British have the weapons, on the one hand, and they have a considerable willingness to extend justice, on the other. On the contrary, if the United States tries to deal with aggression by appeasement it will merely be despised for neglecting its huge potential capacity for armament, and will meet with an inability to understand even what we mean by the liberties we wish to preserve, and ought for mankind's sake to preserve. With no little justice it will be said that we valued the comforts of peace, our automobiles and other material advantages, more than the defense of immaterial and priceless rights to religious, educational, and other forms of freedom. We will seem to care more about wealth or the immediate ease of following our habits of life and thought than about the long-run development of American life in accordance with American ideals.

The true role for pacifism lies in keeping in mind a *goal* for the nations, to be pursued by all means, including force, likely to lead to it, in which a place for all the peoples will be found. Not those who want to stop aggressor peoples as such are the enemies of humanity, but those who want to do it by the unscrupulous method of killing off troublesome populations, dismembering troublesome nations, and the like. The right combination of firmness and generosity which alone can really give lasting peace will require all the social awareness, all the love, that can be mustered. But mere generosity to the aggressor without regard to the need for freeing his victims will only be generosity coming to the rescue of ungenerosity as such, that is, it will be self-refuting. To argue that any victors are bound to impose a vindictive, bad peace is relevant only if it be shown that there is a better alternative than to have another set of even less scrupulous victors impose a worse peace. A " peace without victory " might be the thing, but that is no help until it is shown how it can be achieved as other than a thin disguise for the victory of the wrong side, the side that doesn't even want or profess to do justice.

In a heroic time dedicated to the salvation of freedom and the minimal conditions of human brotherhood, it is of service to recall a being to whom suffering is never alien, and who is the individual of all others the most tolerant of the variety of wills, the most ready to cooperate with their efforts, and the most free from the vain or stupid desire to have nothing to gain from the results of their initiative. Proud, willful, uncooperative men will never understand the gentle passivity of God, as weak and flabby men will never understand the energy of his resistance to the excesses of creaturely will at the point where these excesses threaten the destruction of creaturely vitality. The best expression of belief in God is an attitude of social awareness which treats all problems in the spirit of mutuality except where others insist upon treating them in another spirit, at which point we must in our local way, like God in his cosmic way, set limits by constraint to the destruction of mutuality. " Violence " and the constraints it imposes are surely not in the world merely through the fault of good men. It is better that many should die prematurely than that nearly all men should live in a permanent state of hostility or slavery.

The divine love is social awareness and action from social awareness. Such action seems clearly to include the refusal to provide the unsocial with a monopoly upon the use of coercion. Coercion to prevent the use of coercion to destroy freedom generally is in no way action without social awareness but one of its crucial expressions. Freedom must not be free to destroy freedom. The logic of love is not the logic of pacifism or of the unheroic life.

NOTES

1 From Booth Tarkington, *Seventeen* (Harper & Bros., 1915), p. 131.

2 The most plausible attempt known to me to construe God as the group mind of humanity is presented in R. B. Cattell's *Psychology and the Religious Quest* (Thomas Nelson & Sons, 1938).

3 According to Peirce, rational action presupposes that our interests " embrace the whole community " and that this community " reach, however vaguely, beyond this geological epoch, beyond all bounds " (*Papers,* II, 654; also V, 352–57). Thus logic " inexorably requires " that we live for an everlasting goal.

V

THE THEOLOGICAL ANALOGIES AND THE COSMIC ORGANISM

In the tablet of the universe there is no letter save Thy Name,
By what name, then, shall we invoke Thee?

JAMI, poet of Iran

Deus est caritas. – THE VULGATE

THE RELATION of God to the world must necessarily be conceived, if at all, by analogy with relations given in human experience. To reject such analogies completely would be to adopt a wholly " negative " or empty theology, besides contradicting the basic religious doctrine that man is the image of God. Accordingly, a principal task of any theology is to examine the relations in which things stand in our experience in order to discover the direction in which the indeed superior, but not in every sense incomparable, relations of God are to be sought. (The Thomist view that God is not subject to relations will be dealt with in chapter 7. In any case, things have relations to God, and that is enough for the argument of this chapter.)

We could conceivably experience relations between (a) human beings and other human beings or creatures not radically superior or inferior to them; (b) human beings and creatures inferior to them; (c) such inferior creatures and others of their kind; (d) human beings and what is superior to them; (e) superior beings and others of their kind; (f) subhuman and superhuman beings. Since God is the most exalted of all related terms, (c) is not likely to be very helpful; and (d), (e), and (f) correspond to nothing very clearly given in our experience. Except for God himself, who is to be interpreted through analogy with something else, no definite individual unambiguously superior to man himself is known to us, unless it be the universe as a whole, and the character of this whole is part of what we wish to find out; for the questions, How is God related to the universe? and, What is the universe? must be closely connected. Nor is the universe as a whole given in any clear way. Hence our resources reduce to (a) and (b). Here we meet two conflicting considerations. (A) seems to be the religiously preferred basis of analogy. God is to the creatures as a human father to human children, or a ruler to the ruled, or a beloved to a lover, or a friend to the befriended. But philosophically this is doubly insufficient by itself: it throws no light on the radical superiority of creator to creatures; and it throws no light on the immanence or omnipresence ascribed to God. It suggests that he is merely outside things, operating on them through intermediaries, such as sound waves, light waves, etc., whereas all such intermediaries are also his creatures.

We are driven to (b) as our last resort. And here also we encounter certain difficulties. Our relation to the subhuman, to bear much analogy to the relation of God to the world, must be a relation to a whole of things all of which are radically inferior to us, and in which whole we may be said to be something like omnipresent or immanent. There is one and only one such whole — the human body. Certain objections arise, however. The human body does not, for direct perception, contain distinct individual things, as the world to which God is to be related certainly does. It is a quasi-continuous solid, differentiated, but without clear-cut separateness or independence of parts. Hence it is feared that to interpret the world as though it were God's body would be to deny the reality of individuals as such other than God. And this difficulty joins with the preference of many theologians for the pluralistic version of first-type theism — that is, for a God in every sense independent of the world — to create a prejudice against the fair consideration of the mind-body analogy. Even for second-type theism this prejudice is justified, unless it can be shown that the mind-body analogy can somehow be combined with the analogy of human social relations, upon which religion does insist, and which has the philosophical merit of being the only case of a relation both terms of which are equally well understood by us human beings. We know equally well what it is to be a human individual knowing or loving another human individual and to be such an individual known or loved by another. We have ourselves been both. Thus we must use this uniquely familiar relation as a hypothetical or problematic analogy in interpreting all relations in so far as less familiar — if it is true that knowledge proceeds from known to unknown. Now the main point of this chapter is that the human-to-human analogy and the mind-body analogy can perfectly well be combined if both are adequately generalized.

First of all, modern science shows us (it might have been inferred from philosophical principles) that the seeming solidity of the body is an exaggeration of sense perception, due to the mere fact that perception is (for easily specified biological reasons) on the macroscopic scale, while the real individuals in the body are microscopic. They are not for all that a whit less real. The microscope and other even more powerful instruments of detection no more create the objects they enable us to distinguish than the unaided eye creates deer or horses. Philosophers made a pure error in philosophic method when, from the fact that no organism contains individual parts which as such are clearly perceivable, they inferred that organisms probably or certainly contain no individual parts. The premise of the inference was that what does not appear distinctly to the human senses probably or certainly does not exist. The probabilities should have been estimated just the other way. For we have only to see that we can never, as Hume pointed out, from direct sense perception alone derive the slightest clue to the *future* behavior of bodies to draw the certain inference that the *present* actuality of bodies is very scantily revealed to our perception. For this present actuality must contain part at least of the ground of future behavior, and the fact that, as Hume so well insisted, we directly see no hint of the future in the present state of a body — for instance, no hint of the flame in the match before its being struck — is proof enough that there is something in the body which is hidden from us. Why should not this hidden something involve a multiplicity of invisible parts? And there is no reason to think these parts lacking in real individuality. It is the visible things which are typically lacking in individuality; heaps of dirt, deposits of minerals, bodies of water, clouds — it would be hard to see how anything could be less individual than these! We say the water flows; but what really does the moving — the whole mass of water, the drops, or still smaller imperceptible parts? Only science locates definite individual boundaries, distinct active agents, in these amorphous, "passive" masses.[1] And it infers these individuals not only for inorganic wholes but as parts of organisms also. Thus a body, to the best of our knowledge, is really a "world" of individuals, and a mind, if the body is one having a mind (or one capable of thinking and feeling), is to that body something like an indwelling God.

Let us see how inevitable and apt this analogy is, centuries of prejudice to the contrary notwithstanding.

Knowledge, as we know it in ourselves, has more than

one dimension. It varies as to scope, but it varies also as to immediacy and distinctness. Human beings know, by direct and vivid intuition, only a tiny circle of facts. In this respect they seem scarcely superior to the higher animals. The greater range and reliability of human knowledge is due of course to imaginative and inferential leaps, more or less subjected to criticism, beyond immediacy. But if we could intuit the whole environment simultaneously and distinctly, there would (unless perhaps to project plans for the future) be no need for such imaginative transcendence. Nor can omniscience be conceived except as clear intuition of the entire cosmos.

Similar remarks apply to power. Man has power over many things, if we include indirect forms of control, control through intermediaries, or "instruments" in the broadest sense. But of direct power man has at any time very, very little. Omnipotence could only be direct control of every part of the universe, since indirect control is subject to the imperfections inhering in all instruments.

Our problem is now precise: *Over* what has man really direct control, and *of* what has he really immediate knowledge? For when we have found this area of quite immediately known and controlled objects we shall know that, as our relation to such objects, so, though in a more exalted way, is God's relation to the universe — in so far as the theological analogy has any validity. For if we have any knowledge and power that is immediate, then — since nothing can be more immediate than immediate — the only dimension left for God's superiority is that of scope and completeness with respect to all the objects in the universe.

Over exactly what does man have direct control? Control is the ability to carry out a purpose. Now the immediate effect of a human purpose is just one thing: a change in the mind and body of the purposer. Only after the man has induced in himself a shift in his muscles does any effect of his decision appear in the world beyond him. *The immediate object of effective human volition is a change in the human body.* In cases of paralysis the area of control is greatly limited even within the body; and it is considerably limited in extent even in the normal organism. We thus arrive at the far-reaching conclusion: the power-relation in man which alone can be used as basis for the theological analogy is the mind-body relation, or rather, a part of this relation. However much God's relation to the world may differ from man's relation to his body, it must be more similar to it in one chief respect than to any other of man's relations. For instance, let us consider the oft-cited relation of man as artisan to artificial objects. The watchmaker does not directly control the production of the watch, not in the slightest. He controls the motions of his fingers, and these in turn control the formation of the watch, directly or via intermediary tools and machines. Surely God controls the world not by hands, but by direct power of his will, feeling, and knowledge. Now it is equally not by hands that man himself influences the nerve cells which initiate the train of activities spoken of. By the nervous mechanism man controls other things; but there is no further mechanism between his will and the nerves themselves (unless one agrees with the "occasionalists," with Leibniz, and with certain contemporary "personalists" that God is such a mechanism, that our only direct relations are with God — a position the difficulties of which are well known). Here and here alone we are Godlike in directness of power over individuals other than our own ego. Only after this fact has been adequately exploited will it be worth while to consider the possibilities of the artisan analogy in its indirect aspects.

Admittedly, to say, without further qualification, that God is like us in knowing and willing would satisfy no one. All agree that if he is like us in these respects he is also, just in these respects, infinitely unlike us, for his knowledge and volition are the perfection of knowledge and will. He knows and wills *eminenter,* in a uniquely exalted fashion. So far there is agreement. But some theologians are so afraid that the dissimilarity involved in the eminence will be underestimated that they prefer to hold that God does not really know or will, but that at most we can say he is *not* ignorant or powerless. Most theologians agree, however, that this negative doctrine must at some point be dropped, and a positive affirmation of some sort accepted. But with regard to the possession of a body, the negative procedure almost completely predominated (except in Plato, who could not integrate the " ideal animal " with the Creator, and in Stoicism, which of course suffered from its own defects). Little effort was made to explore the possible meanings of an eminent, a uniquely perfect body; instead, one thought more or less vaguely and loosely about the features of the human body and what was supposed to be known about the cosmic body, thought it obvious that nothing worthy of the divine could result from such conceptions, confirmed this conclusion by appeal to the dogmas of impassivity, immutability, and simplicity, and dismissed the subject with contempt. (Theological contempt and snobbery are proverbial, and have been powerful inhibitors of analysis.)

In particular it was held obvious that bodies, being composite, and mutable, must also be destructible, though how it can really be proved that the sustaining and preserving power which even the weakest minds have over their bodies could not in the most eminent mind amount to an unconditional power to preserve the body always, I think it would be impossible to say. Clearly there is a fallacy of imperfect disjunction here. An organic body is both composite and simple, it is a complexity, but an integrated complexity. That the bodies we know, other than God, all suffer death as well as undergo change proves strictly nothing about the — by hypothesis unique — body of God. If such reasoning were allowed, how could we object when atheists argue that all minds, and therefore God, are more or less weak, dependent for existence upon their environment, ignorant, etc.? If the idea of body is treated according to the same principles as are generally accepted by theologians in regard to mind, it will be found that there is nothing against the conception of an indestructible body. True it is that bodies preserve themselves by developing new parts from time to time, to replace those which have disintegrated; but for the body as a whole to survive it is only necessary that the one process keep pace with the other. Now the fact that all bodies less than the universe seem eventually to fail to maintain such a balance is not inconsistent with the notion that the universe itself does maintain it. To have an external environment is to depend upon factors not under immediate control, and sooner or later these factors may happen to conflict fatally with one's internal needs. But the universe as a whole, if it is an organism at all, must immediately control all its parts; so what is to prevent it from setting unsurpassable limits to disintegration in relation to construction? Not its composite character, for there is also its simple character as *one* "minded" organism (in Mead's phrase). The composition involves mutability; but the unity sets limits to mutability which make corruption of the whole impossible. The assumption that a composite must be *merely* that, at least potentially a mere heap of parts, is unfounded. Again, the argument that in a composite there must be a combining principle which holds the parts together but is itself without parts, proves only that if God be complex there must be *something* in him which is simple and always the same, and this is fully provided for by the A factor in the AR doctrine. The simple something in God is not God, but the abstract aspect or mere self-identity, rather than the concrete totality, of God; his essence, but not his accidents (see chapters 1, 7, and 8).

An objection to our argument might be that the immediate object of human volition cannot be the body; for according to both modern behaviorism and Aristotelianism the mind is a state or form or function of the body, and hence cannot act upon the body as a separate entity. But, however one may seek to identify body and mind, there is one distinction which must be made, that between the body as a single individual and the body as an association of cells (and these of molecules). It is to the bodily whole rather than to the bodily parts — even taking these collectively — that human thought and volition primarily belong, while the nervous changes and muscular processes are almost indifferently ascribable to the body and its parts taken collectively. The cells do not think our thoughts or will our volitions (at least, not as we do), since they are many and the human thinker and purposer is one; but to say the body changes in position or posture is precisely to refer to certain collective changes in the positions of its parts relatively to one another and to the environment of the whole collection. The body as a whole, as a dynamic individual unit (not a collection) or — it is the same thing — as a mind, wills: the parts of the body (which may be minds, but not *that* mind) respond. Analogously, when an army moves, this movement coincides with the sum of motions of its members, but it is not normally the members which initially will the movement. If the mind of the commander were more intimately and immediately effective than it is in setting up the subordinate movements and volitions which constitute the operation as attaching to the parts, the soldiers, and more responsive in its turn to impulses coming from them, the situation would be a more literal analogy to the mind-body relation than it in fact is.

In short, a man directly controls his body, within limits; and there is no clear evidence that he directly controls anything else.[2] Even if you say that bodily control is self-control, it still remains (with psychological self-control) the only clear case of instantaneous, non-mediated control we have, and the theologians who deny that the world, as immediately controlled by God, is God's body will hardly like better the doctrine that the world is God.

What, again, does a man immediately know? The evidence is clear and unambiguous only so far: a man's awareness registers immediately, in addition to his own thoughts and feelings, certain aspects of the changes going on in the parts of his body. If there is pressure on a nerve, this abnormality, or at least a resulting abnormality in the brain, or both, will impinge upon his consciousness (under favorable conditions) without any known indirectness or loss of time. True, the awareness of the bodily abnormality is not distinct, it does not bring out what the detailed situation is for individual cells or cell groups as such, but that something is wrong with the body somewhere the man immediately knows, all inference apart. On the contrary, no event whatever taking place outside the body is, with any comparable vividness, apprehended, except after some measurable period of time. Or, to take another test of immediacy, infallibility: a man can never be certain that an object which appears to him as bent is really bent; but he can be certain, not only that it *appears* to him as bent, but that this bent-appearance has a physiological aspect (such as non-straightness of the retinal image, etc.) which is infallibly present whenever the appearance is. This may be an assumption, but no contrary instance is known, and psychophysics is based on it.[3] There is every reason to believe that the internal bodily conditions are at least more precisely correlated with experience than are the external conditions. For instance, there are some hundreds of thousands, but not billions, of distinct parts of the visual field; but this number corresponds to no real divisions in perceived inorganic objects, but to the " resolving power " of the eye due to its structure. Or again, the polar contrast between complementary colors is purely physiological rather than extrabodily, or at least it is more uniformly correlated with physiological than with physical conditions. Item for item the contents of the visual field, which appears so full of definite information concerning the external world, is full of even more definite information concerning the body (whether or not we are interested in this aspect of the matter, as we usually are not).

The reason philosophers have sometimes failed to see this fact clearly is that all our inherited and acquired patterns of behavior lead us to *use* the visual map as representative of the external rather than of the internal conditions, though it is more faithful to (and is immediately presentative of) the latter. Visual perception is shot through with inference aiming at the external world; subtract this inference, as we must do to conceive the immediacy of omniscience, and it is the relation to the optical nervous system that remains as worthy of use in the theological analogy. Of course even this basis is inadequate, in that there is no distinct awareness of the individual cells (still less, however, of molecules outside the body), but only a sort of blurred outline of the cell structure and activity. God's immediacy is perhaps not more immediate than ours, but it is certainly more vivid and distinct. It surpasses in this respect our awareness of retinal activity as this surpasses our awareness of the viscera, of which we note only vague pains and pleasures.

In sum, then, God's volition is related to the world as though every object in it were to him a nerve-*muscle,* and his omniscience is related to it as though every object were a muscle-*nerve.* A brain cell is for us, as it were, a nerve-*muscle* and a muscle-*nerve,* in that its internal motions respond to our thoughts, and our thoughts to its motions. If there is a theological analogy, here is its locus. God has no separate sense organs or muscles, because all parts of the world body directly perform both functions for him. In this sense the world is God's body.

In preference to the organic analogy theologians have generally resorted to one or more of several others. They have said that the world is the content of God's mind, as ideas are of our mind (Berkeley). But this doctrine seemed to make human beings mere passive ideas of God, without genuine dynamic distinctness. (One may think that " pantheism," as the doctrine of this chapter will perhaps be called, makes man a mere cog in the divine world machine, but after all science does not show that cells as well as molecules and electrons have *no* independence of action, though of course their independence must be far from absolute.) Besides, while we do appear to have some immediate power over our own ideas, we do not appear to have any immediate power over the ideas of others (" telepathy " apart — perhaps even granting telepathy, which need not be immediate). Now it is the ideas of others than himself that God must control, in controlling his own. When we control our ideas, the only immediate effects upon individuals not ourselves are changes in the parts of the nervous system. Thus again we are driven to the mind-body analogy as the basis of any real advance.

Additional to the artisan analogy, the mind-idea analogy,

and the mind-body analogy, there seems to be but one other of any promise, the already mentioned social analogy. We know and control others most intimately by sympathetic understanding, by sharing interests with them. This analogy is obviously relevant in theology. It even has certain superiorities over the organic analogy. For while it is a fact that mind has immediate relations to the body it cannot be said that the nature of these relations is obvious. The paralytic may feel perfectly normal until he makes the attempt to execute a movement. Hume argued from this that we cannot be said to have intuitive knowledge of the connection between volition and bodily movement. What he was entitled to infer is that the knowledge, if it exists, is extremely indistinct, so that false inferences may easily occur. Moreover, the primary nerve-muscles with which our thought interacts are, as we pointed out above, the brain cells, not all of which are ever " paralyzed " while life continues. Nevertheless, the social analogy is in some respects superior even to this aspect of the organic analogy. There is no opaque mystery in sympathy. *Of course* I cannot have a vivid representation of the emotions of others without to some extent undergoing these emotions myself. The attention span is limited, or is an individual whole, and as such, even in God, must restrict itself to what can be brought into one unity of feeling. (In God the " restriction " coincides with that of actuality as such, contrasted with the all-possible.) I can realize how others feel only by doing something like feeling that way, at least " imaginatively," myself. Hence the power of love, whereby what happens in one individual produces partially similar occurrences in another individual aware of this happening, is transparent enough.

But the trouble with the social analogy in its usual form is that it does not explain how one mind is able to communicate its feeling to another *immediately*. Human intercourse is apparently not direct contact of mind with mind, but requires intermediaries, such as vibrations of the air particles between their bodies. And the use of such intermediaries depends entirely, so far as we know, upon the mind-body relation. Thus we have two analogies, each of which is strong where the other is weak, and neither of which alone can suffice. The organic relation is factually immediate but mysterious or unintelligible as it stands. (It is further insufficient in that the relation of God to man which we particularly wish to understand is that of mind to mind, whereas the relation of a man's mind to his cells appears to be the relation of " mind " to " matter.") On the other hand, the human social relation, while intelligible, and a relation of mind to mind, lacks immediacy. What is to be done?

Is it difficult to answer? What could possibly be done except to combine the two analogies so as to produce a unitary variable without either the seeming unintelligibility and materialistic character of the one or the non-immediacy of the other? If this could not be done, then atheism might have to be accepted; but it can be done, and that with no great difficulty — indeed with the support of many lines of argument additional to those we have indicated. We have only to suppose that the mind-body relationship is immediately social. We can indeed hardly suppose that interhuman social relationships are immediate (except perhaps secondarily and in slight degree), since practically all the known evidence is in conflict with that supposition; but there are no facts which disprove the social character of the surely immediate mind-body relation, and some which suggest it. The human body is often called a " machine "; but this is a very inadequate description, since the body is a society of living, organic cells.

We have only to suppose that these cells possess humble forms of feeling or desire to reach the position that the human mind influences and is influenced by them through immediate (there is nothing to mediate it) sharing of feeling, with much indistinctness on both sides (by no means however with the same indistinctness, and in the same respects, on both sides). Is this not the principle, and the only principle with any analogy in our experience, by which divine love (free of the "indistinctness," i.e., imperfection) could know and sway the world?

But can a social relation, even to parts of one's own body, be immediate; or, to put it the other way round, can an immediate relation be social?

As in all philosophical questions, we must try to exhaust the alternatives. All possible human social relations must be: (a) with radically *inferior,* or (b) with more or less *equal,* or (c) with radically *superior* individuals. And in each case we have to consider whether the relations are wholly *indirect* or inferential, or whether the social other is, to some extent at least, an immediate datum. It cannot be taken for granted without inquiry that the three types of relation have the same immediacy, or lack of it. Thus the all too common argument, since relations with other human minds rest upon inference from the perceived qualities and changes in their bodies, therefore all social relations are equally inferential, is thoroughly lacking in cogency, unless it has also been shown that there is no peculiar reason why relations to equals should be at least primarily indirect, as compared to other social relations.

There is such a reason, however — unfortunately for the argument. If human beings, say, saw immediately into each other's feelings and purposes, the independence of individuals would be seriously curtailed, and with it the depth of originality and the power to surprise each other which make up a good part of the value of human life. It is true that Siamese twins have a certain direct intuition into each other's sensations, and that one of them has described the great beauty of their relationship. But it is only sensations, not ideas or purposes or memories, or in the full sense emotions or sentiments, which are directly shared in this case. Nor is such an individual in a position to judge of the comparative value of such interdependence. Perhaps no human being can judge of it. But it is clear that the range of activities in which such individuals can engage is more restricted than in the normal human being. If one of them falls in love, the other has to be also in love with the same person, at the same time and in much the same ways, or else become an enforced passive participant. The solution, in one poignant case at least, was to renounce marriage. And it is hard to see how any other solution could have been desirable.

Clearly there is definite value in the privacy which human beings enjoy owing to their inability to peer directly into each other's states. But it is quite different with radical unequals in the cosmic social scale. Suppose a man could directly intuit the feelings of a one-celled creature, such as one of his own bodily cells. This would not enslave the man or embarrass the cell. It would not enslave the man because a single cell is too slight and weak a thing for its feelings to have any predominant influence. Even should there be multitudes of cells felt at once, still, since these creatures are too limited in knowledge to cooperate to any concerted end such as might interfere with the human being, the latter, by influencing each of them a little in a desired direction, could move the whole more or less at will. Nor could the cell complain that its privacy was invaded, for however the cell may *feel* the human being, it cannot know or think it as such, it cannot say to itself,

" There's that man prying into my affairs." The human being must be incomprehensible to the cell to such an extent as to constitute merely a sort of environment, not a definite term of a social relation. Of course, the human being would have more power over the cell than the cell over it, but that is inherent in the inferiority of the cell, and not an inconvenience, granting this inferiority. Here the idea of members of a social system " knowing their place and liking it " is unobjectionable. The trouble with this idea in its application to purely human relations is that there is no unambiguous inequality between human beings. All are fundamentally the same sort of metazoan animals, filling the same cosmological niche in the system of beings, and while any one may be superior to some other in this or that respect, there are always other respects to be considered, as well as possible advances or degenerations in the two individuals which may obliterate the difference, or reverse it. A cell is once for all not a man, and it is once for all less than a man. But only an idiot is once and for all less than a man while yet, after a fashion, a member of the human race, and an idiot is an exception for which the ground plan of the species as such naturally does not provide.

Again, consider the relations of a man to a radically superior mind, such as God. Suppose this relation were in part direct. What would this imply? The man would not have the divine as a clear and distinct datum; for if he saw God distinctly he would *be* God, himself omniscient. Thus, as the man to the cell, the divine to the man would be a vague environment rather than a definite social other. In exceptionally exalted states, the mystic, greater definiteness might be arrived at, but complete adequacy would be impossible. It is clear that, just as the cell could not tyrannize over the man because of its comparative insignificance, so the man could not tyrannize over God. It is less obvious that the man might not have a complaint to make about the invasion of his privacy. Some atheists seem to dislike the idea of God for some such reason. But is there not a burden of proof upon them to justify this attitude? After all, if God peers into our thoughts, he does not do so in order to further some one-sided and partial ends, or with the likelihood of envying us, or without the capacity to grasp the context into which our thoughts must be fitted if their value is to be appreciated. God is the one being who rightfully can invade all privacies. And the vagueness which inevitably limits the direct vision which we men could possibly have of God gives us plenty of freedom of interpretation of the divine datum, this freedom going all the way to denying that there is a God. An indistinct datum can always be explained away, if not completely, still sufficiently for a good many purposes.

It is also to be remembered that even with equals on the human level there may be *some* direct perception, so faint as to be easily overlooked, and hence the inference from the indirectness of human-to-human social relations to the indirectness of human-to-sub-or-super-human social relations not only is a *non sequitur,* but its premise may very well be an exaggeration of the facts. Finally, the reasons which make an almost complete lack of direct rapport between equals on a complex level desirable or necessary may have diminishing application as one considers equality relations on lower and lower levels, say between cells, then molecules, then atoms. Human beings need wide independence from others of their kind. They do not want to have to share in the thoughts and feelings of others by automatic direct participation, such as binds us to our brains, but they want to be able to select and choose and shut out when desirable the states of mind of their fellows. This is appropriate to their complexity and their ability to survey wide alternatives through language, the ability to abstract and generalize. But cells need no such wide freedom. If they are pervaded by waves of mob psychology coming directly from their immediate neighbors, this is no abrogation of their dignity, of the demands of their type of structure and functioning, so long as not absolutely all initiative is thus destroyed. The appropriate ratio of independence to dependence is vastly different than in man, even infinitely different in a sense, for man can react to the infinite as such. And on the electronic level, where perhaps there is no inner diversity of parts whatever, there is nothing for the electron to do but to interact directly with its neighbors, since internal action is not possible.

Thus we see that the lack of appreciable directness in human social relations is entirely compatible with its being nevertheless the case that not only some but even all direct interaction is social, whether the direct interaction of cell with cell, of cell with light rays striking the body, of human mind with human brain cell, of world mind with all parts of the world body. Thus on every ground we may well consider seriously the doctrine that the world is God's body, to whose members he has immediate social relations, and which are related to each other, directly or indirectly, exclusively by social relations.

Yet what a host of traditional objections arise! The doctrine of divine impassivity will be appealed to, as implying that God could not share in, and in so far be dependent upon, the feelings of the creatures entering into the world body. We have seen, however, that there is no need to admit the impassivity of God in his total or concrete reality. Second-type theism thus refutes the objection. A perfectly loving, a just God must indeed never be moved one-sidedly, by the feelings of some only of the creatures, but always in a way appropriate to all of them at once. This is the meaning of ethical action, response to all on the same terms of adequate sensitivity, and of adequate creative furtherance so far as the various interests of others can be harmonized with the least sacrifice of value. The higher the mind, the more catholic is its passivity, and therefore the less is it enslaved to anyone.

But it will be said that the organic-social analogy does not give us the idea of God as creator. For by taking thought a man cannot add to his stature, cannot create, say, his bones. But then, as we have seen, it is primarily the nervous system and not the whole body that functions in our analogy, and although it seems to be true that no new nerve cells are produced by our thought or volition, it is equally clear that *something* new is produced in the nervous system by our efforts. We do affect the development of the cells, even if not their generation. Cells are continually growing new parts to replace those broken down. In the embryo the elementary mind may actually participate even in generation of cells. And certainly we influence the generation of atoms and molecules; in the nerve cells, for instance, where consciousness has direct effects. Now God is by hypothesis the supreme instance of the principle only imperfectly represented in us; consequently it is necessary to suppose that in him the effect of mind upon bodily growth and generation is of a higher, and even of an infinitely higher, order. If by "creation," then, is meant "supreme influence upon growth," the objection falls. And I see no paradox in interpreting Genesis in this sense, not to mention its almost obvious appropriateness to Plato's *Timaeus*. The whole present pattern of the universe doubtless had an origin, including all the elements of that pattern mentioned in Genesis or in Plato.

What unimaginable earlier stage of the universe they grew out of under God's influence the Bible does not say, and why should it? To turn this reticence into an affirmation of creation *ex nihilo* is a procedure at which many well equipped scholars would protest. It seems reasonable to think that in saying simply, God " made " the existent world, the Bible is merely saying that he somehow brought it into being, and that I am not disputing. Surely no one would want to read a literal use of the obviously inadequate artisan analogy into so noncommittal a word. Nor are we any better off if it be said that what is asserted is that God is the " cause " of the world; for the concept of causality has positive meaning only through some experiential analogy, and until the analogy be exhibited we have only an uncontrolled, vague, composite picture of all the analogies (a picture which is not improved by being called intellectual or super-sensory). If, again, it be said that our treatment has ignored the distinction between created and uncreated being, and has failed to realize that concepts cannot apply " univocally " to God and other things, I reply that the distinction itself has no meaning except thanks to some analogy, and that if there is in *no* sense any univocal meaning then theology is pure sophistry, while whatever sense does admit univocal meaning will justify our argument. " Cause " is an analogy taken from volition, or from the mere rules of regular succession discovered by science, or from the experience of logical implication of conclusions by premises. The first has been dealt with, the second is obviously inapplicable, the third is almost as manifestly inappropriate. God is not a premise, that is, a proposition, nor is the world another premise. Not abstracts but concretes are here to be related. Besides, if the relation be that of premise and conclusion, then Spinoza and the necessitarians are right and freedom and contingency are unreal. As for final causes, we have seen how inapplicable the idea of purpose is to a merely immaterial and immutable deity; and one would still have to know what the bond of connection is by which God becomes immanent as an ideal in the human mind.

The most serious problem confronting the organic analogy, if not all theological conceptions, is that of evil. How can there be conflict, disorder, defects, in the body of God; or, if there are none, what are we to make of empirical evils and of our feeling that we should try to mitigate these? The effort to remove something accords ill with the denial that it exists! We must accordingly admit that in some sense the world body is not an absolute, perfectly harmonized unity. It may be absolutely unified in so far as unity is the basis of co-presence to one awareness, the divine omniscience; but there is experiential warrant for admitting that a kind of conflict and evil is compatible with such co-presence, since otherwise we could not ourselves be aware of conflicting factors. There is intolerable discord that causes lapse of consciousness. Unlike us, God is not subject to such discord. For him and in the world body no conflicts occur except such as are to him tolerable. But this does not mean that for God no conflict and nothing unpleasant occurs at all. The idea that God equally and solely experiences bliss in all his relations is once for all a denial of the religiously essential doctrine that God is displeased by human sin and human misfortune. Without such displeasure, the words "just" and "loving" seem mockeries.

It might perhaps be held that since painful experiences tend to be forgotten, the perfect memory of God could not admit pain. Yet nothing is commoner than painful memories, and it is hardly apparent that pain or discord is anything like coincident with ignorance. Indeed, the vivid awareness of the fact that pain and conflict exist shows that pleasure and harmony are not the sole factors determining awareness. We tend to exclude unhappy thoughts, but this is not our only tendency. Therefore it is not the only motivation involved in mind. Another motivation is the social one; we tend to share in the experiences of others, even if painful, or even if not in harmony with our own (as in jealousy, hatred). Hence awareness is to be viewed as the product of a double selection, on the one hand with a view to harmony, on the other with a view to social inclusiveness. In the supreme or divine case, this would imply a maximal elimination of evil so far as this elimination is compatible with maximal social inclusiveness. Now it seems self-evident, upon careful reflection (there is in philosophy no other self-evidence), that the elimination of evil could become absolute only if the social inclusiveness became zero.

It is to be noted that omniscience must in some fashion know evil. Now to know involves experience; hence God must experience the quality of evil. Could he experience the evil of conflict if there were nothing in his being but sheer harmony?

Does this imply that God must experience wickedness through himself being wicked, as he must experience conflict by himself suffering from it? I reply that conflict is positive in a sense in which wickedness is not. God is himself qualified by what is positive in evil, namely discord, which is not mere absence of harmony, but positive clash. But he is not qualified by the privative element essential to moral evil, namely *blindness* to the interests of others. Let it not be said that "blindness" is here equivocal; for it really does mean some kind of ignorance. There is no such thing as selfishness which does not involve lack of realization of the concrete effects of action upon others. The common word " thoughtless " is indicative. The real ignorance of the poor shown in all societies by the exploiting rich is an example of the essential connection between lack of goodness and lack of awareness.

It may be said that there is an element of positive willfulness in wickedness, which we call perversity. But the answer is that it is not simply as deliberate volition that perversity is perverse, but as the deliberate choice of non-realization over realization. The " greatest " or divine realization cannot make this choice, but can experience it as made by others, because it can itself participate in the positive factors, and can see by comparison the privation or ignorance involved.

It may again be argued that God must participate in negative as well as positive factors. This, however, can in a sense be admitted, yet harmonized with what has been said. In conflict, which we have called positive, there is a negative element. Indeed, in all difference there is negation of similarity, and in similarity, negation of difference. So in conflict there is negation of harmony. But to experience this it is not necessary to experience privation as ignorance, if by that is meant non-realization of a part of what is real. It is only necessary to experience that *a* is not *b*, or that *ab* is not a harmonious whole. Moral and cognitive evil, which in the absolute case are indistinguishable, are in the absolute case equally self-contradictory. Only aesthètic evil, which alone is not privative (it is not the absence of things which harmonize but the presence of things which conflict), can qualify God.

From another point of view this is clear enough, in that aesthetic evil is " suffered," while moral evil is enacted, chosen. God must suffer all things, for he must participate in all things to know them, but he cannot be said to choose all things, for he has granted choices also to the creatures.

The partial passivity implied in knowledge agrees perfectly with the tolerance implied in love, and both agree with the denial of wickedness to God. The good man is not freed by his goodness from dependence for full happiness upon the welfare of his neighbors, but he is, to the extent of his goodness, freed from dependence upon them for the goodness itself. God, being entirely good, is entirely independent of all others for that goodness, which is inalienably and wholly his own choice; but if goodness means love, then God is dependent for happiness upon others to a unique degree; for whereas we are left unaffected by the misery or joy of millions we do not know even the existence of, God has nowhere to hide himself from any sorrow or joy whatever, but must share in all the wealth and all the burden of the world. The cross is a sublime and matchless symbol of this, partly nullified by theological efforts to restrict suffering and sympathy to God as incarnate. The point is that in whatever sense incarnation is required to make God passive, in that sense the incarnate God is the only God that reason, all revelation apart, can give us any conception of, as well as the only God of use to religion.

The Aristotelian conception of the body as wholly passive in relation to the soul is an overstatement of the important fact that the human mind is incomparably more powerful than any *one* of the individuals composing its body, so that the mind has a directing, " forming " power not otherwise found in the bodily system. Had Aristotle known of cells, molecules, and atoms, I cannot conceive of his persisting in the one-sided conception which some of his followers still support. And even did we not know of cells and the rest, there are philosophical objections to the doctrine. Being is power, and any relation in which a thing was wholly powerless would be a relation in which the thing was nothing. This truth was concealed by the notion that matter, while powerless, could produce negative effects merely by virtue of its lack of ability to " receive " certain forms. I fear no way of validating such a distinction can be found. Men act on kittens and kittens act on men; and no matter how lowly a thing may be, if it is a real individual it reacts upon all things, however exalted. Cells, molecules, electrons, exhibit in no way any exception to this principle. It is even harder, on scientific grounds (though not on general philosophic ones), to justify the assertion that men can act on and " form " their cells and molecules, than the assertion that the latter act on and form men.[4]

Since there are no gradations in the intimacy of things to God, though there are, in a certain sense, gradations in the intimacy of God to things (sin and saintliness, etc.), God cannot, as we have already noted, have a nervous system or sense organs, for these are bodily parts with a preferential relation to the mind. And if by " sensation " we mean experience mediated by sense organs, then God has no sense experiences. But if by sensation we mean that aspect of experience which is neither thought nor volition, neither meaning nor action, but qualitative feeling, then God can as little be free from sensation as men. It seems stupid ingratitude to deride the " sensuous " in favor of the " spiritual," when not one of us could possibly choose to exist at all without the contribution which the sensory qualities make to life. (In all the heavens that ever really appealed to men, sensations, of music and color and even smell, have played a role.) God will have not the least but the *most* of the richness supplied by such qualities; but he will derive them from all parts of the world body, not merely from focal points which would constitute sense organs. He will have them also at all times (except so far as future at those times), and not intermittently, interrupted by sleep, sickness, inattention, darkness, as we do; nor will he be overwhelmed by sensations of one type, such as a loud noise, while deprived of intense feeling of another type, but all will be in a rich balance. Thus he really contains "all positive perfections" (so far as actual, and potential ones only as such, as potential).

Let us sum up in terms of a definition. The body of a given mind is *that much of the world which the mind immediately knows and controls and suffers.* It is the locus of attachment to the system of real things. A disembodied mind, as Leibniz said — alas, without applying it to God! — would simply not belong to existence. There is an obvious relativity in the definition, which has for consequence that the nervous system is as it were a body within the body, and that in some diluted sense the whole universe may be included in the body of any mind, just as physics now says a particle may be conceived as a wave-train pervading space. But God is that mind which enjoys the fullest intimacy with all things, and therefore in an undiluted sense has all the world for body. It is an implication of this that the world is not less but more organic than a man, and if the reader doubts this, let him remember that at least the world order persists, no matter what else undergoes destruction. It is a bit strange to regard the most stable order as the least orderly.

But organic order, you may say, is only one kind of order. Granted; it is the order of an individual as such, rather than of a mere group, or of a mere part of an individual. Now the cosmic order is the most individual, the most distinctive, of all. It belongs to this actual universe, not to any of the possible universes. It belongs to every part of this universe, even more completely than the individual gene pattern belongs to all parts of an animal body.

Quantum mechanics and relativity are the gene structures of all things, not of most things, in the present actual cosmos. One might go on. The blindness of some philosophers to the seemingly obvious in this regard is perhaps not easy to explain. Possibly they fail to see that though the cosmic structure belongs to all things in the cosmos it belongs to none of them *as their individuality*, which is rather always a special case of the cosmic individuality, as each of a man's cells is a special case of the man's individual pattern. Cosmic individual unity, that is, organicity, is far *other* than local organicity, but other by being sublimely more, never less — for example, as to " growth," for which the cosmos has infinite time. Nothing proves that the cosmic gene pattern is fixed forever. Indeed, the law of entropy indicates that it has not always been and will not always be. A creative side of nature there must be, and its local manifestations in planetary life cannot exhaust its reality, or there would have been no cosmos to " run down " toward the " heat death." The presupposed " running up " or creation cannot be *less* fundamental as a cosmic function, however hidden from us its larger operations may be. If rigid persistence in an identical pattern were an aesthetic or spiritual value, the fact that the present cosmic pattern is going bankrupt would be disturbing; but all our aesthetic and spiritual experience indicates that such rigidity or monotony would be hideous beyond any nightmare. Every pattern, every style, has its day in art, even in the cosmic art, and it is satisfying that physics actually has evidence of this. (See Whitehead's neglected little book, *The Function of Reason* — a work of pure genius if there is one.) The cosmos grows ever new patterns for itself, and in this way too is organic beyond our imaginative grasp. It *exceeds* any requirements of individuality that we can clearly understand or measure.

There are three religious analogies which we have yet adequately to consider.

1. God has been compared to a poet, and the world to a poem. But the only poem immediately produced by a human poet is the poem in his own mind and brain. To provide analogy for the immediate production of poetic effects in other minds, we must treat the poetic analogy as simply an elaboration of the mind-body-social analogy, an elaboration acceptable enough.

2. God has been compared to a father. In one sense this is supremely appropriate; but it can easily be so construed as to amount to nonsense. The love of a parent for a child is the best case we know of a love having a human being for its object, the subject of which is or may be vastly superior in power and wisdom and goodness to the one loved. But the superiority is still not radical enough to serve as a very clear indication of the direction of divine superiority. If the child is really a human being, and not rather barely more than an embryo, he may in some respects actually exceed his parents in goodness. And as for direct knowledge and power, that is little changed by growing into adulthood, except as the accumulation of memories gives a kind of direct knowledge of ever widening scope, subject, however, to the drastic qualification that nearly all of this knowledge is virtual rather than actual at any one time. To find radical superiority, together with intimate relationship, between two individuals, we must turn to the bodily hierarchy of organisms within organisms, culminating in the universe. To neglect this analogy while putting stress upon the interhuman social analogy is to run the risk of falling into one of two errors: failing to make concrete and firm the sense of the radical supremacy of God (and the abysmal limitations of human parenthood); or, if this danger is avoided (probably by stressing,

as Jesus did, the unique position of God as supreme power and goodness in the universe), we are then likely to make the heavenly Father superior by making him remote and abstract. Jesus, the preeminent religious genius, did neither, but also he was not a theologian open to the temptations of abstract thought. The organic analogy, socially interpreted, gives us intellectually, so far as this is possible, what Jesus had intuitively and practically.

3. Perhaps the most shockingly bad of all theological analogies, or at least the one open to the most dangerous abuses, is that of God as a monarch, a world boss. Political power is indirect power to an even greater degree than human relations generally. It is power over millions by virtue of power over a few immediate underlings, or by virtue of certain institutions not themselves due to the power that uses them. It is not chiefly the power of direct sympathetic interaction, and is less this than is the influence of a great actor or prophet. Of course, some political leaders are great actors, but they are unwilling, usually, to rely solely upon their artistic appeal, but wish also the support of swords or guns. And above all, the political leader is more or less impassive, insensitive to the feelings of others. He sways the passions of others, but tries to insulate himself against these feelings, except so far as it may be convenient to share in them. Thus Napoleon could say a million deaths meant nothing to him, implying his complete non-participation in the feelings of several million persons (more or less all Europe) concerned in those deaths. God may and does have a share in the killing of much greater numbers, but none of these deaths are as nothing to him, or even are less to him than to the human beings concerned. He merely has other values to consider also. God is the only genuine servant of all, who grieves in all griefs whatever, who longs for the fulfillment of all

desires actually entertained, even though he cannot eliminate all griefs or fulfill all desires (because the very idea of this is nonsense). God is the monarch or king of all only through being in a real sense the slave, nay, the scourged slave, of all, infinitely more passive to others, more readily "wounded" even, than anyone else can ever be. Political imagery is as far as it is easy to get from such supreme mercy and companionship as God shows toward all that is — toward the least insect, and toward the lark that devours the insect and in a manner devours God. This is not a mere blanket pantheism, since God is all things in a certain ethical unity, just that unity and no other.

It is plain enough that as the cell is in the man so the man is in the cosmos, and even though God be more than the cosmos, "more than *x*" has definite meaning only if we know what *x* really is, so that we cannot be mistaken in using the cell-man-cosmos relationships, so far as they go, in trying to interpret how man is related to God. But also we cannot be mistaken in so using the relation of man to his fellows. For in that relation only are we on both sides of the relationship with approximately equal understanding, knowing what it is both for a man to know and love and influence, and for a man to be known and loved and influenced. We cannot possibly, with the same distinctness, know what it could be to a man's cell either to love or to be loved, still less how atoms and other subanimal organisms can figure in such relationships. Thus all roads lead to the common result that, inadequate though the resulting conception of God may be, the organic-social analogy must be the best means of constructing such a conception open to us. The fact that one is thereby committed to a certain interpretation of the mind-body relation, and also to the view that all individuals in nature are capable of some lowly form of social relationship, that is, to a relational form of panpsychism, will repel some thinkers. But it may be suggested that if God is essentially love, nothing can be incapable of being loved (as dead matter must be), and that to be rich in implications beyond those immediately sought is one of the most unfailing signs of a good rather than a poor theory. Moreover, for theology to leave the general nature of so-called dead matter, if not the entire relation of mind to things in space, a wholly unilluminated affair would be most inappropriate in view of the absolutely universal relevance implied in the very idea of God.

The idea of the world as a divine organism is at least as old as Plato, and was a favorite idea in antiquity. But the idea could not come into its own until certain other ideas inherited from the Greeks were overcome, such ideas as that the supreme being must be totally immutable, impassive, and self-sufficient, or that some portions of matter can contain no sentience or social connectedness whatever. Modern science and logic show that these ideas are based upon no real evidence. By giving them up we open the way to a more frank and intelligible treatment of the theological analogies.[5]

NOTES

1 Many philosophers fail, in my opinion, to grasp the significance of the Leibnizian distinction between individuals and aggregates. Appealing to the Aristotelian tradition, or allegedly to common sense, they urge that a stick or stone is as much a unitary individual as a molecule or an animal organism. This contention is also advanced sometimes in the name of science. In the latter case it takes the form of holding not that stones have as much, but that they have as little, unity as molecules or organisms, on the ground that *everything* from the atom to man is nothing but electrons and the like interacting according to quantum laws. This makes electrons, protons, etc., the only dynamic individual agents. Thus it violates common sense for certain, and makes any philosophical

understanding of the world impossible. If, however, one admits with most biologists that the vertebrate animal, for instance, involves action of the whole as a unit upon its parts, then surely *no* scientist would suppose that a stick or a stone is a dynamic unit in any such sense, whereas a number of high authorities have suggested that in atoms and molecules we do have rudimentary forms of organic units (Bohr, Jordan, Whitehead, etc.). Thus the Aristotelian attitude, while a wholesome corrective to extreme atomism, has really no standing whatever in present-day science, any more than the notion that the earth is flat. It has indeed been argued that a stick or stone has an individual pattern which is both individually peculiar to it and relatively stable. Now of course *any* aggregate is individual in that sense in which "individual" is used as a synonym for *concrete,* that which is not abstract, rather than as a term for what is primarily *one* rather than many. A group of persons in an elevator has as a group a unique pattern, but there is no reason for thinking of this pattern as an agent which acts on its parts, and upon other things. The pattern is the way in which the parts act on each other and upon the outside environment, it does not itself act. But a genuine primary individual, an organism, does itself act; it is not merely the way its parts act. At one extreme there is the vertebrate organism, which only a minority of scientists or philosophers would deny has dynamic unity. It is agreed, for instance, that a vertebrate is as much a unitary agent as the cells composing it. Toward the opposite extreme is the colony of plant cells, as in nostoc, which form more or less stable cohering masses, without appreciable action as a whole, that is without supercellular activity. In between, a doubtful intermediate case, is the ordinary many-celled plant. Botanists debate whether such a plant is best regarded as a colony of cells or as a single organism or supercell with cells as its organs. Now the criteria here have nothing to do with stability, or with solidity and continuity as suggested by direct visual impression. In fact, mere stability, mere temporal uniformity unbalanced by variety, is contradictory of dynamic individuality, as is mere uniformity or homogeneity in space. Novelty is essential to action and to time as such, and any unity which does not exhibit it is secondary or derivative from its parts. Electrons by this test are more individual than sticks and stones, they have frequent and exciting adventures not completely subdued to regularity by any known or, it appears, even any conceivable laws. Whether an aggregate lasts a long time or a short, this cannot endow it with dynamic individuality while it lasts. Originality, initiative of action, can be perfectly real in a fraction of a second, and absent for an eon. The point, of course, is that stability may be a mere statistical uniformity holding of the actions of numerous entities each slightly capricious or, as Born says, "restless," uncontrollable and unpredictable by man, not only in any actual but in any even conceivable way.

D. W. Gotshalk suggests that a stone has a "supermolecular" structure, but apparently he means, in the sense in which any aggregate has a structure not possessed by its parts. The question is whether this structure has boundaries-and-unity as significant dynamically either as the boundaries and unity of some of its parts, or as the boundaries and unity of some whole of which it is a part. (See D. W. Gotshalk's in many ways excellent *Metaphysics in Modern Times,* University of Chicago Press, 1940, p. 35.)

I suggest that we shall never understand the world, or the problem of God, until we learn to see reality as a system of individuals on many levels and of many kinds, and that individual in the primary sense of *dynamic one* is to be contrasted with mere segments of reality carved out more or less arbitrarily by the beholding mind or by the operations of the sense organs whose biological function is not to reveal individuals as such but rather (a) to reveal those individuals whose kind and level is sufficiently akin to our own to make them individually important for us, and (b) to reveal those aggregates or swarms of individuals which, though insignificant for our purposes in their individual constituents, are effective causes of our weal or woe in the aggregate. It is (b), the illusory or pseudo-individuality which our senses attribute to things as units in the pragmatic sense, units *for* (our) action rather than units *of* action, that leads philosophers into materialism by suggesting the idea of in-organic yet dynamically unitary agents, the pseudo-concept of inorganic " individual," composed of mere lifeless and insentient stuff, whose activity is without adventures, without novelty, without caprice, without effective contrast or harmony. The illusion is being dissipated by science, which shows the non-individual character of most sensory " objects."

[2] Cf. the remark of David Hume, " No animal can move immediately anything but the members of its own body " (*Dialogues Concerning Natural Religion,* Part VIII). Hume goes on to point out that, reasoning by analogy, we should expect God to be the mind whose body is the universe, with the result that God would depend on the world as truly as the world depends on him, for " equality of action and reaction seems to be a universal law of nature." Hume did not stop to note that as between the human mind and any one of its member cells or atoms (he did not know definitely of these, to be sure) there is by no means equality of action, since the human individual is incomparably more powerful than any lesser individual contained within him. Even taking all the parts collectively, there was nothing but a vague speculative extension of the laws of physics to make them apply to subject matters having little analogy to those of which the laws were known to be true to support Hume's notion of a mere equality as between mind and body. What Hume was entirely justified in insisting upon was that a God in every respect independent of the world could not be related to the world in any way to which we have any analogy whatever. The world mind must be passive as well as active. Action and reaction need not be equal in relations between wholes and

parts, indeed cannot be; but action and reaction there must be. Activity is mutual, social, or nothing.

[3] Bichowsky says: " The first law of psychology . . . is: If in introspection, relations are found between conscious content and these relations are of the kind that can exist between nerve impulse groups, then these relations do exist between nerve impulse groups. . . ." See F. R. Bichowsky, " Factors Common to the Mind and to the External World," *Journal of Philosophy*, XXXVII, 477–84.

[4] For an interesting discussion, from the point of view of a Roman Catholic biologist, of the problem of the relations between the organism and the individual forming its parts, see the paper, by Hauber, " Mechanism and Teleology in Current Biological Theory," *Proceedings of the American Catholic Philosophical Association,* XIV, 45–70. Hauber favors a panpsychic theory of cells and other inferior organisms, holding that these have their own simple forms of feeling. But he does not face the evidence for ascribing also some slight initiative or individuality of *action* to the part-organisms, hence for admitting that the total organic individual is passive as well as active in relation to its parts. Naturally also he does not suggest the corresponding problem of the universe as an organism. He misses the essential mutuality of the part-whole relation, its social character. Misled by Aristotelian terminology, he suggests that when it is in a larger organism the lesser organism has no " substantial " form (although it is an individual) but is " merely a quality or accidental form of the larger unit," whereas in an inorganic environment it has " a mental life entirely its own." The absoluteness of this distinction — either the mental life belongs only to an including organism, or it belongs only to the included organism — is characteristic of Thomism (note the word " entirely " in the quotation). The relativity and mutuality of existence cannot be adequately grasped without a more radical detachment from Aristotle and Thomas than even this relatively free representative of Roman Catholic doctrine could attain. Otherwise he would not have thought of included organisms as " strictly submerged " in their including organism, any more than he would have thought of the independence of organisms in an inorganic environment as absolute, or the distinction between organic and inorganic as absolute, or the distinction between an organism as such and the universe. Such absolute dualisms or dichotomies are not scientific or philosophical, since no conceivable evidence could establish them. " Relatively submerged " would fit any evidence that could be alleged for " absolutely submerged."

[5] The perception that the mind-body analogy, so far from amounting to a weak pantheism, or to a denial of the transcendence of the God of religion, is in fact the only way to achieve a just synthesis of immanence and transcendence, the only way to avoid the twin errors of mere naturalism and mere supernaturalism, is excellently expressed in the following quotation:

"It is hard to think of God as being at one and the same time truly immanent and truly transcendent. Perhaps . . . it is better to fall back upon an analogy. We human beings . . . are immanent in our bodies, in the sense that our life is intimately bound up with and expressed through our bodies. At the same time we are transcendent to our bodies, in the sense that we do not remain a dimly diffused energy but somehow, somewhere come to a self-conscious focus and can look down upon our bodies and to a degree master them. In the same way, God may be thought of as being immanent in the universe in that his life is intimately bound up with and expressed through it, and at the same time transcendent to his universe in that somehow, somewhere he comes to a self-conscious focus and is more than his universe. . . . This dual relationship in ourselves . . . we accept . . . every day as a fact; we may as well do the same concerning God. What is true of the microcosm can also be true of the macrocosm."

The author quoted (Nevin C. Harner, professor of Christian education, Theological Seminary, Reformed Church in the U. S., Lancaster, Pa.) points out the serious educational disadvantages of the two alternatives to the view outlined: that is, in either sheer immanence or sheer transcendence (only verbally qualified by an immanence with no definite experiential meaning). The quotation is from "Three Ways to Think of God," *Religious Education,* XXXIV, 217.

Since writing this chapter I have discovered that the relations of God to the world are discussed by the great German psychologist and philosopher, G. T. Fechner, in a manner in most respects superior to anything known to me in theological literature. Doubtless Fechner's seemingly fantastic notion of plant souls and souls of the heavenly bodies distracted attention from his strictly theological discussions. If theologians did read the latter, then I am tempted to say, in the words of the title of a recent best seller, that they could not have known "how to read a book." The combination of logical strictness with sense for the realities of experience in all its more spiritual aspects has seldom been so excellently exhibited. See especially Fechner's *Zend-Avesta* (1851), Vol. I, chap. 11.

APPENDIX TO CHAPTER V

An example of how neglect of the mind-body analogy may persist even in a theology by no means slavishly bound to tradition is afforded by the empirical theology of H. N. Wieman. This writer, for instance, says:

"God . . . is not merely man lifted to the *n*th dimension of perfection. . . . God is different from man. God works concretely. Man cannot do that. . . . Man's plans, his ideals, his purposes, are necessarily abstractions by reason of the very nature of the human mind. . . . The forming of 'internal relations' is creation. A common word for it is growth. It is God's working, not man's. Hence mind and personality would cramp God. . . . He cannot be so limited." (" Some Blind Spots Removed," *Christian Century,* Jan. 25, 1939, p. 116. See also various books by Professor Wieman, who is perhaps the most radical of empirical and third-type theists of our time.)

Now if by " man's working " is meant his way of acting on objects outside his body, the argument is strong. But surely our influence upon the growth of our own minds and bodies is concrete and creative, even though more or less radically weak and intermittent. If this intuitive-organic, not abstract-external, working of mind as we know it be conceived as it would be if it embraced the whole, instead of, as in us, but a fragment, of the universe, does it not imply precisely the supreme power to promote growth which Professor Wieman so justly demands as the divine prerogative? In such a supreme organism abstraction would have no function, except as the contrast between abstract and concrete is inherent in reality as such by virtue of the intrinsic generality or indetermination of the future.

(Purposes in us are abstract for two reasons, or in two ways: (1) we do not intuit organically, directly, and vividly more than a tiny portion of the world with which we have to deal, and so have to rely largely upon abstract generalization; (2) purposes, any purposes, refer to the future, and so cannot be wholly particularized or concrete, since only the past can be so represented. The first ground for abstractness would be absent from God, for it is a mere privation, our lack of complete grasp of reality; the second, which is inherent in existence as such, would be present in God. Absolute concreteness is as meaningless as an up where is no down. To be sure, the abstractness of the future is not literally the result of abstracting from details which are there, but is the non-existence of such details in the partially indeterminate future. Thus God may be the *n*th dimension of mind in its intuitive aspect, as concrete where the past and present are concerned, and abstract in the sense only in which futurity means abstractness in proportion to the degree of futurity, the more remote portions of future time being those less concretely purposed by God.)

It might be suggested also that it would be in conformity with Professor Wieman's advocacy of the method of science in philosophy to weigh the fact that qualitative distinctions, such as the passage quoted above proposes as holding between man and God, have repeatedly been shown to have only provisional significance for science. The problem may be not to allocate " creativity " to the right subject, but to measure the actual differences in degree and direction of creativity, even though in the comparison between man and God the difference in degree may be infinite. Can any empirical test for " absolute uncreativeness " be so much as conceived? Is not any such assertion a priori, metaphysical — and that in the " bad sense "?

However this may be, to have translated this aspect of the old qualitative theology into modern terms and made it a fresh issue is an achievement for which one can only be grateful to Professor Wieman (and others working in a similar vein). Is the contrast between "creator" as such and "created" as such, between creating and being created, absolute, a matter of all or nothing, or is it relative even though infinite? See H. N. Wieman and W. M. Horton, *The Growth of Religion* (Willett, Clark & Co., 1938).

A view close to the one expressed in this chapter is that of Professor Montague, who says that the universe is God's body, and that God is perfect in goodness and knowledge, although his power is "limited." The power might still be perfect if this means the greatest conceivable, and if Montague would grant that no supreme being is conceivable who would *not* be limited by a universe of things "within himself yet not himself," and if he would grant further that God enjoys all the power conceivable, subject to this inevitable limitation. Montague reminds me of Fechner — whose doctrine also was similar — in the vividness, sincerity, and penetration of his thought. Like Fechner he seems not to be sufficiently appreciated, and partly for similar reasons, which in both cases have little to do with the value of their contributions to theology. See William Pepperell Montague, *The Ways of Things* (Prentice-Hall, Inc., 1940), especially pp. 110–23.

Somewhat farther from my own view is that of Fechner's greatest philosophical admirer, William James. James finally concluded that Fechner was probably right in regarding finite minds as parts of some more inclusive mind or minds. Thus two great philosophical psychologists agree on this point. But James seems to me to have strangely erred in his interpretation of Fechner's notion of God. Fechner did *not* slur over, to any great extent, the distinction between God and the timeless absolute. Nor was he so little interested in God as James seems to think. Above all, Fechner avoided two errors from which reading him failed to save James: the notion that without an "external" environment God would be responsible for all that happens, would be sheer power acting upon nothing distinguishable from itself; and the notion that if a being included all space he must include all time also in a single moveless instant. Fechner saw that an internal environment sufficed to establish a division of power and responsibility between God and the included individuals; and he saw that the whole in time is not, like the momentary whole in space, a single, definite whole. He did not spatialize time, and so was able to have a pluralism of events without putting anything outside God, since the new events mean, in a sense, a new God, as a man is a new man every moment. The "pluralism" needed for novelty, like that needed for finite responsibility, is within God not between him and something external. To this question we shall return in chapter 8. See William James, *A Pluralistic Universe* (Longmans, Green & Co., 1909), especially pp. 293–95, 310, 318.

VI

GOD AND THE BEAUTIFUL

As if the efforts of human beings in behalf of justice, or knowledge or beauty, depended . . . upon assurance that there already existed . . . some supernal region . . . where criminals are humanely treated, where there is no serfdom or slavery, where all facts and truths are already discovered and possessed, and all beauty displayed in actualized form.

JOHN DEWEY, in *A Common Faith*

THE MOST generally recognized principle of beauty, in art and in nature, is the principle of organic unity, or unity in variety. We say that variety is the spice of life, but we know equally well that spice by itself is not a satisfying diet. There must be a balance of likeness and difference, of similarity and contrast, if there is to be beauty. Too little likeness between the parts of a work of art results in confusion, discord, chaos. Too little difference results in monotony. The great objective of art is to avoid both the evil of chaos and the evil of monotony.

Suppose a state of pure unity without variety or difference of any kind. Such a state would necessarily be valueless; for value is at least awareness, and awareness involves duality of subject and object, hence variety. Moreover, value involves possible degrees and hence contrasts between degrees; and an " actual " value as such must be contrasted to other at least possible values. Finally, bare unity makes being, as Hegel (in so far without sophistry, I take it) maintained, indistinguishable from non-being. For what but the word could be alleged as the difference?

But a state of pure variety is equally, though for complementary reasons, valueless and inconceivable. It would not be *a* state, or *an* experience, or *a* something, even *a* plurality.

So we have the result that total absence of unity and total absence of variety equally imply total absence of being or value. Now modify the two nonsensical extremes ever so slightly in the direction of sense. At some point reality and value will become possible. But the first value reached in this way will not be maximal value. By infinitesimal steps, only infinitesimal additions to the initial zero of value will be effected. Thus we will have a series of values beginning at zero and going toward either an open or a closed infinity, that is, toward a definite maximum, or simply toward more and more with no possibility of an absolute limit. Since the necessity for some unity and some variety is equal, being in both cases absolute, there can be no reason for favoring one or the other, hence value will be a balance of the two, increasing as both increase *pari passu*. That both can increase together is due to the multi-dimensionality of existence, and in this relation we have an a priori reason for such multi-dimensionality. You can add to the variety of colors, while increasing the similarity of shapes, or vice versa, or in more subtle ways (for color and shape themselves are multi-dimensional) exploit the fact that likeness and difference are not univocal.

Is the universe as a whole beautiful? Certainly it contains more contrasts than anything else, for all contrasts fall within it. And it does have unity. Physics discovers the same kinds of matter, the same laws, even in the most distant heavenly bodies — so far as the present " cosmic epoch " (Whitehead) is concerned.

But there is one contrast in the world which seems unbalanced by any sufficient unity. This is the contrast between living mind and mere dead matter, between that which has feeling and emotion and memory and desire, and that which totally lacks these traits. Now such a contrast as this between the living and the dead, that which has feeling and that which has none, is not beautiful. For it is the contrast between something and nothing, between the mere presence and the mere absence of a quality, whereas the beautiful contrasts are those between widely separated positive qualities. Red contrasts with green, not as not-green with green, but as one positive quality with another from which it is separated by a wide interval. But there is no positive quality opposed to feeling, memory, will. All we can point to in the so-called inorganic world of rocks, fluids, and the like which might indicate the absence of mind is the simplicity of the individuals which science finds compose these entities. Atoms, molecules, crystals, electrons are indeed simple affairs, compared to the higher animals. But simplicity is not a positive quality; it merely means a low degree of complexity, and hence it is contrasted, not to mind and feeling and will in general, but to complex types of mind and feeling and will.

The way to bring the most beauty into our picture of the world is to regard atoms and the other inferior individuals as very simple, low-grade types of minds, or sub-minds, with their own to us more or less unimaginable feelings. Then we have immense but positive contrasts between the various levels and kinds of mind and feeling. Mind in general becomes the theme of which the entire universe is a system of variations. Materialism lacks any such theme, any real unity in the variety of things, and yet it can point to no positive contrast which the opposing view omits.

Minds and their interrelations form the materials of all beauty. The interrelations of minds constitute what in the broadest sense we may call *drama.* Drama is the essential art. All other arts tend to serve drama (including under this term the novel, narrative poetry, pageantry, parades, the cinema, and all arts frankly embodying relations between social beings as such). Abstract completely from the dramatic and there would be negligible or even zero beauty left. Even a simple design can express the personality of the designer; even flowers are "empathized," and seem happy or affectionate; the mere sunshine seems joyous. We see something of life everywhere, and something of individuality — that is, in the broadest sense personality — and something of the interplay of personalities, which is drama, in all life.

What I am urging is that not only would the harmony, the unity in variety, of the world as such be inadequately enjoyed were not all individuals, from electron to cosmos, at the least sentient, but also there would not really be any *cosmic* harmony to enjoy, even by the human spectator. We find unity and rich contrast where we see some striking variant of the theme of personality, and only there. Animals are fascinating because they are subpersonalities; electrons, because they are dimly envisaged as sub-subpersonalities; heroes, because they are superpersonalities; divinities, because super-superpersonalities; "Nature," because it is the mysterious supermind whose thoughts are both other than and akin to ours. The poets personify things because otherwise they would be giving aesthetic problems rather than solutions. The only difficulty is that the ranges of personality remote from the human are not adequately expressible in human language, or easily ascertainable by human science, still less by common sense.

But you ask, Has the contrast between the personal and the impersonal no aesthetic value? I answer, yes, as a contrast between and within personalities. There are "unpersonal" persons, that is, their personalities are relevant to a wide range of other personalities, actual and possible, and hence they seem unpersonal to one who wishes for support to his own lack of such catholicity. Also, there is the contrast between individuals, personalities, and groups; and a group may be called unpersonal. A rock is a group of crystals or molecules. But a group is nothing except in and through persons, including not only its members, but its spectators, whose attention and interest unite the members into one object of reference.

Not only does materialism fail to unify mind and matter, but by leading to atheism it also deprives us of some of the principal contrasts of life. No contrast can be so great as that between the creature and the creator, between limited imperfect minds and the all-knowing mind. For this contrast is infinite in every sense in which infinite contrast is possible. The dramatic relation with God is unique among dramatic relations. No other can be a substitute for it, for all other relations are between finite individuals.

But besides losing this unique contrast, atheism also loses equally in unity. For the highest type of mind, the divine, contrasts with all other minds just in its infinitely superior capacity to unify the diverse. The way to find the most unity in the world is to see it as the expression of a single plan, and the only such plan conceivable is the love of God for the various forms of life and feeling, a sympathy flexible enough to appreciate simultaneously the joys and sorrows of all the multiform individuals inhabiting all the worlds. Thus the divine as love is the only theme adequate to the cosmic symphony.

An electron is a principle of unity-in-contrast on a very small scale, or over a negligible portion of space. An atom is a unification of greater contrasts, covering a larger area. A man is the unity of the region occupied by his body. Thus the higher types of being integrate more of the variety of the world. Only the highest conceivable being could integrate the universe as a whole.

The world as a whole would be infinitely ugly (if, *per impossibile,* it could even exist) should it fail to exhibit a universal " theme," of which all contrasts express " variations " — as, for instance, all of a man's acts express his personality. What is this world theme, for atheism? Matter in motion? Or just " being "? The one is too narrow, the other is only a word for the problem, since what is sought is a clue in experience to the common nature belonging to being in spite of its variations. Matter in motion is too narrow, for it is structural, not qualitative, and the contrast between qualities, and between qualities and structures, is aesthetically positive. Simply to add to the structural aspect of matter the qualities we know is not to explain the unity of relations and qualities. In experience this unity is the unity of experience as such, and as essentially social, that is, at once relational and with private qualitative characters by virtue of which relations have terms. Matter as the universal theme of existence, really one and really many in all its variations, can only be God in disguise. It has lost of the lower status, and gained of the higher, everything but the word (see chapter 8). The only adequate theme of all variations is the maximally flexible or divine sympathy.

But materialism and atheism are not the only ways in which one can fall into ugly views of the universe. There are forms of theism which are no less incompatible with the principles of beauty. Since the beautiful must contain contrast, it is as necessary that there be variety, multiplicity, in God as that there be unity. Yet theologians have commonly insisted upon the unqualified simplicity of God, his absolute lack of parts and inner complexity, as though that could be anything but unspeakable monotony. (It does no harm to conceive the unchanging or abstract aspect of God as simple, for the beauty of abstractions is not solely in themselves but also in their relations to other aspects of the concrete whole which includes them. But it is this concrete whole which possesses the value and hence deserves the name of God.) First-type theism endeavors to persuade us that God has all the value of variety except variety. The reply is that the value of variety is variety, just as the value of unity is unity. Even the Trinity gives no sufficient, even if so much as conceivable, contrast. What is required is maximal contrast, not only on one level, as between persons of the Trinity, but between levels within the unity of God — for instance, between the contingent or changing and the necessary or immutable.

An attempt to impute variety to God without departing from first-type theism is found in the following passage from Cardinal Newman:

> Order and harmony are God's very essence. To be many and distinct in his attributes, yet after all to be but one – to be sanctity, truth, justice, love, power, wisdom – to be all at once each of these as fully as if he were nothing else but it, and as if the rest were not; this implies in the nature an infinitely sovereign and incomprehensible order, which is an attribute as wonderful as any, and the result of all the others. Such is the unity and consequent harmony and beauty of the Divine Nature.[1]

In so far as the variety of attributes is real variety, second-type theism is at least equal to first-type. It asserts the unity of the attributes in the same sense. But it does not reduce God to a mere unity of abstractions, all on the same level of generality. It also includes in him the integrated contrast between the particular and the general, and between the multiplicity of divergent particulars. Surely the beauty of a man's life is not equivalent to the mere concordance of his justice, love, wisdom, and the like with each other; but rather is this concordance a mere aspect of the essential harmony of the man's particular experiences with each other and with the experiences of other persons in whose life he participates. The terms of harmonic relations are concrete as well as abstract. In spite of Newman's eloquence, the absolute inner poverty of God as Thomistic theology conceives him cannot be concealed.

The denial of parts and of change to God not only deprives God of contrast within himself, and so of beauty, but it also robs him of unity, and so of beauty in his relation to the world. For if this relation is to be beautiful, then, in spite of the infinite contrast between creator and creature, there must also be a no less profound similarity. The creature must really be the image of God, and that in all his being, for man must be a variation on the cosmic theme, which is divinity. Here traditional theology tended to sacrifice unity to diversity. Within God the diversity of contingent things was lacking; but between God and things there was little but the sheer contrast between the uncreated creator and the uncreative creature, the purely necessary and the contingent. Man changes; God simply does not. Man has a body; God has none. Man alters, but cannot, like God, create substance. Thus while God within was ugly by defect of variety, reality, as composed of God and the world, was ugly by defect of unity, and the two defects were clearly two sides of the same defect. For the only wav to unify God with his creatures is to regard the unity of God's being (the supremacy of which lies in its inclusiveness) as the unity of reality as such. And the only way to give maximal diversity as well as unity to God is to allow that his unity genuinely embraces all that is, with all the variety which it really has.

The Scylla and Charybdis of aesthetic failure, monotony and discord, are represented in the two horns of the theistic dilemma so wonderfully set forth by Hume. Either God has nothing in common with man, in which case we can have no conception of him, and theism and atheism are indistinguishable (for what is the idea of God if not that of an analogy between man and the supreme power who made man in His own image?) ; or else God is frankly conceived anthropomorphically, as infected with human weaknesses, and then the idea becomes suspect from the opposite angle. Now the relation of God to man is infinitely ugly unless it is equally true that the two are alike and that they are different, and the relation is infinitely beautiful only if both likeness and difference are in some sense infinite. The aesthetic problem is the same as the metaphysical, except for emphasis upon the conditions of value in the most concrete form, rather than in the merely abstract form of logical coherence.

If God can be conceived as the infinite degree — or such form of maximality as is in each case possible — of whatever variables are applicable in finite degree to man, and man as the finite degree of whatever variables are infinitely applicable to God (see *The Universal Orthodoxy*), then the problem is solved both logically and aesthetically. If, for instance, God is not unchanging while man changes, but rather God changes in a manner as different from change in man as is possible while yet really change — that is, if change is varied as much as possible between the two, while yet retaining its generic identity as change — then both unity and diversity in the relationship will be provided for.

Moreover, the unity may be as great as the contrast. For a changing God may by sympathetic participation completely experience the positive qualities of the human being. The aesthetic supremacy of harmony in contrast between persons over lesser harmonies is in the sympathetic parallelism through which what is on one side of the contrast may, more or less completely, appear also on the other.

And the infinite or all-apprehending mind is the one in which the parallelism reaches completeness. In spite of, indeed because of, his infinite difference from man, God repeats in himself all positive qualities and qualitative contrasts that are present in man, including the quite positive contrast between actualization of potency and potency itself, as this contrast is unified in change. God is the mirror of countless finite individuals, endlessly varying the theme of personality, whose range of variations only his uniquely sympathetic, flexible personality can span.

We have then exactly as good motive for insisting upon " univocal " applicability of properties to God and man as for insisting upon maximal contrast within the unity of a property. What is needed is a definite provision for maximal flexibility of concepts, not the substitution of some vague or ambiguous " analogy " for strictly common variables.

Aesthetics equally condemns the ideas of a merely perfect and of a merely imperfect deity (first- and third-type theisms). For in either case there is failure of contrast not only not compensated for by more adequate unity but — as we have seen already for first-type doctrine — aggravated by an equal failure of unity. In a wholly imperfect deity the contrast of perfect and perfectible would be lacking; and also such a deity by definition could not represent maximal (perfect) unity, or adequate unification of all that is. He must fall short somewhere in his unification of reality. His sympathy could not integrate all the riches of the world and could not parallel all of its variety.

On the other hand, in the " pure actuality " of first-type theism all contrast vanishes. In God so defined there is either no contrast or, what comes to the same, all possible contrast. For to compose a pattern of all possible contrasts, rejecting none, is to compose no pattern and to lose all contrasts in the sheer continuity of the merely potential (not "actual" at all). It is the possible (grounded in the primordial or abstract nature of God) that is above definite diversity and composition. We get definiteness by restricting the possible, and that restriction *is* definiteness. You may in a picture combine blue with yellow of some shade, but to combine all hues of yellow with all hues of blue is the same as to do nothing aesthetically. You may go on to other parts of your picture and use more and more hues in these additional parts, but the rejected possible combinations of hue and shape in the first-named parts are rejected once for all, since other parts are other parts because in some characters they fail to duplicate the given parts, either as they are or as they might have been had certain choices been made otherwise. God may enjoy Shelley and Keats together in a manner quite impossible to Shelley or Keats; but what no aesthetic experience can do is to combine the Keats or Shelley that actually was with the Keats or Shelley that might have been, had choices of these men fallen otherwise. For the incompatibility of alternative possibilities is the meaning of possibility, and of all distinctions whatever. The poems Keats could have written no one else in all past or future cosmic history ever could write; for other individuals must, by the very meaning of individuality, lack the personality which is the theme expressed potentially in all the possible states of Keats. The once potential Keats is now forever impossible, and impossible even for God, in the same way as round squares are impossible for him, that is, because it is nonsense that something should be known by omniscience as both actual and not actual, or known as not actual, yet as yielding all the contrasts it would have exhibited had it been actual. That would merely be to say that the actualization of the potential is aesthetically superfluous, and to really believe that would be to cease to actualize, to cease to live.

Thus aesthetics seems to be adequate to decide between the three types of doctrine, provided only one admits that a thoroughly or infinitely ugly view of the cosmos would be a more radical sacrifice of values — including intellectual values, for what is truth *as appealing* but intellectual beauty? — than anyone can really make except in words; so that we must regard atheism or first- or third-type theism as pretenses, not real beliefs. One can admit ugly aspects of the world; but to make ugliness the essential pervasive feature, as atheism implicitly does — is that more than a gesture, in beings who continue to go about their business in the world? Or if they do not do so, then how is one to argue with them, if their business be philosophy?

But aesthetics throws yet other light upon theology. Theologians have often done some justice to the beauty of the world, so far as it was defined through structure as correlated with intellect. The world as relational is the satisfying object of mind as the sense for relations. Also, even simple qualities were sometimes admitted to have aesthetic value, as in their simplicity clearly apprehended and so satisfyingly accessible to our awareness. Thus Thomas says " clarity " is a feature of the beautiful, including brilliance or vividness as an aspect of clarity. And God, as supreme knower, corresponds to the world as clear, as God as will does to the world as active. But knowing as sense for relations is distinguishable from knowing as mere having of qualities. There seems but one way to know a quality, and that is to feel it. There is nothing in it to think, if by thought is meant relating; for a simple quality is not a relationship, but the term without which relations would not be possible, as the complex presupposes the simple. God must equally know qualities and relations, and how he could know a quality except by having it as a feeling-tone, a quality of his experience itself, we have not the faintest clue in experience. There is no intellectual content whatever to the blueness of blue except such as presupposes the non-intellectual, the purely sensory content. A God who knows but never feels, who has no feeling-tones, but only superintellection, or superintuition entirely above the contrast between terms and relations, is an aesthetically hideous or empty conception.

Aesthetics is the study which has finally brought philosophy to take feeling and quality seriously as positive excellences, not defects. It is time that we incorporated this insight into our speculations about God. Either feeling is or it is not reducible to a special case of thinking or willing (or to mere matter in motion) ; and if it is not, then being as such involves it. For being as such is simply the irreducibles in their unity. Only the idea of God exhibits the unity plainly and vividly, and this only if God be conceived not as without feeling but as more rich in feeling-tones than any other being, not as without the experience of potency but as equally supreme in achieved actuality and in potency of actuality to come. We must preserve contrasts, all of them (except those between something and nothing, e.g., knowledge and ignorance, and even such contrasts as vicariously enjoyed) , in God, while ascribing to him a matchless power to hold these contrasts together (so far as intrinsically compatible) in one experience.

It is sometimes said that aesthetics is concerned with essences, not existences, as though possibility were enough for beauty. But I have yet to meet a man who enjoyed merely possible symphonies as much as actual ones. I fear there is a confusion here between two kinds of existence. So long as sensations, or sensory images, of the required kind exist, it does not always matter to us what the physical stimulus of these sensory states may be. But the sensory states exist, and not merely in the mind or experience; they exist also in the sense organs and in the whole body. This is actual existence in the complete sense, it is merely more narrowly localized than some other forms. The distinction between the possible and the actual is of quite another order.

Of course Keats does say that

> Heard melodies are sweet, but those unheard
> Are sweeter; therefore, ye soft pipes, play on;
> Not to the sensual ear, but, more endear'd,
> Pipe to the spirit ditties of no tone. . . .

But this seems to mean that actual melodies are not the best possible ones, not that possibility as such is equal to actuality. Or perhaps it only means that music is incapable of expressing the profoundest harmonies. Keats was a poet, not a musician.

It may be held that to a strong enough imagination possibles would be as beautiful as actuals. But this raises the question whether or not the completely imagined would be any different from the completely perceived, that is, the actual. It is not to be assumed that " imagination " is in essence a dealing with the " possible " but only accidentally a dealing with it as more or less indefinite, and hence aesthetically unsatisfactory. If the possible is not distinguished from the actual by deficient definiteness, how is it distinguished? And if the possible is as good as the actual, then why actualize?

At the opposite extreme, if a " pure actuality " or timeless absolute could contain all possible value as actual, then why should there be a world consisting partly of unactualized potencies? The reason there is a contrast of actual and potential is that both are positive and hence afford a valuable contrast. Possibility is not the mere absence of actuality, it is the non-actual which *can become* actual, and this can-become-actual is a positive something irreducible to anything else. Moreover, actuality is essentially the has-become-actual of the previously could-become-actual, it carries this previous having-been-potential within itself. (God, as necessary being, is not the being whose actual state is necessary, hence without previous potency, but the being which at all times actualizes in *some* generically but not determinately specified way an antecedent potency expressive of his unique generic nature.) The contrast between the *is* and the *might have been* belongs to the *is* and is essential to its beauty. Without it, all of being would collapse into a single entity which either had no pattern whatever, no beauty, no harmony, no wealth of variety in unity, or else had but one everlastingly fixed pattern without the hint of an open alternative, the nightmare of monotony carried to the absolute, the " block universe " with which modern man has appalled himself.

The contrasts which give life its value need not be sacrificed in forming the conception of the highest value; rather, we must give to " highest " just such meaning as will express and preserve, not annul, these contrasts, so that the unity of the highest will be a unity *of* something — not just bare unity. As Fechner so well said, the God of traditional theology (A) is empty unity, as the world of traditional theology is ununified plurality. The " form of forms " lacked content, the content lacked an inclusive form. The cosmic art is the content-with-the-form, the form-with-the-content. It is the one living experience, sublime in its infinite past and present, sublime in its potencies for the future, sublime in the contrast between these, sublime in its multiplicity and variety of parts, sublime in the wholeness to which their partiality is relative. God is neither a poem containing all possible poems — a hideous nightmare of the incompossible — nor is he the mere sum of all actual poems, nor yet merely one poem among others, nor finally is he sheerly above all definite patterns and forms. He is rather the never ending poem of which all actual poems are phrases, all cosmic epochs yet elapsed are verses, and whose " to be continued " is the promise of infinite poetic creation to come. He is the poet as enjoying this poem, the poem as the life of the poet down to the given present. But the phrases of the cosmic poem are themselves poets enjoying their poems. In this respect many aesthetic analogies are false. Thus in poetry words are mere carriers of meaning, they do not possess, enjoy, meanings. Much human art manipulates materials similarly regarded as not themselves enjoying any of the aesthetic experience they make possible. The chorus director or stage manager is in a way closer to God than the poet or painter, who is not an artist dealing, as God does, with lesser artists, recognized as such. (The molecules of pigment or of ink may indeed be sentient, and enjoy rudimentary harmony as well as suffer from rudimentary discord, but this is of no interest to the human artist.) God's art is superior to man's not because he " controls " his materials more absolutely, but almost the contrary, because he knows how to set the limits within which the living units of his work are to control themselves, to do as they happen to please, not precisely as even he could foresee. Of course this means that the resulting art work cannot exhibit " perfect " harmony (whatever that would be), and certainly discord, evil, hatred, suffering exist in God's world if anything exists there. The play of the world is a tragic as well as comic play, for players and for playwright. The social nature of existence makes tragedy in principle, though not in particular, inevitable.

God is the cosmic " adventure " (Whitehead) integrating all real adventures as they occur, without ever failing in readiness to realize new states out of the divine potency, which is indeed " beyond number " and definite form, yet is of value only because number and form come out of it. God is not the super-staleness of the never new, the never young, the monomania-like poverty — vainly called super-richness — of the merely absolute (just as he is not the blind chaos of the merely relative). As Fechner said, every child that comes into the world and brings a new note of freshness, every youth for whom the world looks young, contributes this freshness — this slightly novel beauty of feeling as well as this feeling of novelty — to God, who is literally the youngest and the oldest of all beings, the richest in accumulated experiences, and consequently the most equipped with suitable background for diverse new ones, as the man with a varied past is apt to have the most capacity to assimilate further variety.

If such a cosmic adventurer did not exist, we should from an aesthetic point of view be compelled, in Voltaire's phrase, to invent him. The ideal by which the artist is inspired is not any notion of " absolute beauty " as either a supreme sample or a fixed total of possible beauty. The artist wishes, taking the past of culture as given, to add something new which is both intrinsically valuable or enjoyable, and is appropriate to, enjoyable together with, that past, though by no means deducible from it. He wishes in a small way to simulate the cosmic adventure, to create a note in the next phase of that adventure as visible from his corner of the world. The reformer seeking new beauties of social relationship is essentially in the same attitude, but his " corner " is somewhat different. The only static " beauty as such " or timeless absolute which the artist ever contemplates, even subconsciously, is purely abstract, such as the principle of unity in contrast; not any definite unity in contrast or any absolute sum of such unities (which would have neither unity nor contrast since it would be nothing), but the purely general requirement, Let there be as much unity in contrast as possible, both within the new pattern and between it and the old patterns — so that the pattern of ongoing life shall be unified and diversified. (I have adapted this thought in part from Van Meter Ames.) This is the aesthetic imperative which the artist feels laid upon him by the scheme of things, and it is the voice of God as truly as any other imperative. As Berdyaev says, the service of God consists, not in rule-conforming correctness of behavior, but in that creativeness of new values together with respect for old ones by which man can most truly imitate the everlasting creator.

But the artist has also a concrete ideal, which is by no means timeless. This is his glimpse of the concrete, ever newly enriched beauty of the present actual world; for of what avail would it be to contribute beautiful parts to a whole which was mere chaos or monotony or nothingness in terms of value? Indeed, if the beauty of experience which the artist creates for men is to really "exist" in the universe, this universe must as a whole possess a value which exactly provides for his contribution (see chapter 8). Thus an abstract eternal principle of cosmic search for beauty, and a concrete ever growing totality of beauty actually achieved, provide the two senses in which "absolute beauty" can rightly be spoken of. Neither one sense nor the other nor both together constitutes an entity absolute or perfect in every sense which these words have sometimes been supposed to bear, but they represent so much of perfection as can really be conceived.

NOTE

1 Quoted by John Rickaby, S. J., *General Metaphysics* (London: Longmans, Green & Co., 1890), pp. 153–54.

VII

THE DIVINE SELF-CREATION

Immobility is an imperfection . . . dramatic movement and tragedy are born of the fullness, not of the poverty of life. . . . Creation of the world implies movement in God, it is a dramatic event in the divine life.

NICOLAS BERDYAEV, in *The Destiny of Man*

A POSSIBLE objection to the temporalistic view of God defended in this book is that it conflicts with the classical idea of creation as creation *ex nihilo*. One can no longer contrast God as purely eternal with his creation as temporal, and if God is to be viewed as essentially temporal, one can no more admit a beginning of the temporal as such than of God himself. Does not the world then become a second primordial and everlasting entity over against rather than created by God? The answer is that the question is full of ambiguities. "The world," if that means the system of atoms and stars we see, or anything in any particular respect like it, is not everlasting but a created product. It is created, to be sure, not out of nothing — whatever that would mean — but out of an earlier world and its potentialities for transformation. This earlier world was similarly created. The world as preserving its identity through all these transformations is something infinitely protean and infinitely endowed with power to assimilate variety into unity. Indeed, the world in this sense is identical with God, not a second entity. God is the self-identical individuality of the world somewhat as a man is the self-identical individuality of his ever changing system of atoms. The only everlasting (and primordial) entity upon which God acts in creation is himself; all individuals, other than himself, which are influenced by his action are less than everlasting, or at least less than primordial. To contrast the world as creation to God as creator is one of three things: it is to contrast the multitude of non-primordial individuals with the single primordial individual which alone makes of this multitude a single inclusive individual with self-identity throughout all time; or it is to contrast the concrete totality of God's being — his " consequent nature " (Whitehead) — as at a given world moment with the abstract essence of God as purely the same at all times, all accidents being left out of account; or finally it is to contrast God at one moment with himself as in a preceding moment about to create for himself an appropriate subsequent state.

The term creator can perfectly well be used by one who denies creation *ex nihilo*. For to " make the world " out of a preceding world is not only no abuse of language but the very meaning that language supports. All making we ever encounter is transformation, enrichment of something already there. The word creation is standard usage for all the more exalted examples of such transformation, for instance, for composing music, writing poetry, imagining striking characters in a novel. Of course divine creation is intended to be a unique case, but the uniqueness of God is his maximality. He makes on a supreme, that is cosmic, scale; he makes the whole, not just certain parts; and he makes not for a limited time but during infinite time. These functions are strictly unique and unrivaled, not a whit the less so because the making is still transformation, enrichment. And it is not as if the given world which is utilized in creation were simply imposed upon God from without as something alien, for the given world too is his creation, though made from an earlier world which he created out of an earlier one, and so on. The highest authority in traditional theology, Thomas Aquinas, admitted that this conception is open to no objections except those derived from revelation. And since Protestant views of revelation render these objections thoroughly questionable, the issue reduces to the Roman Catholic issue, which is irrelevant to the subject of this chapter. Thus there is no reason why the " creator " need be supposed to have created out of nothing.

From another point of view theologians ought not to have been so averse to the notion of transformative creation. For they were committed to this notion in another guise. Namely, creation was not really out of nothing, but out of the potentialities, essences, or natures of all things, as embraced eternally in the divine essence. These were transformed or transferred from their status of mere possibilities, in which some of them, the uncreated but possible creatures, remained, into the status of actualities, whatever the difference between the one status and the other may be. We are more inclined today to say that the natures of things which come into existence are really created *de novo,* utilizing only the natures of other things already in existence. Thus there is *more* genuine creation in this view than in the old. For there is hardly any meaning to the idea that God " made " what is (on the usual older account) part of his necessary essence, the eternal essences of things. Just in knowing himself he knew his possible effects. On the new view God chooses not only what is to be but even what is to be a definite possibility. Of course he could not have chosen to make definitely impossible what he has made definitely possible, but he could have left possibility indefinite in certain respects, so that there would have been no truth about either the possibility or impossibility of the thing in question. Descartes's famous view that God made possibilities as well as actualities by a free act of will may thus be given an acceptable interpretation. This is an example, out of many, of the power of second-type theism to reconcile age-old oppositions of doctrine.

The final defense of the idea of creation not *ex nihilo* but out of a pre-existing state of affairs is that the idea of a beginning of time is self-contradictory, as Aristotle pointed out. Even a beginning is a change, and all change requires something changing that does not come to exist through that same change. The beginning of the world would have to happen *to* something other than the world, something which as the subject of happening would be in a time that did not begin with the world. God as changing furnishes such a subject, since he is in one respect (in Whitehead's terms, his primordial nature) ever identical, in another (his consequent nature) ever partly novel, and yet also — by the indestructibility of the past — containing all that he ever was as part of what he at any subsequent time becomes.

One might, of course, argue that a beginning or first state of the temporal process would not be a change from anything anterior, and so would require no subject of change. But at least it would realize a possibility, which however, as not separated from it in time, would, self-contradictorily, have to coexist with the actuality. Also the first state would have nothing in common with later states, it would have no memory, achieve no antecedent purpose, etc. Would it be anything we could mean by a "state"? As Edmund Gosse's father saw, God could not have created a first state of the world that looked like a first state. Each animal would have appeared as if it had come from parents (except in a few quasi-comic details, such as the absence of an umbilicus), the hills as if formed by geological forces, etc. A first moment of time would be an ontological lie through and through, a joke of existence upon itself. True, the alternative is the — to us unimaginable — infinite regress of past events, but all attempts to show this idea to be self-contradictory seem to have failed. We cannot " complete the synthesis," starting from the present; but the universe did not start from the present, and, as Couturat, in his book on the mathematical infinite, seems to me to show, the mathematical idea of infinity is not a mere successive synthesis, in spite of Kant.

It is worth noting that the equivalent of the contrast between primordial and consequent natures is inevitable in any theology, the question being only whether it shall be a temporal distinction. For God is always to be considered in two aspects: (1) in himself, or apart from having created just this world as it now exists, or any other particular world that might be thought of (and both medieval and contemporary logic agree that the details of the world might have been otherwise than they are) ; and (2) as having in fact created the particular world in question. Thus there is God in his essential, and God in his accidental, functions. The only way such distinctions can be made conceivable is in terms of time; the essential being the purely eternal, and the accidental being the temporal or changing, aspects of the divine. The unity of God is preserved in principle in the same way as that of a human person, but here, as always, the difference is between a partial and a maximum realization of the principle. God identifies himself as the same in basic purposes through all the details of the past and all the general traits of the future (the farther in the future the more general) ; whereas we finite creatures have only an extremely partial memory of even the limited time during which we have existed, and are densely ignorant of what is ordained for the future, that is to say, of the partial limits set in advance to the freedom of the creatures.

The accidental functions of God — without which he could be of no importance to the accidental being, man — were a scandal in traditional theology. The world embodies God's glory, but according to Von Hügel, quoting some Scholastic, it embodies his "accidental glory." That creates a dilemma. If the glory is accidental and is God's, then God has accidental properties. If it is not God's (or is not accidental), then how is it God's glory (or the glory which he has in relation to the accidental)? Apparently, the glory belongs to the world, to the contingent, not to God!

Thomas Aquinas actually goes so far (some other Schoolmen do not) as to say that the relation of God to the contingent world is a relation with respect to the world but not with respect to God. How could one make clearer that Thomism, whatever it is, is not a religious doctrine? In it God says to man, "I love you, but so far as I am concerned I am not related to you in any way, my relation of love to you is literally nothing to me."

Yet what Aquinas says here is in a sense true. There is such a thing as an external relation, a relation which "does nothing" to one of its terms, or even to both of them. The doctrine that relations are exclusively internal, that every object of thought involves every other, has been sufficiently criticized in the last half-century. It too is an oversimple extreme. But external relations are subject to two conditions, the neglect of which constitutes the opposite and equally oversimple extreme. First, every relation is internal to *something,* either to one at least of its terms or to some entity additional to these. Second, the entity to which the relation is internal is a *concrete* whole of which the externally related entities are *abstract* aspects.

Let us take the second point first. If I think of whiteness, whiteness is not made anything other than it was before by this relation to my consciousness, and this relation is thus external to whiteness, but my consciousness is altered to just the extent of the relation. It is clear in this instance that the externally related term, whiteness, is abstract and the concrete term, my consciousness of the whiteness, is inclusive of the relation, is an internally related term. Or, suppose we consider the relation between the whiteness and my personal identity as a certain human individual. I can enter into this relation without becoming a numerically different individual. But I cannot do so without alteration in the concrete state which I as such an individual enjoy. Had I thought of blueness instead of whiteness, I might have been the same individual, but this means that I might have enjoyed the same past (if one admits, as I hold we must, a contingent relation between past and present), and I might even in the present have had the same general, more or less abstract, characteristics, but my total concrete being would have been slightly different.

Thus external relations are possible only on condition that the terms to which the relations are external should be abstract and relatively unindividual. " This red object " is nothing to " redness " as such, which would be the same for thought without the object. The abstract is what is not meant to be wholly determinate in its relations, or indeed in its quality. Redness as such or in the abstract is a somewhat vague conception. If one substitutes for it " the red of all objects *exactly* the same in color as this one," it then becomes a question whether any other objects with exactly the same color are so much as possible. After all, any other objects would be in different circumstances. How then could exactly the same color result? Can our memory and powers of comparison and imagination verify such absolute sameness? It is hard to see how they could do so, and hence, so far at least as is at all obvious, the abstract entities which we can detach from their relations must be regarded as unindividual, not wholly determinate, in nature.

Let us apply this to God. If there is a legitimate way of taking God abstractly, if there is an aspect of God objectively distinguished from God as a whole and hence abstract, then this aspect may be related to the remaining aspects, and to the world, by a relation which does not enter into the being of the abstract aspect. Now as we have seen, second-type theism distinguishes between the immutable abstract quality of being benevolent and the concrete state of experience constituted by this benevolence as particularized in relation to definite objects. Of the former what Thomas says is certainly true. Not merely that we conceive God in an abstract aspect, but that he himself must distinguish between (1) his eternal and unchanging aspect, his purpose as laid down before all the worlds, or rather before each and every world, and (2) the more and more particular purposes which mark the approach to, and (3) the achievements of purpose which mark arrival at, any given point of time. These distinctions are, for second-type theism, what is objectively meant by ascribing purpose to God, not in the least merely our subjective way of conceiving purpose. And only by means of an abstract or indeterminate aspect, contrasted to a concrete, determinate one, can an individual be conceived as identical through changes.

It is, then, the meaning of the universal, the abstract, as such, that it is capable of external relations, that it can be identified without considering all the relational contexts, the concrete cases, in which it might be embodied. But on the other hand (to return to our other requirement for external relations), the relations of abstractions are made possible by the fact that both universals and particulars are embraced in, or are internal to, concrete experiences, or individual events, as wholes. Otherwise, such external relations would be self-contradictory. For an individual relation is a *single* entity which is nothing without its terms, and hence its entire unitary actuality must include that of each of its terms and must qualify some whole of which the external terms are parts or aspects. This whole may be one of the terms, as inclusive of the other (my body as related to its height), or a still more inclusive whole (as when my height and my weight are considered as related by both belonging to me), perhaps the entire universe. The point is that a relation between several things is not several things, but one thing, and yet it includes its terms in this unity. My-love-for-Rachel is not a mere aggregate of me and Rachel, nor is it a mere abstract general relation of "love" between us, but a single unique something of which both of us are internal essential constituents. The interaction between two molecules is slightly peculiar to those molecules, yet it is one thing even though they are two, or rather, it is one thing with various aspects. In this oneness is expressed the unity of the world. All relations, internal or external, involve a substantial unity embracing the relata. (Whitehead's perception of this requirement is one of his points of superiority to most pluralists, with whose defense of external relations as such he heartily agrees.)

If the relation of the absolute to the world really fell wholly outside the absolute, then this relation would necessarily fall within some further and genuinely single entity which embraced both the absolute and the world and the relations between them — in other words, within an entity greater than the absolute. Or else the world itself would possess as its property the relation-to-God, and since this relation is nothing without God, the world, in possessing it, would possess God as integral part of its own property, and thus the world would itself be the entity inclusive of itself and the absolute. On any showing, something will be *more* than an immutable absolute which excludes its own relations to the mutable. It is therefore necessary to distinguish between the immutable and the absolute, if by absolute is meant the "most real," inclusive, or concrete being. The immutable can only be an abstract aspect of God, who as a concrete whole must contain both this aspect and its relations to the novel and contingent. The tissue of relations between the world and the immutable aspect of God constitutes a sublime pattern inclusive of all that is, whether mutable or immutable, and therefore *cannot possibly be less than the pattern of God himself* in his total being or "consequent nature," or as involving both a necessary essence and an infinity of accidents. This total pattern — here we must, I think, agree with Thomism and disagree with Spinoza and Bradley or Royce — cannot possibly be unchanging or internal to anything immutable.

Thus when Thomists say "God," they really mean, we should suppose (though over their protest), "God in one aspect," and when they speak of the relations of God to the creatures they mean "as embraced in God in his total reality, though we prefer not to call this total reality God." If this is understood, then nearly every difference between Thomistic theism and that, say, of Whitehead, disappears. For instance, the primordial or abstract aspect of God, as conceived by Whitehead, is "infinite . . . free, complete . . . eternal."[1] But even the "consequent" aspect of God is in a sense "infinite." For, since at all times God enjoys an infinite past, the wealth of happiness which he possesses is never less than infinite. Though not completely beyond tragedy or the possibility of increase in happiness (nor the risk of falling short of the maximal possible increase), yet is he superior to us in happiness, with a unique, incomparable superiority, as the gap between the finite and the infinite is unique. (How an infinite past can yet be added to will be considered in *The Universal Orthodoxy*.)

Thomists say that finite minds, in knowing, acquire a relation to the object, while the object acquires none to them. From this they conclude that external relations are possible, although the external relation they wish to represent by this analogy is the exact opposite of a relation of object to knower, but is that of the knower (God) to the known! But apart from the amazing (I had almost said brazen) paradox of this upside-down analogy, it is also to be objected that the external relation of the object to the human knower is possible only because the latter, as internally related, is the more inclusive or concrete entity. This is seen in the clearest case of knowledge we have, that of knowledge of the past through immediate or true memory. This is the one case in which we have equally good knowledge of knower and known, and hence the best chance of grasping their relation. The past in immediate memory is not outside the knowing present, but is integral with it — if, that is, memory is really direct intuition at all; and, however much unconscious inference may be mixed with apparent memory, there are grave difficulties in the view that all memory is really inference, not direct apprehension. The present is here the absolute, the more concrete and inclusive, the past the partially abstract, exclusive — and immutable!

Of course Thomists say that it is the weakness of human knowledge that forces us to conform to the object instead of conforming the object to ourselves. God, in knowing, does the latter, the opposite of what we do. He does not adjust himself to contingent objects, but adjusts them to his own purposes. This is true — of the abstract or long-run purposes of God — except that what actually does the adjusting is not the mere abstract nature alone, but the whole concrete deity who, in molding objects which he knows and loves, also makes for himself a new state inclusive of the new states of the object. There is nothing whatsoever in all our experience to furnish the slightest basis for the idea of a knower who as a whole or in his concreteness would be unqualified by his relations to what he knows. Here the resort to experience which, in some respects, is well carried out in Thomism, simply disappears, and we are told that it is the relations of the object of human knowledge which are analogous to God's relations as knower — a clear substantiation, it seems to me, of the accusation often made against Thomism that it treats God " as an object, not as a subject."

Nevertheless, we should respect a doctrine which becomes profoundly defensible the moment a rather simple device of reinterpretation is applied to it. There may very well be a divine Something which is immutable, unaffected by its inclusion in ever more concrete relational contexts — the primordial abstract essence of the uniquely complete, and hence both necessary and accidental, being, God, the ever changing, and hence, as necessary aspect of this perpetual change, forever identical with itself.

Of course, inferential, symbolic, indirect knowledge, " knowledge about," not " by acquaintance," has as its object something relatively external to the knower; but (1) this knowledge is admittedly and in principle incapable of perfection, clearly not the model for omniscience; and (2) even this knowledge conforms the knower to the known, although in a limited, indirect way. To think adequately about six objects I must set up some representative of the number six in my own experience, such as an image of six dots. Mathematical symbols involve an essential element of abstract or structural similarity between the symbolic sets and the ideas thought about.

It seems almost self-evident that a wholly necessary and immutable being cannot know the contingent and changing. Grosseteste wrestles with the problem, How can God know the future — which is contingent — though his knowledge, like all his being, is necessary? [2] (The usual Scholastic doctrine, if I am not mistaken, is that God, simply in knowing his own essence, knows all things, presumably the contingent as contingent, the necessary as necessary, the merely possible as possible, though in the essence there is nothing but sheer actuality!) Grosseteste tries to throw light on the paradox by distinguishing between conditional and absolute necessity. Thus if I saw Socrates run yesterday, this seeing followed from or was necessitated by the running, not vice versa. So God's knowledge of the contingent is necessary in the sense that it is impossible God should be ignorant of it, granted that it occurs. (Yet God, being impassive, is not determined by what he knows!) But of course the presupposition is that Socrates *might* not have run, and that, if he had not, I should not have seen him run; and similarly, if an event known by God is contingent, then it might not occur (or might not have occurred), and should it not occur (or have occurred), then God would not have known it as occurring. That is, he *would have known otherwise* than he actually does. If p (the contingent event) implies q (God's knowledge), and not-p (the contradictory of the contingent event) implies not-q (God as not knowing the event as existent, since in this case it would not exist to be known), then if not-p is possible, not-q is possible — by any known logic. But not-*p* must be possible, or *p* is not contingent. Grosseteste seems to admit this when he goes on to say that ordinary logical ideas, being based on temporal phenomena, do not apply to God, who knows all things in the simplicity of eternity, in which, apparently, contradictions may be realized. The only other course Grosseteste could have taken here is to deny, with the Thomists, that God's knowledge is God's knowledge, that is, that his cognitive relation to objects is anything at all to him, whether it be knowledge of the possible as possible or of the actual as actual, or possible knowledge of something as actual which is possibly actual. In short, God's doing and knowing are nothing, bare downright nothing, in terms of his own reality. Believe in this as a solution who can!

It is all very simple, provided one gives up the notion that God as simple (and changeless) is the whole of deity, instead of merely the abstract side of a being greater than any one-sided conception can grasp, a being both changing and stable, both passive yet secure from all corruption, and in both respects infinitely more illustrative of the categories employed than any other being.

It may seem a troublesome paradox that the absolute as the "complete," and therefore changeless, should be held less than the concrete, changing, and forever incomplete whole.[3] But this is because there is an ambiguity in the idea of completeness. It might mean to lack nothing that is possible. But of course God's completeness was supposed to be more than the full realization of antecedent possibility; for God was above all possibility. Yet was it not overlooked that these properties are possessed by the realm of possibility itself, taken as a whole? This is not itself possible, it just is. And it is complete, since "all that is possible" can lack no possibility. But the realm of possibility, for a theist, is the power of God, God as able to do, rather than as doing. In God, merely as able to do, no item of possible being is missing. But, in another sense, no item is present in God so conceived. For what is present is mere potency, without a single item of actuality, except the actuality of God's ability, conceived in abstraction from its determinate exercise. Thus God as mere power is both everything and nothing. He is everything in the deficient form of potency, nothing in the form of actuality. Hence the " complete " realm of possibility is yet infinitely incomplete. And no other way of conceiving absolute completeness is possible, since it is the essence of actuality to be non-exhaustive of potency, even though the most trivial item of actuality is in some sense more than the most tremendous possibility which remains merely that. Other authors have pointed out the troubles Scholastics had over the distinction between essence and existence. That the distinction is really that between the determinate and the indeterminate-but-determinable, and that the primordial completeness of God consists in his containing the ultimate *dimensions* of determinateness (rather than all possible determinations), could never be clearly indicated by a doctrine which attempted to transcend time. For time is the way in which essence and existence, possibility and actuality, are related, as space is the way actuality is related to actuality. In God's primordial power is no determinate lack, but also no determinate possessions.[4]

God alone is " complete " in potency. But completeness in actuality (" pure actuality ") is meaningless, and the attempt to conceive it only results in a concept whose object must be less than the least of actualities because it is not actual at all. " The most inclusive actual whole " enjoys the only completeness that is conceivable beyond the mere completeness of the potential as such. On the one hand we have that to which nothing determinate or actual can be added because it must be conceived in abstraction from determination or actuality; on the other hand there is that to which infinite new determinations can forever be added, though none can ever be outside it. These are the only totalities of being we can conceive. A worthy conception of God regards both of them as unique properties of deity.

The notion that the immutable is also the determinate is the great error of the Greeks, and results partly from their not having seen that the peculiar definiteness of mathematical ideas is due to the fact that their indefiniteness, though infinite, is uniform and for certain purposes can be neglected. Two and two are definitely four, but two what, and four what? Nothing could be more indefinite: two apples, two dots on paper, two children, two atoms, two ideas, two lines, two colors. Indefiniteness could scarcely be more extreme, but the point is that the other ideas involved are equally indefinite, and hence the interrelations of the ideas can be specified with complete definiteness, or completely uniform or homogeneous indefiniteness, as you wish to put it. The dimensions of the ultimate degree of indefiniteness might almost define the mathematical, and the immutable absolute arrived at in this way is nothing but the bare outline of possible actuality, the mere anatomy of God as able to do rather than as doing. Everything which is in the least particular, such as " light blue," or " sour," we have no reason for regarding as eternal, not because there was or could ever be a time when blue was not blue, or when blue was green, but because there may have been a time when blue was the subject of no truth whatever, since no such item was included in the whole of reality, or in the content of omniscience. Not that it was then true that " blue is not included in reality," but that it is *now* true that the whole of what was then real failed to contain blue, since no color which then was real was what we now know as blue. (In the foregoing I am departing somewhat from what appears to be Whitehead's doctrine of eternal objects.)

I am aware of the axiom that a cause cannot impart what it lacks; but I know of no experiential basis for this axiom that will bear examination. It simply denies creative interaction, and experience exhibits nothing else than such interaction. *No* cause has *precisely,* in advance, what it imparts. And if it did, why impart it? Why the effect, if the whole form is already in the cause? The only answer must be that to the form as possible is added " actuality," which however is formally nothing, or that to the form as in one thing is added the same form as in another. But this duplication itself must add some form or quality not in the cause, or it is useless.

One may well hesitate to base a doctrine of divine creation upon an axiom that there is no creation, save as mechanical passing about of pre-existent predicates.

But if God creates new forms additional even to his own being, is he not potential and actual, " teacher and taught," in the same respect at the same time? Not at all, for the potentiality of the form (a less determinate form) is temporally earlier, and its actuality (which includes the earlier indeed, but as such, as the immortal past, and so as constituting a different moment of time) is temporally later. To ask for a further " cause " of the actualization of a potency than the power to achieve such actualization is merely to suppose that being is prior to becoming, the very question at issue. Similarly question-begging is the notion that the final cause at which the actualization or change aims has to be " there " to be aimed at, and so actual already. A purpose, as we have seen, is indefinite by contrast with any of its realizations, and the ultimate purpose (to create beauty and the enjoyment of unity in contrast) can never be " reached " in the sense of exhaustively actualized, for it is inexhaustible by any determinate multitude, even infinite.

The Thomistic query, Is not actuality prior to potentiality rather than vice versa? suggests the retort, Why should either be the case? Is up prior to down or is down prior to up? Prior to both actuality and potentiality there may be " existence," as having the two contrasting modes of achieved actuality and power to achieve further actuality. This power exists, it does not merely have power to exist as a power to exist. What may have misled some thinkers here is the truth that there is indeed such a thing as the potentiality of existing, as when we say that a man is the actualization of a prior potency, which potency must have existed, not just have been possible. But to say existence is prior to potentiality of existence may only mean that there must be *some* existent whose power to create further existence has never itself " come into " existence, this ungenerated existent being indeed that into which things " come " in coming to exist (see chapter 8). Such a presupposed or necessary existent will not for all that be purely actual, to exist as an individual essentially involving an identity of selfhood which may be preserved through more than one course of possible experience and action. The actuality of a person is in essence *impure,* since it is a blend of the having actually done and experienced (something definite) and the about to do and experience something not yet wholly defined out of what is possible. To say that this is *not* the essence of individuality, since actuality is in principle prior to potency, is an assertion which, in my opinion, has yet to get beyond the assertion stage, and is so far from self-evident that its falsity is, I suggest, apparent upon careful inspection of the context of the problem, provided one is not under hypnotic control of what past thinkers have said. If it were impossible to conceive perfection, unsurpassability, of existent individuality defined as essentially a blend of actual existence and potential existence, then one would have to choose between atheism and first-type theory — a hard choice. But the conception is not impossible.

It is notable that though an externally related term is indeterminate and " unindividual," this is only so in the sense in which the *maximally* determinate or most individual thing is the enduring entity *as at a given time,* or as integrating past and (indeterminate) future in one state. Taking the enduring thing abstractly, as identical at different times, neglecting the increments of content coming to the thing at particular times, one still has something which is individual to the thing in the sense of not belonging to other enduring things. Now the abstract, externally related, aspect of God is individual to him in this sense, and furthermore it is unlike all other externally related yet individual entities in being identifiable by a definition. It is the only " perfect lovingness," the only " omniscience," there is or can be, and any instance of it (taken as a universal) will simply be some state or other of the same enduring individual, God. The reason for this is that the perfect or maximal case of love is not a mere species under the genus of loving individuals, but the presupposed standard of what it means to love, love without negation of itself, sheer love; in short, not the genus plus a specific difference, but the genus without the limitations of the specific cases. Yet it is not the genus as a mere subsisting abstraction, for perfect love is by no means the common class character of loving individuals. As we shall see later (in chapter 9) only a real perfectly loving individual can provide the concrete base for the abstraction of sheer lovingness. God is indeed "above genus and species," and is the only individual distinguishable from other individuals by a definition. But the tradition was involved in the paradox of denying any distinction (in the "simple" nature of God) between the abstract property of perfect love, and the perfectly loving one as more than merely abstract. The paradox disappears if one recognizes two grades of individuality, in God as in all concrete realities: the abstract or outline individuality which the thing has indifferently at diverse times of its history, and the fullness of individuality which the thing has in a given present, as containing its history up to date and in outline foreshadowing its future. "Divinity" as a property is not identical with God (though only God has this property), for it is by abstraction from determinate states of himself that one is aware simply of the common character of all his states, minus the infinite richness of detailed contents of his determinate enjoyments and sympathies. Thus one more paradox proves to be the result of the inadequacy, not of the human mind as such, but of the orthodox theological tradition.

Those who ask, Is God personal? might perhaps agree to define a person as an *individual* conscious being. Now were it in every sense true that God is not in a genus, then in no sense could it be true that God is an individual. The first-type notion of pure actuality, a being which is actually all that it is possible for it to be, a being that comes, therefore, under no genus of alternative cases of which it is one, is not the idea of an individual. Between the *actus purus,* which is the colorless and formless pure and simple, and the individual God who made, and knows as having been made, individual human beings and other creatures, when he might have made something else, and might then have known that something else as having been made, as actual, there is a great gulf. For second-type doctrine God is truly individual and personal. He may indeed be said to come *under* no genus, but only because he is, as individual, his own genus or principle of alternative states, by which he is differentiated generically from other types of individuals and individually from himself as he — and only he — might have been.

NOTES

1 Whitehead, *Process and Reality* (The Macmillan Co., 1929), p. 524.

2 See Richard P. McKeon, *Selections from Medieval Philosophy* (Charles Scribner's Sons, 1929), I, 285 ff.

3 Paul Weiss says, "Whatever is abstractly complete or perfect requires the aid of the concretely imperfect in order to be at all; whatever is concrete is imperfect and requires support from an abstract completeness to be itself." See Paul Weiss, *Reality* (Princeton University Press, 1938), p. 153. See also R. A. Tsanoff, "The Notion of Perfection," *Philosophical Review*, XLIX, 25–36.

4 For an extended discussion of the indeterminateness of possibility as such see my essay, "Santayana's Doctrine of Essence," in *George Santayana*, "Library of Living Philosophers," edited by Paul A. Schilpp (Northwestern University, 1941).

VIII

THE SUBJECT OF ALL CHANGE
(*Cosmological Argument*)

He knew, "I indeed am this creation, for I created all this." Hence he became the creation, and he who knows this lives in this his creation. THE UPANISHADS

THERE ARE as many arguments for God as there are conceptions of absolute generality, that is, conceptions with a cosmic range of application, relevant to "all time and all existence." Such conceptions are "actuality," "possibility," "knowledge," "value," the conception of God itself. Since these conceptions are more or less arbitrarily divisible into aspects or nuances, there is no one final list of arguments. There is also no simple answer to the question, Are the arguments independent of one another? For the more one explains the conception upon which an argument turns, the more one must elucidate the conceptions central to the other arguments, and such elucidation will bring out more or less distinctly the point of the other proofs, while still not developing them perhaps to the full. It is indeed meaningless to speak of independence, in the sense in which this term is used in science, when the question at issue is as to the necessary being, arguments for which must involve necessity not probability. Any one argument for God is either fallacious or proves God to be necessary. No number of arguments can add to necessity. And necessary truths mutually imply one another, are really aspects of one and the same necessity, namely, God. The only value of a multiplicity of arguments is that it diminishes the probability that we have overlooked fallacies in the reasoning, somewhat as performing a mathematical operation by several methods helps to insure that no blunder has been committed; but the value of varying methods holds to a greater degree in the theological case, since philosophical ideas are less clear than mathematical, and acquire their maximum clearness only when developed into a system. The various proofs are, then, only ways of focusing such a system. In the inductive sciences independent proofs serve not merely to clarify, or show up blunders in reasoning, but to establish degrees of probability where no necessity could be established by any evidence, however correctly estimated. If there is no such distinction between truths of contingent existence and truths of necessary existence, then there is equally no distinction between God and not-God. Theological proofs are all fallacious, or else they have only relative and subjective independence from one another.

The premise of the argument from existence is: something exists (or, the term existence has a referent). The premise of the argument from possibility is: something is possible; of the argument from knowledge: something is known; of the argument from value: something is in some sense valuable; while the argument from the idea of deity itself has this as premise: "God" is a symbol which as defined in some specified way is neither simply without meaning nor is its meaning self-contradictory (or, in positivist phrase, merely "emotive"). Of these premises, only the last would ordinarily be contested by non-theists; although a question might be raised concerning the meaning of the term "possible." The premises state no mere facts, their denials are not genuinely conceivable, which is the reason they can lead to the assertion of a necessary being.

There is one common form of argumentation omitted from the above list, the argument from the empirically observed order and goodness of the world. The reason for omitting it is that the very form of such an argument seems questionable. It reasons from the difference between the world as we find it and worlds which we imagine and by comparison with the real world find less admirable. The objection is that God, if he exists, is the ground not only of this actual world but of any possible world, so that the imaginary worlds with which we have compared the real one either are impossible, and hence not really imaginable, or else they involve God no less than the real world, and the comparative merits of the latter are irrelevant. If we could consistently conceive a world so bad that it could not be "God's world," then this alone would suffice to disprove God! Of course one can vaguely imagine something apparently corresponding to "a Godless world," a world without order or beauty or goodness; but that this is a distinct and self-consistent conception, that, for instance, "world," or even "existence," retains any consistent meaning in such a case, is not to be taken for granted. The various remaining arguments for God, indeed, maintain precisely the contrary.

The foregoing considerations lead to the conclusion that even apart from the existence of evil in the world it would be absurd to try to prove God from the observed goodness of the world. However, this conclusion follows only for one convinced of the soundness of the argument which bases all possibility upon the existence of God. And yet, who could believe in God (unless a wholly imperfect one) while denying this relationship?

It is true that one who finds the world in the large to be bad (or valueless) rather than good cannot, without abandoning this persuasion, consistently believe in God. In so far there is logic in the attempts of skeptics to make believers aware of the evil in existence. Yet they would have to go further than they usually do if they wished really to refute theism; for they would have to prove that no possible world could be appropriate to a Creator. If the would-be theist is led from the evil of the world to doubt God's existence, he must, if he is logical, equally doubt even the possibility of a God, for, as we shall see in the next chapter, nothing can be the " potentiality of deity," the phrase being self-contradictory. The theist who finds the world on the whole good can rightly feel that this fits the implications of his faith, but not that it proves it, nor that, if the world seemed to him bad, faith would be disproved. Nothing could be decisive here but the insight into the impossibility of a world embodying spiritual perfection. It must be shown that the very idea of value contradicts the idea of perfection; but to show this would simply be to accept the argument from the concept of value — though in inverted form — as an argument *against* God. There is no way to escape the necessity of arguing philosophically or from general categories, rather than inductively, pseudo-scientifically, from particulars, if one wishes to make out anything concerning the existence of God.

There is a further weakness in the " argument from design " which has often been pointed out, notably by Hume and Kant; namely, that while the evil in the world may, for all we can prove, be consistent with the belief in God (as these men are too careful and candid to deny), it is even more obviously consistent with the atheistic doctrine that perfection is impossible, since good is essentially relative and limited, so that in the absence of evidence drawn from categories we could not decide the question at all.

Another familiar argument seems to be lacking in our list: the argument from motion and causality. It is, however, not really omitted, since it may be regarded as a way of combining the arguments from actuality and possibility. The premise, "something exists," can be experientially established only in the form, "something exists in space and time." Existence, at least as an indubitable datum, is spatio-temporal, that is, it is motion and change. That something not actual is "possible" can also be established only in connection with change and the experience of open alternatives with respect to the future. The limits of such possibility are identical with the scope of causality. Thus even in a pure argument from categories we cannot avoid dealing with the old argument for a First Mover and a First Cause. But we must not take "First" to mean temporally first, in the sense of a beginning in (or of) time, nor must we assume that the Divine as Mover must be unmoved, or that the First or Supreme Cause must be immutable. What we must assume (hypothetically, as the conclusion whose truth is to be decided one way or the other) is that perhaps it can be proved that there is and must be a Mover or Cause which is perfect in the way and only in the way required by the religious idea. The question is whether there is a real cause which is ideal in its degree and kind of power. What such perfection can mean in terms of causality and motion must be deduced from our analysis of these categories, not assumed from traditional analyses whose results are in doubtful harmony with the religious idea they are alleged to support, and in doubtful harmony with logic as refined and purified and generalized during the last hundred and fifty years.

In outline the argument from existence is: Temporal existence implies everlasting (not timeless) existence; everlasting existence can belong to but one individual, which can only be conceived as God. Everlasting or "eternal" existence is not the negation of temporal existence, but its perfection. It is the negation of existence having a beginning or an end in time, the negation of birth or death, not necessarily of change.

If temporal existence is characterized as "changing," then it will hardly be denied that the meaning of this concept includes the idea of something which changes. Change involves a diversity of states, which, in spite of their diversity, belong to one and the same thing, the subject of the change. The subject of the change is not at all the unchanging, but the changing; it is that which alters, and in altering remains itself. Alteration and permanence are the two aspects of change, each implying the other. It is the changing which endures and in so far escapes the "ravages" of time. It is the thing in so far as it does *not* endure but perishes that is ravaged.

There is, however, one kind of change which we may be tempted to think an exception to the foregoing. This is the change involved in the generation or destruction of a subject of change. The generation of an entity cannot be conceived as a change occurring to that entity. For the passage from non-existence to existence is not a shift from one state of the thing which is to exist to another; rather is non-existence the absence of the thing with all its states. It is not the generated thing which changes in coming to exist, but "existence" or "the world" which comes to acquire a new member, and thus a new state. The changing subject of that change which consists in generation is always a pre-existent subject, which through the generation acquires the new subject as, with all of its predicates, a state of itself (though not a "mere" state, or not the kind of state which would prevent the new subject from being really a subject, an individual on its own account).

The only way to avoid this conclusion is to hold that before actually existing the thing is not a mere non-entity but a potentiality, which passes in generation from the potential to the actual state. But the potential is discoverable, has definite meaning for us, only as a power characterizing something actual. A man is something which may exist in so far as there are human beings capable of being his parents — or his grandparents. The potential is an aspect of the existent, or it is nothing identifiable. And so our proposition stands: The fact of generation consists in (and does not merely imply as its "cause") a change in something which exists before the generation.

Similar remarks apply to destruction or death. The decease of a man is not a change in the man as a personality (except as the latter may survive death in a manner of which all the details are hidden from us); for the state of a thing's no longer existing is not the positive presence of a certain state in that thing but the complete absence of the thing along with its states. Death seems indeed a state of the man's body, as a system of molecules which after the event is no longer vivified and guided by human thoughts and feelings as it was before the event. Similarly, birth (or the formation of the embryo at least) is something which happens, not to the new mind emerging but, apparently, to the physical particles which begin to achieve a new organization, expressive of the informing power of mind. We have now reached our decisive question: Is "matter," conceived as only accidentally infused with mind, or if you prefer, only accidentally functioning in thinking and feeling organisms, a sufficient subject of the generative, destructive, and all other changes in the world?

It is clear that no subject or subjects of change are sufficient unless at least one of them is eternal, that is, ungenerated and undying. For a generated subject can appear as a new state only of a subject not at that moment generated, and if this pre-existent subject were itself generated earlier, then it could itself only constitute a state of a still earlier subject, which must still endure, and thus there must always be at least one subject to whom no beginning or end can be assigned.

This is not the usual argument against a regress of causes. For the subject of change must endure through all the changes of which it is the subject. If *a* "changes into" *b,* losing its identity as *a,* then the subject of this change must be *c,* and if something has changed into *c,* then the subject of this change must be *d,* and *d must endure still* as the subject of all the changes to date, unless *d* itself is only something into which a more fundamental subject has changed while retaining its identity. For when *c* came into being, its entire being was a state of *d,* or of whatever changed so as to constitute this coming into being.

It is notable that a man does not fully possess his changes. Not only do his beginning and ending escape him as such, but falling asleep is a process which he does not fully experience, since it is (apparently) the cessation of experience.

Materialists, seeking to make matter ultimate, have generally recognized the force of the foregoing argument, and have claimed that matter is indeed eternal, and the subject of all change. Man's birth, living, and death, the very life of any gods there may be, according to Epicurus, are nothing but the adventures of the everlasting and ungenerated atoms.

In another form Aristotle upholds the same view, except that his eternal matter, *materia prima,* is formless and without definite number, a mere abstract aspect of things, but an everlasting one. However, Aristotle did not believe that this mere abstraction could constitute the sufficient explanation of change. A second eternal principle, God, was also required. But this second principle was not the subject, but merely the " formal cause," of change. In itself it did not change. Thus if we ask Aristotle what it is that permanently, everlastingly changes, and of which all generations and destructions are states, he answers only with two mysterious words, " matter " and " potency." And if we ask him to identify such an everlasting entity in experience, he can, I suspect, give us no very helpful answer. Matter is that utterly flexible something which can assume all forms, but if we ask what its identity through these transformations may be, he can only answer, its unique flexibility. But the flexibility means only that identity is preserved; identity is presupposed rather than clarified. Is it not really God in whom the identity of the final subject of change consists? It is, I am about to argue, God who can be all things to all things, whose all-sympathetic teleology assumes all the changing states of the universal striving. Hence David of Dinant did well to identify matter with God, even though Aquinas regarded this view as " crazy."

The medieval Aristotelians rejected Aristotle's view of the eternity of matter (on supposedly biblical grounds), but refused to make God the subject of change, with the result that the generation of the world is either a change without a subject, or else not a change, and hence — it would seem — not a generation.

The main question is whether either the Epicurean or the Aristotelian view of matter can furnish a sufficient subject of change. Both have for this purpose a defect in common, and each has in addition a defect peculiar to itself. The common defect is that in both cases the identity through change is asserted, not positively conceived. The atom is ever the same wherever it may wander, but what positively remains the same about it? Perhaps its shape and size and weight? But these are purely relational properties, and relations require terms. The atom can possess shape only because there is in it something which distinguishes its boundaries from the empty space surrounding it. What is this something which fills certain parts of space? The Epicurean can only answer, "being," or "stuff," or "matter." But we want to know what it is that distinguishes the filled being of the atom from the empty being, or "not-being," of space, the "void"! It will not do to say that since we have here an ultimate conception no explanation is possible. For conceptions, however ultimate, have to be identified somehow and by more than a mere word, and it is perfectly plain how we identify the being in question in experience. We identify it by qualities, and by the similarities which qualities, in spite of all their diversity, present to our feeling. A certain shape is given to us visually as the boundaries of a given color, meeting some other color. But the atoms were said to be without color or quality of any kind in their eternal being. Even a blind man does not in fact so represent them, but rather he thinks of them more or less consciously in terms of the qualities of tactual sensations which things give him. Apart from quality nothing positive can be thought under the term being or matter. And the purely negative is nothing and the definition of nothing. Hence if being must have identity-in-change, it must have this identity in qualitative as well as structural terms.

Now we do have direct experience of identity in the midst of, and even by virtue of, qualitative contrast. "Beauty" is something unitary which exists not in spite of, but even thanks to, qualitative contrast. Feeling is a positive unity of which various qualities may be integral aspects. Through memory, this unity spans past as well as present. Here is the only experiential clue whatever to the qualitative side of permanence in change. The alternative to the merely negative, or at least the merely structural, view of being is an aesthetic-psychological interpretation of change. Aristotle, in his insistence that everything has its end and value, vaguely and rather crudely hints at such an interpretation, but it is flattery to say that he furnishes it.

The defect peculiar to Epicurean materialism is that it makes logically contingent characters, such as the shapes and sizes of atoms, pervasive of all time, and therefore temporally indistinguishable from necessary factors, although, as we have seen, time alone is the concrete embodiment of categories such as possibility and necessity. What need not have existed at all, exists not only in one of the infinite periods of history, but in all periods. What need not have happened at all, goes on happening forever. This creates a dilemma. Either the eternal factors are constitutive of being as such, and so ontologically necessary; or they are ontologically, as they certainly are logically, contingent (any particular shape or size can be conceived as non-existent). If ontologically necessary, then their conceivable non-existence is a paradox; if ontologically contingent, then their temporal universality is a paradox. It must also be unknowable, for the only way to know that something always exists is to know that it must exist. (To run through all the moments of time to see what they happen to contain is impossible by the nature of time, since future moments do not exist in determinate detail.) Thus the everlasting atoms with fixed forms would constitute arbitrary limitations upon being coincident with being as knowable, and so, it would seem, not arbitrary. If, on the other hand, the atoms have no fixed forms, then their identity through change vanishes, unless there is a pattern in the succession of forms, and then we would want to know how this pattern can be really in the atoms as at any one moment with any one form, just as we want to know how "having been at point *a*" can belong to an atom as at point *b,* how matter can constitute the being of motion. Whitehead has, I think unanswerably, expounded these paradoxes as appearing in modern physics so far as taken to imply the notion of mere matter.[1]

The defect peculiar to Aristotelian materialism, or "hylo-morphism" if you prefer, is simply that it escapes the defect of Epicureanism (endowing eternal matter with logically contingent properties) only by the desperate expedient of depriving matter as eternal of any form, even structural, of any positive identity, thus aggravating the common defect of all materialism — insufficient provision for identity in change — to the highest possible degree.

It is true that Aristotle, as anti-evolutionist, apparently believes that the specific forms of things are also eternal, along with matter and God. But if so, that only means that he has fallen into the error of eternalizing, necessitizing so to speak, the logically contingent; that is, into the same error in principle as that of which we have accused Epicurus. In any case he has no real, positive subject of change, inclusive of generation and destruction.

As for modern scientific materialism, taken as a philosophy and not merely as a legitimate methodological limitation, it is merely a compromise between Epicurean and Aristotelian doctrines, a compromise which does nothing to remove the fundamental defects of the two. If atoms are no longer eternal, are electrons? Apparently not. If they were, we would again have the logically arbitrary exalted into temporal absoluteness; if not, then matter as eternal has no identifiable characters, even structural, except perhaps the fundamental laws of quantum and relativity physics. But these laws are logically as contingent as the shapes of atoms (in both cases there are constants, magnitudes to which there are an infinity of mathematically conceivable alternatives); and there is certainly no evidence of their eternal validity. No experiment can show that something will always happen, since the experiment tests only what happens in the present era of cosmic development. It is true that unless there were aspects of nature which change at most very slowly we could learn nothing from experiment; and hence it is an obligatory assumption that some features of the world are stable within the limits of our imperative practical and scientific needs; but it is the merest dogma that some features of the world, in themselves logically arbitrary, are absolutely changeless for all time. Every evidence from analogy supports the view that, just as the more complex biological species change, though more slowly than the simpler ones, so those still simpler species with which physics deals change, but far more slowly still, and since laws are merely the ways of behaving of various classes of things, the non-eternity of these classes means the non-eternity of these laws.

In any case, even were the physical laws eternal, it still would not be possible to see in them the identity of matter as the sufficient eternal subject of change. For qualitative changes are not identical with structural ones, and cannot be exhaustively expressed in terms of the laws of physics. And, once more, no materialism can escape the dilemma: either its conception of the eternal is purely negative, or it is a conception some of whose positive aspects are logically arbitrary and therefore cannot be eternal.

The most plausible evasion of the dilemma seems to be that of S. Alexander. Pure space-time is the eternal stuff, the permanently changing subject. There is nothing logically arbitrary in this conception of the everlasting. But is there anything positive in it? Certainly there is nothing positive on the qualitative side. Even on the structural, is not pure space-time, apart from anything further, merely a system of *potential* shapes and sizes and changes rather than anything actual? Have we not here the inversion of the true conception of possibility, which is that it is identifiable only as a capacity of the actual? Space-time is said to be equivalent to pure motion, but is motion anything unless something not just motion either moves or at least exists with a capacity for moving?

Alexander himself seems really to concede the case when he describes time as the mind of space, and also when he grants that even electrons have some to us unknown qualities of feeling.[2] The issue can be put in this way: Granting that space-time is eternal and the everlasting subject of change, are the relational aspects of space-time sufficient to characterize it, and, particularly, how are we to distinguish between spatio-temporal relations as mere mathematical possibilities, and shapes and sizes and changes really happening? Space-time is after all only a four-dimensional version of the indeterminate " void " of Democritus, Epicurus, and Lucretius; we still want to know what the " being " is which fills this void in definite ways to furnish definite configurations. Space-time may very well be conceived as eternal, since beginnings and endings seem to fall within it, and to affect it not as beginnings and endings, but as changes in its own being. But mere space-time as such cannot be more than the structural aspect of the eternal; indeed, not even all of that, for qualities involve structures in their relations of similarity and dissimilarity, which mere space-time does not include. To add " matter " to space-time is merely to say that a required something is added to it, it is not to say what the required something is.

What then is the sufficient subject of all change? What is it which is so flexible that it can preserve its identity through all the variety of real predicates in the world? Surely the most flexible positively known thing is mind in so far as it is sensitive, and broad and quick in its sympathies. True, there are inflexible minds, but we know this precisely because we know or can conceive of minds not inflexible. All predicates of which we have definite knowledge express possible forms of mind. The identity of a man's mind, in spite of the variety of sensory, emotional, volitional, and intellectual qualities which his experience includes, is the obvious clue to the cosmic identity we are seeking. But equally obvious is it that no merely human mind will serve. Every man has his prejudices, in such fashion that there are qualities of experience in the lives of other men that he would not allow himself to realize, even given the opportunity. And the limits of our attention span preclude our embracing all *actual* predicates together (all possible predicates could not, except as indeterminates, mere possibles, be combined by any mind). Only a mind completely free of selfish prejudice, ready to enter with instant sympathy into all existent forms of experience, to participate without reserve in every last fragment of feeling and thought anywhere, and able to harmonize all this variety of experience into one tolerable aesthetic whole, can constitute the subject of all change. Precisely this is also the religious idea of God, to whom all hearts are completely open because his sensitive sympathy is absolute in flexibility.

Nor is this a merely negative conception. It does not mean that God has no positive character, that he simply tolerates everything. He tolerates variety up to the point beyond which it would mean chaos and not a world; but his intolerance of what would lie beyond that excludes nothing real from his fullest participation, but rather prevents the "beyond" from becoming real, that is, prevents reality from losing all definite character. What God ignores he equally, and thereby, destroys or prevents from occurring.

Another way of putting the difference is that we human beings are never entire and single-minded about our sympathies; we always remain more or less deliberately unconscious of the full content even of those lives with which we most intensely sympathize; while God relegates nothing of other lives to the dim background, the subconscious of his life, but is either fully aware of things or dismisses them from his awareness and (it is the same thing) from reality. Of course God opposes some of our desires, but not by imperfect participation in these desires, as though he did not distinctly feel them, but by balancing them against the main desire-mass of the world of creatures, somewhat as we may check some among our wishes by force of other opposing ones. We men are not strong enough, not catholicly sensitive enough, to trust to such balance alone to resist the desires of our immediate neighbors; and therefore we must resort to the inferior device of unconsciousness, of insensitiveness. We control in the negative way, God in the positive. But the difference is not in every respect absolute, since the best men are distinguished by something of this very positivity of control. There is therefore nothing absurd, or contradictory of the nature of mind, in the idea of divine sympathy.

The idea of love is a positive idea of flexibility in still other respects. However the content of love may be conceived to vary, certain identical dimensions must persist throughout, and these dimensions serve both as the measure of the variety and as aspects of the self-identity of the love. Love is always feeling, whatever else it may be, and feeling has at least the universal dimension of intensity. But equally universal is the dimension of good and bad, of enjoyment and suffering. Further, there is the dimension of self-and-other, and also the dimension of complexity, due to the number and kinds of other beings loved.

The variety of qualities in sensory and emotional experience seems to be derivative from these dimensions of love.[3] At any rate, no one could fully love all minds and not fully realize, participate in, all qualities enjoyed by those minds. And that would be all the qualities we know or can conceive.

The conclusion is that when it is said that nothing can have all predicates (all actual predicates as actual, all possible as possible) and yet have distinctive character of its own, the statement may be accepted upon the one condition that the idea of love is excluded from the debate. From the moment this idea is considered, the negation appears no longer convincing. The " being " which all qualities embody is either nothing further describable, or it is cosmic love. And conversely, cosmic love is either nothing conceivable or it is the distinctive character of " being " itself.

Of course even divine love cannot embody all qualities without regard to any distinction between actual and possible ones, or those completely and those incompletely determined. It is by neglecting this distinction that men convince themselves that " being " can have no character. The character of being is expressed in the process of choosing possibilities to be actualized. Unactualized possibilities are also in being, in God, but in a deficient way; they constitute the less determined aspects of God as being.

The foregoing distinction is made paradoxical if not useless by philosophies which deny change to God. For in changeless eternity things are either present once for all, or absent once for all; there is no function for the possibly present or absent. Since we are speaking of God as the subject of change, not as the unchanging, we can escape these (and many other) paradoxes.

There is another important respect in which mind

rather than mere matter answers the requirements of the final subject of change. Mind involves memory, memory is the presence of " past " qualities in present experience. If past meant simply not present, this would be a contradiction. That it does not mean this is shown by the difference between events known to have occurred in the past and events which have not occurred at all as yet. The latter are certainly not present; the former, in a manner, precisely are present. Memory is the making of them palpably present. They form the old, the familiar part of the content of the present; as distinguished from the new, the just occurring part. They are there, but also they " have been " there; the others are there, but have not also been there. The identity of personality is this union of more or less consciously remembered past with the merely presented or new. (Psychoanalysis is here a better metaphysician than some metaphysicians.)

The identity, the personality of the world (I use the phrase with care), is the supreme example of the same union. The world memory is sufficiently conscious fully to realize forevermore all past qualities whatsoever. In this stupendous sense God is literally infinite. He is not, however, infinite in the self-contradictory sense of realizing determinately all future (that is, partially undetermined) qualities as well.

If there is no such world memory, then all truth about the past is a blind mystery; if there is, it is an open or intelligible mystery, that is, something we can grasp in principle though it infinitely eludes us in detail.

The argument from time to God as the eternally enduring unity of the world can be stated even apart from the concepts of change and the changing. Suppose we assume, not change, but simply events " following " each other. It still has to be considered what the relation of following identifiably is. In experience this relation is directly given in this manner, and in no other, that *a* is experienced to follow *b* when *a* is given as influenced by *b* but *b* is given as independent of *a*. The first note of a melody is given as a quality which is what it is whatever is to follow, but the succeeding note is given from the outset as in relation to the preceding, and cannot be completely abstracted from this relation. Later notes receive part of their musical character from the earlier, not the other way around. More precisely, by memory, immediate or remote, earlier events, as particulars, modify later; by anticipation later events, not as individual realities, but only as more or less generalized outlines, modify the earlier. This difference is the identifiable meaning of before and after. Develop this truth into full explicitness and you will arrive again at the conception of divine (sympathetic) memory and anticipation, that is, cosmic love. There is no dependence of the argument upon " substance," as an assumption which may be discarded; and indeed two of the greatest critics of the old idea of substance, Whitehead and Bergson, are temporalistic theists. It is time and not thinghood that leads us to God as the self-identity of process.

So far we have neglected the question of the number of ultimate, that is, everlasting, subjects of change. Atomistic materialism believed in an infinite number of such subjects. The objections to this are two: first, to fulfill its functions each subject must have properties which would make it equivalent to and indistinguishable from every other; and second, atomism implies that the ultimate subjects of change have less unity than the temporary subjects, which is absurd. To take the latter point first: according to materialism a man is, in terms of ultimate subjects, numerous atoms and their interrelations. But the atoms are many and the man is one. To ascribe the man's thoughts to the atoms as subjects in the plural would be to deny the man's unity, though this unity is a primary datum for philosophy compared to which atoms are secondary (though overwhelmingly secure) inferences. The man's nature, which is one thing, would be parceled out among the atoms, or ascribed *in toto* to each and every one, both these alternatives being absurd. You can say it is ascribed to the whole interconnected group of atoms, but the question is precisely, To what final changing subject is the change consisting in the generation of this group as a unitary entity to be ascribed? " Emergent wholeness " must, after its emergence, belong to some subject of change which both antedates the emergence and survives to possess it as its new state. This required subject cannot be the atoms, for they remain many, not one. Surely a man's atoms do not adequately possess his thoughts! What subject, like the atoms pre-existent to the man, does so possess them?

You may try to make the problem very simple by saying that it is " the world " or " nature " which possesses the new whole constituted by the emergent man or animal. Against this answer I have no objection, provided the world or nature be admitted to have the character required for the assigned function. The world as the final subject of change cannot be a mere aggregate or collection. The appearance of the man is not simply his addition to the world, as a set of items, for only after he has appeared and belongs to the world is he anything real to be added to the sum of things. " Reality " cannot be a mere external relation to other real things, a further item of an aggregation, since the relation in question constitutes the reality of the thing related. The world may be the final subject of change only on condition that it have a unity in some sense maximal, absolute, and exceeding the unity of any of its parts. For the world unity is the ground of all plurality as well as of all unity in the world parts. No " real " aspect of anything can be omitted from the final unitary subject of change.

A plurality of eternal subjects seems excluded by the mere consideration that all must " exist," and that the unity implied by the common factor of existence must finally override the alleged plurality. But apart from this perhaps seemingly too verbal argument, there is the necessity that every eternal subject possess properties identical with every other. Each must be able effectively and absolutely to possess some share at least of the new predicates continually arising. But absolute participation in the predicates of even a part of the world is inseparable, because of the interconnections of things, as assumed for instance by science, from participation in the predicates of every other part of the world. In terms of mind — and we have seen that it is in any case impossible to meet the requirements apart from mind — omniscience of even one thing is indistinguishable from omniscience pure and simple. Nor has anyone ever, so far as I know, tried explicitly to conceive a localized omniscience (though some philosophical doctrines may have unwittingly implied such a notion).

(The temporal concept of God might be accused of localizing omniscience in the present. The answer, of course, is that it is only by " spatializing," detemporalizing time that the present is made to seem a locus, a mere part, of time. It *becomes* such a part when it is no longer present but past, but *then* omniscience is no longer limited to it but enjoys a new present which is the whole of actual existence in time precisely while it is present and not past. This is the " modal " structure of time, its metaphysical ultimacy as the unity of actuality and potentiality, that " existence as a whole " has a partly new meaning each time the phrase is uttered. " Existence " in this sense is a demonstrative pronoun, meaning " *this* whole of things," the one to which the act of using the term belongs, and which will as a whole be identical with a part of all the wholes that ever come into existence, and is already identical in a part of itself with any preceding whole. Thus *the* whole, the one that is the same for all references, the ever identical universe, is constituted by such actual and potential identities with past and future. To argue that a growing whole is an incomplete complete and thus absurd is to commit sophistry. The whole is " all that exists " when this " all " is referred to, and that is the only completeness it claims or needs. He begs the question who insists that " the totality of existence " must include as actually existent all that ever will or may exist, for that is the question: Does the " may exist " or the " will exist " actually exist, is its existence as such full and complete — and determinate? Why should not " existence " be a demonstrative pronoun? Pointing is prior to naming and describing. Different acts of pointing may reach different total referents, if the acts belong to different non-coactual *states,* rather than coactual parts, of existence. To reject this distinction is to spatialize time and falsify all our categories. If it be said we must do this to talk about God, I reply that the contention seems to me the perfect affirmation of atheism. It is non-sense to say that non-sense may be true, and the concepts by which we inevitably think are the concepts by which we always do think — no less so when we insincerely or self-delusively pretend to do " better.")

Plurality of eternal subjects could not be conceived in terms of time, since temporally all eternal subjects as such are identical. The distinction could be made definitely only in terms of space. But space has its unity no less than time. We say things in different places are outside each other; but this outsidedness cannot be absolute, for there are no degrees of absoluteness, while there certainly are degrees of separation in space. The minimal degree is given if two things almost completely coincide in spatial area, the maximal degree if they are at opposite ends, so to speak, of the world. There are all gradations between these extremes. The relativity of spatial outsidedness is palpable enough from these considerations.

When Newton, impressed with the obvious unity of space, called the latter "the sensorium of God," he expressed a thought to which his own age could not possibly do justice, but which our own may well take to heart. So long as anything that would possibly be suggested by the term pantheism was considered beyond the pale of respectable theology, there could be no serious analysis of the relations of God to the world. Leibniz objected (in his letters to Clarke) that to make the unity of space an aspect of God meant to make God dependent upon happenings in space, as the human mind depends upon happenings in the human body. It meant to make God "passive" to material forces. But contemporary theology ascribes to God, with full deliberateness, supreme sensitivity, that is, passivity, not as contradictory of supreme activity, but as a necessary aspect of it. To act upon something spiritually, one must be sensitive to it; for that to which a mind is totally insensitive is non-existent to that mind. God is the perfection of action-and-passion, who escapes the defectiveness of our passivity not by impassivity but by the all-inclusiveness, the catholicity, of his sensitiveness, which gives him the balance, the all-sidedness, the fairness, the justice, which are precisely what our passivity lacks and the only ground for its appearing to us as a defect.

The upshot of the argument so far is then: if anything exists in time and space, God exists as the eternal and omnipresent unity of space-time, without which that unity is not positively conceivable. By God is here meant an eternal, omnipresent being, " flexible " enough to possess the infinity of qualities which the whole of process up to now has brought forth, this " whole " being simply the life of God in which we, the speakers, now share. Only mind as love makes the flexibility in question identifiable as a positive characteristic. There is always and everywhere just one alternative to theism, the contentment with negation, that is, nothingness, emptiness, as the final meaning, at some point, of universal conceptions.

A shrewd objection to our whole argumentation might be that the allegedly quite negative conceptions to which theism is the alternative cannot be purely negative after all, since we have drawn positive conclusions from them. Thus the " flexibility " of being as such must have some positive content or we could not say that matter, for instance, is inadequate to this content. But we must distinguish between purely intuitive meaning, such as words like " unity " possess, and " identifiable " meaning, that is, relation to some aspect of direct experience which particularly clearly illustrates and makes explicit what we really, though more or less subconsciously (from memory of previous more or less vague identifications) , intend by our words. The identifiable positive meaning of general conceptions turns out, when made as vivid and distinct as possible, to be some aspect or application of the intuition of deity which is the secular or universal element in the mystical awareness. All proofs for God depend upon conceptions which derive their meaning from God himself. They are merely ways of making clear that we already and once for all believe in God, though not always with clearness and consistency. With no belief in God no belief could be arrived at; but the question at issue is as to the comparative self-knowledge of

" believers " and " unbelievers." Both employ ultimate conceptions which unbelievers tend (or so it seems to believers) to leave unanalyzed.

It is time to ask about the once so popular argument from " causality." We have spoken of an ultimate subject, not an ultimate cause, of change. One reason for this choice of approach is that change is a more obvious and unmistakably identifiable factor in experience than causality. The latter indeed is so elusive that many philosophers can identify it only as a seemingly baseless demand or postulate of reason. Another ground for emphasizing change rather than causality is that it is more obvious that the ultimate subject of change must itself change than that the ultimate cause of change must itself undergo effects; and it is to me nearly self-evident that the religious idea whose truth we are seeking to test is not that of immutable activity (whatever that may be) or of purely one-sided causality, wholly non-social, non-mutual.

However, let us now consider the causal problem. By implication we have already done so. The subject of change is also the cause of change. The human person endures the changes in its experiences; it also, as a *will,* is a cause of them. It is not the only or even the chief cause, but then neither is it the only or even the chief subject, of these changes. The chief subject as well as chief cause is always God, the eternal subject; and in addition to God and the human person there are also the subhuman individual factors in the person's body, each of which in its ineffective, deficient, but real way, endures the changes in the person's experience, and contributes causally to them. Also there are finite factors in the environment. The hierarchy of subjects and the hierarchy of causes of change is the same hierarchy; in the latter case it is considered from the standpoint of one of the two correlative aspects of activity and passivity, or in terms of the relation of earlier to later states so far as rendering them predictable. It is precisely the changing which causes change, both in itself and in others. The changing human person certainly does act upon his own experience, his own changes, and not even a Thomist wishes to deny it. The human person also, as evidently, acts upon changes in his body, thus producing changes in the environment. In support of the dogma that the cause of change must ultimately lie in the unchanging (except as abstract, as less than the entirety of an individual) there is no shred of evidence in experience.

The insufficiency of the changing causes of change, apart from God, to fully constitute the world process (which last phrase is simply a dim, " unidentified " reference to God in his concrete totality) lies not in their being changing causes, that is, subjects of change, but in their not being sufficiently catholic, flexible, or universal subjects. Each finite subject of change is the *effective* subject of only a narrow circle of changes, narrow both in space and in time; there must be a cosmic subject effectively enduring all changes in space and time, and the active aspect of the unity of this subject will constitute the ground of orderliness in the world. Things other than God change far too little, rather than too much, to constitute the comprehensive cause or active subject of all existence. How vastly much more change is found by physiology and physics to go on in the human body alone than the human mind clearly endures in its experiences! During a thousandth of a second practically no change is consciously experienced by us, yet myriads of bodily changes go on in that time.

The argument from " existence " is only a slight variant upon the argument from space and time. It can be made concrete to the reader if he ask himself what can be meant by the fact that he is a part of reality. It cannot be meant merely that the list of real things includes himself; for apart from belonging to the list he would be nothing, not even a " real " possibility. The world is a collection of items, membership in which entirely constitutes the items, measures all the difference between them and nothing. If the items are all of an accidental character, the situation is surely nonsensical. Evidently there is something, relationship to which is the universal measure of reality, and which itself is real by its own measure, is self-existent. Now mere matter cannot possibly measure the difference between the existence and the non-existence of a mind. Matter, as mere stuff which fills space, is indeed in itself a purely empty conception, so far as experiential meaning goes; but waiving that, it throws no light whatever on how mind *also* can fill space-time, that is, enter into existence. Matter may be thus and thus organized in the human body, but organization of shapes and sizes and motions (all that matter is positively) is only just that, organization, shapes, sizes, and motions; it is not quality of feeling, memory, fear, etc. Yet these too are real. Their reality must be clearly measured, recorded as an addition to the total reality, the whole of what has come into being, by more than matter.

The fantastic notion that the ultimate subject of change is mere matter is given brilliant and perhaps ironic expression in E. D. Kennedy's remarkable poem entitled, " To a Molecule." I quote a few lines:

> You are mankind and all its works . . . .
> And men and gods are dust and dream
> While your eternal seconds pass.
>
> The star and snail are one to you,
> The snail and star alike must be,
> And life and death are filtered through
> Your idiot identity.

> You are my death, for in you I
> Admit myself a transient thing,
> Behold what lingers when I die,
> My end and your continuing.[4]

Of course, this is poetry not science. Today we do not regard any molecule as strictly " eternal." And the abiding " identity " of electrons seems not to be involved in contemporary physical theory. Nothing, it seems, abides forever except the cosmos, space-time as a whole. And no characters of the cosmos are unalterable for physics except its basic mathematical structure as expressed in the laws of quantum mechanics and relativity physics. This unalterability, however, is a mere a priori assumption, not an experimental result. No experiment can show that nature will *never* change her pattern of behavior. But even granting the fixity of laws, this cannot possibly constitute the ultimate permanence in change. We should still have an empty, abstract, or " idiot identity," for which the strange adventure of taking on the forms of a man's thought and feeling, or an elephant's, would subsequently become even less than a dream. Indeed, the mere adventure of motion, so far as past in time, would for the mere physical cosmos as in a given present be as nothing. Or else, the cosmos must be viewed as a single changeless entity inclusive of all past and future events, and thus change will be explained by denying its reality. Philosophers know just how thoroughly this " explanation " of time has been tried out, and how little it has in the end commended itself to the philosophic community.

Of course I shall be told that matter acquires in this case the " emergent " property of feeling, etc. But there is not the least suspicion of an identifiable connection between dead matter and feeling matter, such as could give meaning to the notion that the former *acquires* the properties of the latter. All that can really be got from the materialist is that space, formerly filled (and thus shaped) with we know not what, has become filled with something we do know, namely, feeling and thought and volition. Space-time must be such that the presence of feeling makes a difference to space-time, which difference measures the whole difference between feeling and not feeling. What positive character in space and time furnishes this measure? Surely not their geometrical properties. Feeling is clearly more than geometry. If space-time is, in Newton's phrase, the "sensorium of God," the unity of an all-sympathetic mind, then clearly every new feeling makes a difference to space-time which exactly measures the content of that feeling. It is this explanation or nothing! Whatever feeling is, space-time involves a measure of all feelings and values, for it distinguishes between them and non-existence. Therefore space-time involves an absolute standard of feeling and value; and such a standard can only be a perfect mind, the all-embracing and thus "righteous" love of God.

If space-time is not a mind, or an aspect of one, then still less am I! Space-time is "merely physical" only in whatever sense you and I are so. Behaviorism does not touch the real point. If feeling is only matter, still the world whole must as a unity possess all the feeling there is, and that is just the idea of the supreme love. God is thus more or less self-evidently contained in the mere idea of one's own existence, the degree of self-evidence depending upon the degree of clarity attained by the latter idea.

God is contained in our existence, not merely as cause of our "coming to be" but as constitutive of the very meaning of "coming to be." It is also to be emphasized that the necessity for God is not due solely to our existence as minds, as though matter would explain the world were there no higher animals on the planet. Matter as dead, insentient, mindless, explains nothing whatever, not even itself, since it has no identifiable positive meaning. The moment we identify matter in experience it turns out not to be dead, but to be a part of our own aliveness, or of the aliveness of other subjects directly disclosed in ours or indirectly inferred from it by analogy. Otherwise matter remains a word whose meaning is assigned to the depths of unidentified intuition in which, for all the materialist knows, there is nothing but other finite minds or God, as dimly apprehended by us, to constitute its referent.

The reason we have come to use the term matter is easy to explain. There are entities identified as minds; there are entities of which we have only unidentified, that is vague, intuitions. To express this vagueness we can either say that what we are dealing with is mind of almost completely undetermined specific kind; or we can imagine that when determined it will reveal itself as having nothing in common with mind at all, or at least we may wish to leave the question open. The word matter was hit upon for this purpose. It stands for "being" where no determinate characters are known, or no characters except spatio-temporal configurations. The latter presuppose characters of a qualitative kind. To call these presupposed characters merely material, and to say they are we know not what, is all one.

It is true that one may try to give dead matter quality by ascribing the sensory qualities we experience to material things. It may be said that sulphur is really yellow, and that yellow is not necessarily subjective, or expressive of life and feeling. But the spatio-temporal *unity* of matter in the flux of qualities is not in the least identified by this type of view, whereas the mnemonic-social structure of mind illumines the whole structure of space and time.

And there is the embarrassing problem of the microscopic and submicroscopic material things and their qualities. Surely the electrons of sulphur are not yellow. Have they no quality? Are they mere constructs? Then so are books and crystals. And there is the introspective fact, one of the best attested of experimental introspective facts, whatever one thinks of experiment in such matters, that color is given as a feeling-tone, something through and through subjective, emotional, alive.[5]

The argument may be summed up in this way: Try to understand how matter can serve as the ultimate subject of change, and you will find it distinguishable from an all-sympathetic mind by just the extent to which you fail to understand its ability to perform the required function.

But if God is the subject of all changes, does this not mean that he is the only real individual, the one substance of which all things are mere modes? Have we not arrived at a sheer monism? If we depend for existence wholly upon God, how can God depend even for some of his accidents (as second-type theism asserts) upon us? Or how, as Maritain asks, can we contribute to his being when even our being is purely derivative from his? Now let us note carefully in what sense we have shown that God's assumption of our changing states constitutes their occurrence. We have not said that our states are merely his states; but that their occurrence to him is necessary to their occurrence to us, and that this applies to every item in the states, so that in that sense they are completely and nothing but his states. On the other hand, every item in our states also belongs to us. This is mutuality, the shared nature of existence. But individuals other than God (1) do not effectively or with full awareness realize even their own qualities, still less those of other individuals, and (2) do not last through all time in order to constitute all the changes preceding and following their states of a given time. Thus all being is God in that only God participates adequately in all lives, and in that without this participation " being " would have no definite or public character, and " I am " (or, " there is a man of a certain type ") would have meaning only for the speaker, that is, no meaning. But there is nothing in all this to make the dependence of others upon God a purely and in every sense one-sided relation.

Without God we should be nothing at all, for to be would be nothing. (It is not true that there is no strict refutation of solipsism; for if everything were nothing but my dream, then even the real possibility of other individuals would be only my dream, and thus either I should be not simply the only actual but the only *possible* individual, or else I should be the very ground of actuality and possibility, that is, God himself. In either case " I " in " I alone exist " would lose its meaning as referring to a finite, contingently existing self, and the very terms " exist " or " real " would be no more meaningful than nonsense syllables.)

But also without us God would not be the same as he is. He would exist, and existence would be generically what it is now, namely, the self-identity of his all-participating life. But it is obvious that the details of the participation would be different if the things to be participated in were different, and that thus the divine dependence and independence are inseparable aspects of one mutual relationship. The dependence of God is his " passivity," and this passivity truly belongs to him, according to second-type theism, so that it is by virtue of his passive being, his sensitivity, that our activity can exist, and the divine passivity is the one passivity upon which all activity is unfailingly exercised, whatever other passivity may also from time to time enter into the mutualities of the world. Thus activity has as its only universal correlate the adequate, unstinted, unique sensitivity of God, just as passivity has as its only universal correlate the activity — equally unique in scope — of God. We " give " God his passive being in the sense that, by definition, this being, which is social, can receive determinate form, aesthetic realization, only in partial dependence upon others. But it really is his being we give him, since we do not " act " in a public sense (in the sense in which reality is not a solipsistic concept), that is, we do not really act, except as we act upon God, no matter what else we act upon. It is his response to us that makes our act real, in the sense in which we can call the acts of others also real, and that is the sense of " reality." [6]

The idea that it is God's (partly passive) participation in our lives that makes them real is not without analogy to features in our experience. Does not the sense that one's experiences are occurrences also to others, through their passive sympathy, contribute to our sense of reality? One can scarcely exaggerate the degree to which we actually live and feel as though we were nothing unless what we are becomes a part of what others are, and vice versa. One *can* exaggerate this, so far as human-to-human relations are concerned; for one does not quite believe that the appreciations of others are absolutely essential to and fully measure one's own being. But the tendency is there to view ourselves as *essentially* participating and participated in. Only in relation to God can the tendency go the whole way. There we can say literally, we are as we love and are loved. (We can oppose the will of God, but only because we carry God passively with us, and secretly know that we do. He wishes us to do what we do not, but he willingly experiences what we do do as fully, though not so happily, as if it had been what he wished.) The *almost* completely social character of the finite mind in relation to its fellows (including subhuman minds) escapes being complete only because in another relation it is complete. We have self-reliance because we rely secretly upon one mind that is utterly reliable, that is, one mind that is always passive to the full measure of our potential activity, one mind that will listen no matter what we say, and thus lift our utterance above the merely private (which, as the positivists rightly say, is meaningless, is nothing) and make it relevant to other finite minds who also share in the same atmosphere of all-appreciation, that is, of "being."

To look at a fly, or at a crystal, and say, "That too exists," is to refer to "existence" as neither oneself nor the fly though common to both, and such that without it neither oneself nor the fly would be anything at all. What is that something? What could it be but God? Candidly, I cannot see another answer.

God, it should now be clear, is not, according to our argument, the "one substance," the sole real individual, but simply the one substance or individual which is *necessary* to reality, or which is constitutive of being as such, all other individuals being part-constitutive only of accidental aspects of being. Individuality and necessity of existence are not the same, nor is accidental reality unreal reality.

But if God is involved in everything, must he not be viewed as a part of each thing, thus making the inclusive reality also a part of its parts? We must here distinguish different meanings of part. If to be a part of means to be less than, then God is not less than one of his creatures, except perhaps in their own illusory estimation, as when the sinner takes God's will to be of less import than his own, and as even the saint may at times relegate God to the background of his awareness, as though the principle of all things were a minor detail. Never can we escape wholly from this duality of attitudes; we can only find some adjustment between them which promotes harmony and growth. The problem of sin and radical perversity, the " diabolic " or " satanic," lies in the necessity and difficulty of this adjustment and the sense of relief which follows a more or less unconscious determination to escape the issue by acting as though one really were, for practical purposes, the sum of existence, at least as intrinsically valuable or admirable.

The sense in which God is part of each thing is that generalized sense better expressed as " factor of," meaning something in abstraction from which the thing would be less than it is. Now in abstraction from God, were such abstraction possible, we would be nothing, and that is certainly less than we are. So in that sense, God is a factor of everything, and he is precisely that one factor which alone sums up all that each thing is, and infinitely more besides. He is distinguished from his parts wholly by being more than they, but this more is not simply outside the parts, yet a factor of them, as a man is more than any of his cells; it is a factor of all of them. If this is a contradiction according to some modes of speech, so much the worse for these modes as applicable to philosophical problems. But indeed even physics seems to admit that the merest particle is essentially the whole universe from a certain standpoint.

If to be a substance meant by definition not to be a factor of any other thing, then indeed there could be but one substance or none. For all real relationship would be excluded, since the unity of a relation cannot belong to no term, and whatever term it belongs to, the other term or terms will also belong to this term, for they belong to the relation. There can indeed be external relations, but only as some one term is involved in without involving the other, and this is possible only if the involved but not involving term is more abstract than the other, for this is what is meant by abstract. But substances, so far as they are equally concrete, can be related only reciprocally. Note well that to " involve " does not mean to possess as lesser part of an including whole, but merely to have as that without which the thing could not conceivably be itself.

There is only one condition under which a substance, an individual, related to another, can be more abstract than that other, and so fail to involve it. This is when the more abstract substance comes earlier in time. For time, as Peirce and Bergson seem to me to have discovered and the philosophic world may eventually come to realize, is in Peirce's phrase " objective modality," *the* way (Peirce said, I think misleadingly, *a* way) in which things can have both necessity and freedom in relation to each other. The present can influence the future, especially the near future, but it cannot necessitate its precise character. The world grows in determinations, that is, in concreteness; the futurity of the future is its mixture of abstract and concrete. If then *a* is related to *b* as in an earlier state, then this earlier state of *b* did not involve *a*'s relation to it, for the past contained the future only as a more or less abstract outline, that is, an entity tolerant of relations it does not include. This solves the problem of the infinite regress which has been urged against the idea of internal relations. (*A* is related to *b* as related to *a* as related to *b*'s relation to *a* as related to *b*, and so on.) This problem may seem to be involved in the simultaneous relations of substances. But since the two terms are simultaneous, we can say that there is no question of taking the terms in order, first *a* and then *b* as related to *a*, and so on; for it is only the weakness of thought that prevents us from seeing the two terms in their relations as aspects of one reality. In direct intuition this is just what we do see, a single *Gestalt*, of which the " elements " mutually involve each other, as Peirce and James and Bergson and Bradley and Whitehead and the *Gestalt* psychologists have been endeavoring to make clear. Such a one-in-many or many-in-one can be approximated to in thought by adding items and relations one by one, but never quite attained. God's vision of the world at a given moment can only be of a single organic reality, the content of his unitary intuition. But there is no need that he should see all the moments of time past, present, and future as one mutually implicative whole, for the simple reason that the future moments do not exist, and hence need no relation, internal or external, to the present — except as outlines, which of course are internal (but being indeterminate do not make the details of the future internal) to the present. After the future becomes past, then we can say that earlier moments of time which are also past are involved in it, but not vice versa: for the *earlier moments are abstract* so far as they contain their futures in outline only, as boyhood contains even in retrospect a general plan only of maturity, while maturity contains the details of boyhood experience as remembered (mostly subconsciously).

Suppose one were to say that individual entities neither past nor future to each other could be (mutually) externally related. Relativity physics does seem to say this (though Bergson seems to show that this is only a manner of speaking), and so does Whitehead in his metaphysics (though in conversation he appeared to suggest the need for mitigating the doctrine). But if this supposition be taken absolutely, the result is a vicious regress, pointed out by Bradley, and the one form of vicious regress emphasized by this author against which there is no defense. For if entities are mutually external and are both concrete, then their relations can belong to neither of them nor to anything more concrete which embraces them; and we can only say that the terms have to the relations the relation of being actually related by them, and this obviously involves an endless regress of the kind which is vicious because it must end if the terms are to be related. And there is no chance this time of escaping, as we have done in the case of internal relations, by adducing intuition as capable of seeing the terms and their relations as one simultaneous unitary reality, for just this unity is contradicted by the externality alleged of the relations. Nor does it help at all to urge, as has been done,[7] that the error is in trying to analyze "relation," a conception which, as ultimate, should, it is thought, be accepted as "not further analyzable." For the notion of purely external relations is precisely an attempt to analyze a situation into terms and relations, the whole being taken as absolutely without inclusive unity. As we have said, a relation between two things is itself one entity, and in this oneness both terms must be included. It does not follow, Bradley and absolute idealists to the contrary notwithstanding, that the relation must be internal to both terms; but it does follow that it must be internal to one of them as embracing the other, which is more abstract, or else to some third thing embracing both, in which case both terms must be abstractions.

This reconciliation of organic unity with an open future is the solution of the problem which agonized William James and is in itself a proof of God. For only a divine intuition could really know such a unity, or render it conceivable except as an empty logical demand. And the demand is inescapable on pain of a vicious regress.

The foregoing treatment of the problem of relations is by no means complete, and may not do justice to the arguments of Whitehead, James, or Bradley. I shall return to this subject in *The Universal Orthodoxy* (in the chapter on "The Meeting of Extremes in Second-type Theism").

It has been frequently maintained that an omniscient mind could not contain lesser minds as parts of itself since, knowing what these minds do not know, it could not entertain their partly erroneous beliefs.[8] This assumes that the only way to contain a belief is actively to believe it. But perhaps one can passively suffer it. Belief has been defined as readiness to act. The omniscient would not be ready to act upon our erroneous ideas, and so would not believe them, but it could feel our readiness to act, and so this readiness would become part of its content.

It must be remembered that, whatever problems seem to be solved by putting lesser minds " outside " the supreme mind, the essential problem, that of throwing at least some remote, dim light upon how the lesser minds are yet perfectly known in spite of their externality, is not exactly helped by this procedure. The external, it appears, is known by signs which are internal, that is, it is known imperfectly, abstractly, partially. God infers his objects! If, on the contrary, he enjoys these objects as one with an aspect of himself in this enjoyment, then we have in principle a clue to the perfection of his knowledge. We ourselves seem to have immediate awareness of the feelings of our own cells, which enter into the content of our own experience, but without this making what they do *not* feel, their ignorance, identically our ignorance. The positive aspects of false belief (and even pain is positive, unlike ignorance as such) become positive predicates of the including mind, the negative aspects become predicates of that mind only so far as constituted by the part or included mind which has the negative property in question, while as constituted by other parts, the including mind is without just those negations. To regard this as contradictory might only mean that to have parts at all must be seen as contradictory. For the properties of the parts belong somehow to a whole which in its wholeness does not have these properties so far as they express deficiencies of the parts in their distinction from each other and from the whole as *more* than they. The whole is the parts and more, it is their positive content, not their negative (their partialness), except as this contributes to or defines the positive. It does not prevent God from experiencing dramatic value in the clash of more or less ignorant wills that he does not share in this ignorance by being ignorant. He experiences the full positive feeling and meaning of the state of ignorance, even though in contrast to the experience which he also has of the things of which lesser wills are ignorant. I suggest that when the reasons for denying that other minds are parts of God are examined it will be found that they fail to conform to the conditions by which alone parts and wholes are possible at all. One might as well say that a whole with parts moving in opposite directions could not really contain these parts, for then it must move in opposite directions at the same time, as say that a mind could not contain the false belief of *a* together with the true knowledge of the object of this belief. The property of the part is the property of the whole with a systematic qualification.

We should not assume that we know offhand what is meant by part, and from this assumed knowledge deduce the status of the idea that we are parts of God. It is just as problematic what part and whole are as what God is. All the problems of metaphysics are on the same level. The world whole is made such by the divine inclusiveness, it is love that explains cosmic structure, or the two are aspects of the same thing. What binds many into one is social realization.

The notion that if we are within God our activity cannot be really ours but must be only his supposes that God has nothing that is his but his activity. For if passivity is also his, then the part's activity can be also the whole's suffering of this activity, its feeling that and how the part is active. Passivity seems definable as the activity of one individual so far as possessed or enjoyed by another, and this holds even where the first individual is part and the second is whole, provided the " whole " has some unity of its own and is not a mere sum whose oneness depends upon the mind of some external spectator. (In the latter case the whole is not an individual as either active or passive, it is not a primary unit of reality.)

I should like to pay tribute again to the genius of Fechner, who was perhaps the first to see clearly that the choices of lesser minds, the voluntary acts, must appear in the highest or all-inclusive mind as involuntary " impulses " upon which the choices of the highest mind, its volitions, will operate. By sympathetic union with our volitions God wants, not by choice, what we choose to want. Though it is his choice — or rather, his willingness, for he considers no alternative — to be thus open to influence from us (or from *some* creatures or other), it is not his choice that we give this influence just this or that direction; for, if it were, then we could not really choose at all. God's choice (and not simply his willingness, but his moment-to-moment decisions among rival possibilities) comes in deciding at what point to check or encourage or redirect this or that among the impulses or involuntary movements which we set up in his life. (He does not choose between good and bad ways of doing this, for no bad way is possible to him, yet there is no one predetermined or uniquely right solution to the problem posed by the conflict of interests, but only a general class of valid solutions, no one of which — at least as I conceive it — is wholly definite except the one brought into actualization. The determinate right solution adopted belongs perhaps to no set of equally determinate alternatives, but it does express a " determinable " which could have been determined otherwise and equally well. This is the nature of creation and of time and of all determinate existence, that no " sufficient reason " why it must or ought to be just as it is, is possible. The particular cannot be deduced, even by God. It has to be decided by fiat, the " play " of creation of which the Hindus speak. The " righteousness " of this play consists not in its deducibility from any rules, but in its conformity with the rule — to which an infinity of other possible solutions would also have conformed — that whatever is decided should be with a view to all interests, fully appreciated as they are, and with a view to the principle of combining unity with contrast, of achieving beauty.)

I suggest that this neo-Fechnerian view of the passivity of the inclusive mind to the activity of the included mind is (a) an exact and concrete way of saying what religion has been trying for centuries to affirm, and (b) a philosophically more defensible view than any conception incompatible with it. Activity, volition, cannot work upon nothing or merely upon itself; and that upon which it is exerted will not be there for it unless it is accepted with some appropriate degree and kind of passivity. Choice is among impulses or desires, not among " ideas," mere inert pictures or forms. God has a definite problem to solve only because he actually wants conflicting things through his participation in conflicting desires and volitions. He wishes that others should have their wish; it is their wishings that furnish the matter for his choice by becoming a set of desires within his life. *Love makes control self-control by communicating desires.* Every orthodox theologian admits that wickedness consists not in having impulses, but in consciously and wrongly encouraging or discouraging impulses. So the holiness of God's will is not in his freedom from desires, but in the certainty that none of his desires will be unduly encouraged or discouraged, that is, treated without adequate regard to all other competing desires in the universe. God passively wishes with and for the creatures what they wish for themselves, but his activity lies in *deciding* how to resolve the conflict of interests which he has thus taken into himself. Our problem of conflict with each other is thus through the divine sympathy made God's problem of self-harmonization. This is Fechner's anticipation of the " patience," the " fellow suffering," the " tenderness " which Whitehead ascribes to God. It may be no accident that just such personalities — themselves full of gracious sensitivity — should recognize the divine responsiveness which thinkers generally cannot easily understand or admit.

To say that activity is inferior to passivity is rather like saying that right is inferior to left, for there is as much activity as passivity in any being and vice versa. What is inferior is activity-and-passivity on a mean rather than a grand scale. Nothing and no aspect of anything can be acted upon except by precisely the passivity which is required to *adjust* the activity of the one to the activity of the other; and to nothing can one be passive save by possessing precisely the activity which is required to make the passive adjustment *one's own,* part of that unity of self which is always a creative self-synthesis, and which not even God could do for one. We are passive toward the entire universe, yet we act on a cosmic scale too after a fashion; but both the influence we receive from, and that we exert upon, the whole of things (and God as the individual unity of that whole) are deficient. There is as much that God cannot make us do or be as there is that we cannot make him do or be, and the former " cannot " expresses our deficiency, not God's. He can change us, from our point of view radically, but by his or the cosmic standard the change will be slight. We can change him, by our standards greatly, for we can make him think our thoughts sympathetically with us.

That God cannot " make us do " certain things does not " limit " his power, for there is no such thing as power to make nonsense true, and " power over us " would not be power over *us* if our natures and actions counted for nothing. No conceivable being could do more with us than God can (if theism of the AR type is true), and so by definition his power is perfect, unsurpassable. But it is a power unique in its ability to adjust to others, to yield with infinite versatility of sympathetic desire to all that has desire, and to set limits to the fulfillment of desire not as to something merely alien to himself but as to what he himself would like to enjoy in and with the subjects of the desire.

Does this not introduce the tragedy of unfulfilled desire into God? Yes, it does just that. And no less a theologian than Berdyaev, not to mention others, tells us that God suffers, that existence is tragic for God. It is tragic for *any* being that loves those involved in tragedy. And this is why men can literally love God, because he even more literally loves them " as he loves himself," since by direct sympathetic union they are parts of his internal life. Spinoza's saying that we love God with the love with which he loves himself has thus a truth which he did not quite intend. Not that God loves exclusively himself and no other individual, but that God through loving all individuals for their own sakes makes them one with himself, with phases of his own life. Consequently, when we for our part love God this love is a factor in God's enjoyment of himself, that is, in his self-love. Spinoza and the orthodox theologians seem to have divided the truth between them here. God is neither the whole in which all parts lose their value as distinct individuals — so that there is only the one loving the one — nor is God so exalted that he is not a whole at all, and so that our feelings and conflicts are not his feelings and conflicts, but rather God is the *socially differentiated whole* of all things which only love of all things can explain. God is not in every sense "beyond tragedy," but he is beyond, utterly beyond, the evasion of tragedy, wherever and for whomever it be.

To deny that we are parts of God implies that God as a unity in variety contains less variety than exists, or it implies that an exact duplicate of every item of existence is part of God. Either way is not promising, the first alternative having no point unless first-type theism is accepted, with its denial of variety to God, or unless God be conceived as very "imperfect" indeed, and the second alternative being a reduction to absurdity.

In general, once the essentially negative theology of first-type doctrine has been renounced, it is alone consistent to follow systematically the procedure of regarding *every* positive conception as applicable in some sense to God, searching for the sense in which it is applicable, rather than cutting off discussion by asserting its inapplicability in any and every sense.

Also, if we deny the inclusiveness of the divine unity, we will either have to admit that relations between God and the lesser minds belong to no individual, no real substance, or have to admit a superdivine individual to which they belong. (It would be nonsense to suppose that God embraces his relations but not the terms of these relations, for however "external" relations may sometimes be to terms, no term can be external to its relation. A "relation to" is just nothing.) The paradox of the world-and-God as *more* than the supreme being should be left to first-type theism, which glories in such contradictions.

For the Aristotelian view that substances are not factors

in each other, there was a legitimate motive. There is a sense in which no " subject of predicates " is itself a predicate. If by predicate is meant an abstraction, such as can be known by an image serving as its model or " icon," that is, as a sample of the predicate, then no substance is ever such a predicate. The total personal quality by which each of us qualifies God, or the cosmic life, is knowable only by direct, though for us vague, intuition, and identifiable only by pointing, never by description or abstract imagination. In the terminology of Peirce, substances are indexically, not just iconically, known; and the full nature or quality of things is known only by intuition, which is icon and index in one. Neither the full *what* nor *that* anything is can be known by mere abstract description. In their abstract or more or less general predicates things do not contain particular other things; but in their concrete being things qualify each other reciprocally; and this is the social nature of reality. To point to a thing is to point to its neighbors as factors of that thing, and vice versa; for things are irreducibly social, " members one of another." If under " predicate of " we include " concrete factor of," then things are certainly predicates of other things.

Since even God is " factor of " other things, there is no denial of the reality of finite subjects in calling them " states " of the eternal subject. God appears in us as an aspect of our states. This makes him passive as well as active, and we are active as well as passive as parts of him. Substantiality is mutuality, not simply independence. It is love, the synthesis of the categories.

It is an ancient contention that the number of substances can neither increase nor diminish. This is true only if by substance is meant not merely a real subject of change but the one universal and necessary subject of change, which indeed can neither come into nor go out of being, for it is being. In any other sense the contention seems merely the denial that change is real, that anything can come to be which previously is not, and this denial is an arbitrary limitation of change. What has been overlooked by many (for example, by Kant) is that there is no need whatever and even no room for more than one necessary substance, substance as furnishing identity through *all* change. Contingent substances furnish relative identities through limited changes (though even this identity must be measured by the alone fully effective and public self-identity of the necessary substance), but the changes of the coming to be or ceasing of these substances require a subject of change which always changes, and which is therefore not contingent. Failing to make these distinctions, thinkers naturally also failed to see that the one necessary subject of change is God. There is even a certain comic element in the unconscious ascription of the characters of deity to alleged mere matter, at the bottom of the scale of being.

Men do not easily see the superiority of that "being" with which they can do anything that they can do at all — save only deprive him of the will and power to treat others with similar compliance and to integrate all into the one conscious life — because in human relations a certain stubbornness must atone for the finiteness of human sensitivity, for man's inability to be passive to more than a small portion of the active agents in existence. We worship that second-best form of power which puts influences in balance by deficient, lukewarm response and do not readily recognize the superior power which, more humbly than the humblest of men, even perhaps than the one born in a manger, yields with exact adequacy to every pressure of creaturely activity. The most trivial of physical particles will go where we push it, but will it feel our joy or sorrow, echo our thoughts, assume the *qualitative* forms we wish some fellow being to share with us? Not to any noticeable extent. It resists with superhuman " power " of self-sufficiency, with admirable persistence, in its own course of activity. None but God, the opposite extreme from the particle, can be infinitely passive, the endurer of all change, the adventurer through all novelty, the companion through all vicissitudes. He is the auditor of all speech who should be heard because he has heard, and who should change our hearts because in every iota of our history we have changed his. Unchangeably right and adequate is his manner of changing in and with all things, and unchangeably immortal are all changes, once they have occurred, in the never darkened expanse of his memory, the treasure house of all fact and attained value.

NOTES

1 See especially Whitehead, *Modes of Thought* and *Science and the Modern World.*

2 See S. Alexander, " The Historicity of Things," in *Philosophy and History,* edited by R. Klibansky and H. J. Paton (Oxford: Clarendon Press, 1936).

3 See my *The Philosophy and Psychology of Sensation* (University of Chicago Press, 1934), pp. 190–242.

4 E. D. Kennedy in the *New Republic,* CI, 139.

5 See C. Spearman, *The Nature of Intelligence* (London, 1923; 2nd ed., The Macmillan Co., 1927), chap. 14 and pp. 241–50, 354; also Spearman, *Creative Mind* (London and Cambridge, 1930), chap. 11. On the emotional quality of sensations, see also F. R. Bichowsky, " The Mechanism of Consciousness: Pre-sensation," *American Journal of Psychology,* XXXVI, 586–96.

6 See Whitehead, *Modes of Thought,* p. 140.

7 See Ralph Barton Perry, in *The New Realism,* edited by Edwin B. Holt (The Macmillan Co., 1922), pp. 106 ff. For an admirable discussion of internal relations see Dewitt H. Parker, *The Self and Nature* (Harvard University Press, 1917), pp. 212–73.

8 See E. S. Brightman, *Philosophy of Religion* (Prentice-Hall, Inc., 1940), pp. 219–20.

IX

THE NECESSARILY EXISTENT

(*Ontological Argument*)

Where would such an idea, say as that of God, come from, if not from direct experience? . . . No: as to God, open your eyes — and your heart, which is also a perceptive organ — and you see him. But you may ask, Don't you admit there are any delusions? Yes: I may think a thing is black, and on close examination it may turn out to be bottle-green. But I cannot think a thing is black if there is no such thing as black. Neither can I think that a certain action is self-sacrificing, if no such thing as self-sacrifice exists, although it may be very rare. It is the nominalists, and the nominalists alone, who indulge in such skepticism, which the scientific method utterly condemns.

Charles Sanders Peirce, in *Collected Papers,* Vol. VI

The ontological argument turns logically upon the unique relation between the possibility and the actuality, the " essence " and the " existence," of God. With ordinary finite ideas the task of knowledge is to decide among three cases: (1) the type of thing conceived is impossible, and hence non-existent (e.g., a moral being totally without " freedom ") ; (2) the type of thing is possible, but there is no actual example (a Euclidean space?) ; (3) the thing is possible, and there is an example (a speaking animal). The ontological argument holds that with the idea of God only two of these three cases need be considered, since one of the three, (2), is meaningless. If, the argument holds, there exists no God, then there also can be no possibility of the existence of a God, and the concept is nonsense, like that of " round square." If, further, it can be shown that the idea of God is not nonsensical, that it must have an at least possible object, then it follows that it has an actual object, since a " merely possible " God is, if the argument is sound, inconceivable. *Where impossibility and mere unactualized possibility are both excluded, there nothing remains but actuality, if the idea has any meaning at all.*

The ontological argument itself does not suffice to exclude the impossibility or meaninglessness of God, but only to exclude his mere possibility. Or, as Leibniz said, it must assume that God is not impossible. (We shall consider presently whether the argument can be extended so as to justify this assumption.) The inventor of the argument, Anselm, took it for granted that the man with religious experience, to whom he addressed his discourse, though he may doubt God's existence, will not easily doubt that in hoping that there is a God he is at least hoping for something with a self-consistent meaning. Now, given a meaning, there must be something which is meant. We do not think just our act of thinking. What we think may not be actual, but can it be less than possible — unless it be a self-contradictory combination of factors, singly and separately possible? In short, when we think, can we fail to refer to something beyond our thought which, either as a whole or in its elements, is at least possible? Granting this, the ontological argument says that, with reference to God, " at least possible " is indistinguishable from " possible *and* actual " (though, as we shall see, " possible " here means simply " not impossible " and has no positive content different from actuality) . Let us now present the reasons for the contention that " at least possible " and " actual " are indistinguishable in the case of the divine.

According to one theory of possibility, a given type of entity is possible if the most general features, the strictly generic characters, of existence or of the universe are compatible with the production of such an entity. Thus, there is no contradiction of the most general features of reality in the supposition that nature has really produced Mr. Micawber. There is contradiction of the details of nature (such as the detail that Micawber is a character in a novel written by a highly imaginative author), but these may be supposed otherwise without destroying the meaning, the generic content, of "existence." But the idea of God is the idea of a being everlasting in duration, and independent, in a certain aspect of his being (in his individual "essence"), from everything else. Such a being could not be produced, since he must then be both derivative and underivative, everlasting and yet not everlasting. To create the omniscient, one must endow him with a perfect memory of the past before he existed; to create the omnipotent, one must endow him with incomparably more power, a metaphysically different order of power, than that which created him. It is hardly necessary to prolong the discussion: no theologian holding either type-one or type-two theism has ever rejected that portion of the ontological argument which consists in the proof that *God could not be a mere possibility;* and (as we are about to show) it is demonstrable that in order to reject this proof one must construct a theory of possibility which would not be required for ordinary purposes, so that the tables may be turned upon those who accuse the argument of making God an exception to all principles of knowledge. The argument does make God an exception, but only in the sense that it *deduces* this exceptional status from a generally applicable theory of possibility together with the definition of God. Nothing else is required. The opposition, on the contrary, sets up a general principle which, but for God and the desire to avoid asserting his existence (as following from his possibility), would be without merit.

It might, however, be thought that " possible " need not mean the consistency of the supposition of the thing's being produced, or of its coming into existence due to some cause. Only with one type of thing, it may be held, does " possible " mean this. With another type, consisting of things with universal extent in time, a thing either just always exists or just always lacks existence, either status being possible, although no temporal cause could conceivably effect the difference.

I submit that this is a view so paradoxical that it would hardly be considered at all but for two reasons. One is that it invalidates the ontological argument. The other is that it lends color to the supposition that the laws of nature discoverable by science are eternal laws, although their non-existence is logically possible, and although, as eternal, they could never have been produced, constituting, as they do, the very machinery of all production, the presupposition of all events. The alternative to this supposition about laws is the idea that the laws of nature with which physics deals are themselves produced by the cosmic process, the most general principles of which are beyond " law " in this sense. (There must be some sort of law governing the production of laws, but this higher law is of another order, and may be conceived as the aesthetic principle of the value of order as such, and of the no less real value of a certain element of freedom and disorder, of surprise and novelty, as well as repetition and predictability.) On this view, nothing is possible and at the same time not actual unless at some stage of the cosmic evolution the forces were such that there is no contradiction in the idea of their having taken a turn which sooner or later would have led to the production of the thing in question. Thus, if nature had developed other habits — and who shall say she could not have? — other " laws " would have obtained. But clearly God could not be possible in this way, and he is the *only consistently conceivable object which must be conceived as unproduced,* a reality always existing or never existing or even capable of existing, either in essence uncaused or a mere nonentity.

The old objection that if a perfect being must exist then a perfect island or a perfect devil must exist is not perhaps very profound. For it is answered simply by denying that anyone can conceive perfection, in the strict sense employed by the argument, to be possessed by an island or a devil. A perfect devil would have at the same time to be infinitely responsible for all that exists besides itself, and yet infinitely averse to all that exists. It would have to attend with unrivaled care and patience and fullness of realization to the lives of all other beings (which must depend for existence upon this care), and yet it must hate all these things with matchless bitterness. It must savagely torture a cosmos every item of which is integral with its own being, united to it with a vivid intimacy such as we can only dimly imagine. In short, whether a perfect God is sense or nonsense, a perfect devil is unequivocally nonsense, and it is of no import whether the nonsensical does or does not necessarily exist, since in any case it necessarily does not exist, and its existence would be nothing, even though a necessary nothing. Clearly, again, an island is not in essence unproducible and self-sufficient. Of course one can arbitrarily put concepts together and suppose that an island which could never be destroyed and had never been produced would be better than one capable of production, since some form of eternal life might go on upon it, undisturbed by any possibility of an end to such a world. But it is not apparent what would make such a world an island, if the " waters " which " washed " it never wore its shores, and if it were not a part of the surface of a body in space surrounded by other bodies capable of smashing it to pieces, and were not composed of particles capable of ultimately separating, etc. The question is if such a conception would in the end be distinguishable from the idea of the cosmos as the perpetually renewed body of God, that is, not an island in the least, but an aspect of the very idea of God whose self-existence is upheld by the argument.

The question is, Can a possibility be real, unless it would, *if* actual, be an effect of a cause which is real, or the effect of a possible cause which, if actual, would itself be the effect of a cause which . . . (the series ultimately terminating in a cause which is real)? Otherwise, possibility is something wholly apart from actuality, something no experience could ever reveal or evidence support.

I may be told that "logical possibility" is simply self-consistency and that no further reality than this consistency is required. But the reply is that the meanings whose consistency is granted must mean something, and this referent of the meanings is not the consistency but the presupposition of there being any meanings, consistent or otherwise. If a consistent meaning means something, but something not even possible, then it means something very odd indeed. If it means only its own consistency, then it is really meaningless.

Let us be empirical. I may think of any object of any color I choose; will it be denied that an object of this color is consistently conceivable as a production of "nature"? In fact, of course, objects of at least approximately the same color have been actually given in my experience. The step "from thought to reality" is merely the reverse reading of the step from reality to thought without which there is no thought, as the very logicians who attack the ontological argument on the ground that it seeks to "derive existence from a mere idea" would be the first to grant. We are always in contact with the forces which produce realities, and hence we can think both actual and possible objects. Or, in other terms, we can distinguish, in the reality some portion of which is always given to us, between the essential or generic features and the details, and can see that this distinction implies that mutually incompatible details are both or all compatible (separately, though not together) with the generic features. But God is not a detail, and only contradiction results from trying to make his possibility conceivable in the fashion in which alone mere possibility is ever really conceived.

We may go further. The reason God is not a detail, whose existence would be one of two equally conceivable alternatives, is that he is really the content of " existence," the generic factor of the universe. To conceive God is not to conceive what might exist, but what " existence " itself must be — if the idea of God is not meaningless. Either God is nothing at all, or all else that exists exists in and through him, and therefore contingently, and he himself exists (in his essence, though not in his accidents) solely in and through himself, that is, necessarily. The cosmological argument showed that only " God " makes clearly conceivable the flexibility of the generic features of existence by which alternative details of existence can, as alternatives, be real. Alternativeness is one way of looking at creativeness, and the essential or cosmic creativeness is the divine, and nothing else.

Thus to make God's existence exceptional in relation to his conceivability is a result, not a violation, of the general principle of existence. Whatever is merely possible, this possibility as such is real, is other than nothing, only thanks to something which itself is not merely possible but is reality itself as self-identical, or as that which, being the ground of possibility, is more than merely possible. It is an implication of the idea of God that he is that ground.

At some point potentiality and actuality must touch, and

at some point meaning must imply existence. God is the general, the cosmic and everlasting, the essential or a priori case of the unity of essence and existence, and he is this because he is supreme potentiality as existing power, a real agent who eternally does one or other of various pairs of alternatives which he " can " do. All meaning implicitly asserts God, because all meaning is nothing less than a reference to one or other of the two aspects of the cosmic reality, what it *has* done or what it *could* do — that is, to the consequent or primordial natures of God.

It has been objected to the ontological argument that existence is not a predicate, and hence cannot be implied by the predicate " perfection." But if existence is not a predicate, yet the *mode* of a thing's existence — its contingency or necessity of existence — is included in every predicate whatever. To be an atom is essentially to be a contingent product of forces which were also capable of not producing the atom, and doubtless for long ages did not do so. Again, contingent existence (the equal compatibility with existence or its negative) is implied by such predicates as those describing a man. His weaknesses imply that it is not true that he is the master of existence, able to exist through his own resources. The strength of God implies the opposite relation to existence. " Self-existence " is a predicate which necessarily and uniquely belongs to God, for it is part of the predicate divinity. It is part of the nature of ordinary causes that they are themselves effects of causes which antedate them. It is part of the nature of supreme causality that it is coextensive in time with all causal action. (Not that God's action is in no sense affected by causes, for the law of action and reaction may apply to God; but simply that God, as an individual, cannot have originated out of pre-existent individuals. His existence is uncaused, whether or not all his properties are. Or, otherwise expressed, his essential properties, being one with his existence, have no ground in other individuals; but he may be subject, in spite of the Thomists, to accidents whose explanation is in part to be sought in the accidents occurring in other individuals.) To be God is essentially to be the supreme productive force itself, unproduced and unproducible (except in its accidents) by any force whatsoever. Hence either God is actual, or there is nothing which could be meant by his possible existence. Thus that God's essence should imply his existential status (as contingent or necessary) is not an exception to the rule, but an example of it, since the rule is that contingency or non-contingency of existence follows from the kind of thing in question.

There is another way in which the argument illustrates rather than violates general principles. The argument is not that God's individual nature implies his existence, while other individual natures do not. It may reasonably be held that every individual nature implies existence, and indeed is an existence. By regarding possibilities alone, one can never reach any truly individual character. Individuation and actualization are inseparable by any test, since individuals as such are known only by pointing. Description of contingent things gives always a class quality, unless in the description is included some reference to the space-time world which itself is identified as " this " world, not by description. But " perfection," as we shall see presently, is the one description which defines no class, not even a " one-membered " one, but either nothing or else an individual. If, then, it is true, as it seems to be, that mere possibility is always a matter of class, then the perfect being, which is no class, is either impossible or actual — there being no fourth status.

But if every individual quality implies existence, must

not all individuals exist necessarily? The answer is that contingency is not a relation of existence to a thing, but of a thing to existence. To say a thing might not exist is not to say there might be the thing without existence. It is rather to say there might be existence without the thing. To pass from the actual to what might be is to generalize, ultimately to refer to the uttermost generalities. It is the world (in its generic features) which does not imply its contingent inhabitants, not the inhabitants which do not imply the world with themselves as its existing parts. They do imply it. Without it they, as individuals, would not be, even as possible. There is an unutilized possibility of individuals, but not an individuality of the unutilized possibility. Mr. Micawber is a quasi-individual, with some of the aesthetic properties of an individual, but not an individual in the strict sense. He is a class, specific enough to simulate an individual for the purposes of the aesthetic illusion or "make-believe."

The unique status of God is that no distinction can be drawn between any individual having perfection and any other. Every perfect being must have the same space-time locus (omnipresence), and must know the same things — all there are to know. If there had been another world, the God of this our world would have known it, for the very possibility of another world can be related to God only as something *he* (not some other God) could have done or can still do. Hence "the perfect" is no class of possibilities, all of which might be unactual, but only an individual character belonging to nothing, not even potentially (for the only individuality that could be involved is already involved), or else belonging to the one real perfect individual.

The necessary being is, then, that individual which existence implies, and which itself implies, not simply existence (for every individual does that), but implies, through the identity of its generic with its individual character, that (so far as its primordial nature is concerned) there is in its case no separation between possibility and actuality, the class and the individual. In other words, "perfection" implies that existence itself necessarily contains a real perfection, or that existence, in its cosmically essential features, *is* perfection as existent, as the unity of being and possibility. Or, perfection implies that existence, any and all existence, implies the existence of perfection as its ground.

Again, to conceive a thing in two alternative states, actual and possible, is to conceive something common to these two states, as well as something different. But between the world with God and the world without God no common feature could be found. For the world with God is the world completely dependent upon the existence of God, for both its actuality and its possibility, and hence it follows that in the absence of God nothing of the world as it would be with God could be identified.

Doubtless these are all ways of construing the one simple principle: nothing but existent perfection could make perfection possible, or rather, perfection cannot have the dependent relation to other things implied by the status of mere possibility, but must have either the status of an impossible idea or pseudo-idea, or else must be simply actual, with no alternative of non-actual possibility at all.

If it be thought suspicious that the ontological argument argues from a unique relation of God to existence (though one deduced from the normal relation plus the definition of perfection), let it be remembered that, by definition, God's relation to every question is unique. He is the unique being, unique because maximal, the only unsurpassed and unsurpassable being (in senses A and R).

Naturally, God's relation to existence is maximal also, that is, he exists under all possible circumstances, times, and places, in other words, necessarily. That which would exist, if at all, necessarily, cannot be non-existent and yet possible, for this would mean having existence as a contingent alternative, and a contingent alternative cannot be necessary. To object to this is to object to the idea of God, and not merely to the affirmation, "There is a being corresponding to the idea."

If all individuals are contingent, then the whole of existence is contingent, and it might be that nothing existed, or it might be true (though nonsensical) that there was nothing of which any proposition would be true. Furthermore, what could constitute the identity of existence as such, if not an eternal and necessary individual manifested in all individuals? We human beings tend to carry our own personality with us in all our hypotheses, in so far as we say to ourselves, Suppose *I* were to experience so and so. This gives an aspect of identity by which we might try to define existence as such. But the definition would be solipsistic. Hence there must be some further aspect of identity, like ourselves in being a concrete existent, but unlike us in being able to constitute the unity, the all-embracing register of existence itself, without limitation upon conceivable variety and independence. This is what God is, the all-embracing register of existence, perfect in his flexible and tolerant ("merciful") sensitivity to all experiences, who can see things as they see themselves, also as other things see them, and also as they are related without distinct awareness on the part either of themselves or of other imperfect things.

It is to the credit of the ontological argument that it has to be opposed by making an absolute disjunction between meaning and its referent, reality, or between universals and individuals, a disjunction *at no point* mediated by a higher principle. Only if there is *one* actual individual whose presence is universal, have universals an intelligible ground in actuality. Otherwise we have to relate mere universals and mere individuals by — what? Ordinary individuals, being non-universal in their relevance, cannot explain the identity of the universals as such. Aristotelian objections to disembodied universals can be sustained only if there be a universal embodiment, a " concrete " universal so far as present actuality is concerned, though a universal which is also (contrary to Hegelianism) abstract so far as the future and potentiality are involved.

Thus there is not from any point of view good reason to object to the exceptional status of God's existence, every reason to welcome it as the completion of the theory of meaning.

It is often said (and with an air of great wisdom) that a " mere idea " cannot reach existence, that only experience can do that. But there is no absolute disjunction between thought and experience. A thought *is* an experience of a certain kind, it means *through* experience, even when it reaches only a possibility. A thought which does not mean by virtue of an experience is simply a thought which does not mean. Therefore, if we have a meaning for our thought of God, we also have experience of him, whether experience of him as possible or as actual being the question. It is too late to assert total lack of experience, once meaning has been granted. The only doubt can be whether the experience, already posited, is such as to establish possibility only, or existence also. But in the case of God no distinction between " not-impossible " and " actual " can be experienced or conceived. Hence we have only to exclude impossibility or meaninglessness to establish actuality.

Moreover, since God is conceived as all-pervasive of actuality and possibility, if we do not know God as existent, it cannot be because we have been denied some requisite special experience, since either *any* experience is sufficient, or else none could possibly be. Or, once more, either God is a meaningless term or there exists a divine being.

In still other words: either the idea of God is less than an idea, or it is more than a " mere idea " such as might designate an unactualized possibility, and is a direct awareness of an actual deity — as not only the mystics, but most theologians, have maintained. " Deity " may be nonsense, but a mere idea it cannot, without nonsense, be. To paraphrase Kant's final remark on the subject, all disputation about this, the real, point of the ontological argument is labor lost, as much as disputation about arithmetic. To say God cannot be a mere potency and to say two and two cannot make five differ in the degree of clearness of the ideas involved, but not in the a priori, or (relatively) self-evident, character of the reasoning.

That the ontological argument is hypothetical we have admitted. It says, "*If* ' God ' stands for something conceivable, it stands for something actual." But this hypothetical character is often distorted out of all recognition. We are told that the only logical relation brought out by the argument is this: The necessary being, if it exists, exists necessarily. Thus to be able to use the argument in order to conclude " God exists necessarily," we should have to know the premise " God exists." This makes the argument seem ludicrous enough, but it is itself based on a self-contradictory assumption, which says, " If the necessary being happens to exist, that is, if as mere contingent fact, it exists, then it exists not as contingent fact, but as necessary truth." Instead of this nonsense, we must say, " If the phrase ' necessary being ' has a meaning, then what it means exists necessarily, and if it exists necessarily, then, a fortiori, it exists." The "if" in the statement, "if it exists, it exists necessarily," cannot have the force of making the existence of the necessary being contingent — except in the sense that the argument leaves it open to suppose that the phrase "necessary being" is nonsense, and of course nonsense has no objective referent, possible or actual. Thus, what we should maintain is, "that which exists, if at all, necessarily," is the same as "that which is conceivable, if at all, only if it exists." Granting that it is conceivable, it then follows that it exists because it could not, being an object of thought at all, be a non-actual object. Or once more, the formula might be this: The necessary being, if it is not nothing, and therefore the object of no possible positive idea, is actual.

Kant confronted the ontological argument with a dilemma: either the argument is analytic, and then it begs the question by defining God as actual while pretending to derive his actuality from his mere possibility; or it is synthetic, and in that case actuality is added to possibility without warrant. But the argument consists in showing that "mere possibility" is meaningless with respect to God, and the inference is indeed analytic; but its premise is that God is not impossible, which — since God cannot be merely possible — leaves as the only case analytically allowed, that he is actual. It is not true that all things have two conceivable states, possibility and actuality. To assume this, and on the basis of this assumption to accuse the argument of begging the question, is for the accuser himself to beg the question. "Not impossible" or "conceivable" involves three different cases: (1) no such thing exists, but existence is or has been capable of producing it; (2) such a thing exists, but existence might have failed to produce it; (3) such a thing exists, and it is impossible that it should not have existed. In the third case, to conceive the thing as merely possible is to conceive nonsense. The argument for existence in that case will not be that the conception of this nonsense implies the thing's existence, but that the impossibility of conceiving the thing not to exist leaves but two alternatives: the thing exists and hence can be the object of the conception of its existence, or the thing neither exists nor is a possibility of existence and the conception of it is nonsense, is the conception of nothing, unless of mutually contradictory elements (as is God conceived as sheer A). Thus we should not say that God is "possible therefore actual," as though he were in one of two states because conceivably he is in another, but we should say that God is not impossible, i.e. inconceivable, and therefore he is in one of the three states given above, but since he is not a contingent but if anything a necessary or self-existent being, eternal, unproducible, etc., therefore only state (3) can apply. There is no question-begging, provided it be admitted that "God" stands for more than an impossibility. If he is not less than a possibility, he can only be more, that is, an existent. The general case of possibility, which does not decide between the three cases, may be called compatibility with existence or conceivability. God is either impossible, or he is compatible with existence in such wise that both the generic and the special aspects of existence imply his existence, but do not imply his non-existence. Other things than God are conceivable if the generic aspect of existence implies neither their existence nor their non-existence, but is compatible with both.

The famous Kantian example of the hundred unreal dollars (as exactly one hundred, and as precisely dollars, even though they do not exist) is also beside the point, if our analysis is correct. With dollars the distinction between potentiality and full actuality is obviously meaningful;

with deity it is, almost as obviously, irrelevant. This is not because existence is one predicate among others, which God, having the maximum fullness of predicates, cannot lack; but rather because the status of non-actualized potency of existence, that is, contingency, contradicts the predicate of deity.

It is in one sense not quite true that unreal dollars can have every predicate of real dollars. For if individuality or determinateness is a predicate, then there is no reason for ascribing this predicate to imaginary dollars. No one could show that an imaginary dollar has any exact shape or color, except by arbitrarily defining it to have, and this would start an endless process. (How to define a precise hue and shade of color?) The " real " might be defined as that which alone is definite, apart from human acts of definition, and transcendent of the utmost that these acts can attain. Now the predicate of deity is unique in that, as Kant himself notes, it is *self-individuating a priori*. Its definition determines the individual possessing the predicate sufficiently to distinguish it from all other individuals, actual or possible. What is left undetermined refers merely to the alternative accidents of one and the same God. In Whitehead's terms, the definition determines God's primordial nature, though not his consequent natures (it should best be put in the plural, for there is a new consequent nature every moment). But it is the same individual being which pervades all the consequent natures which have been or even might have been; just as the adventures of a man, including those he might have had if he, or his friends or enemies, had chosen differently, are all *his* actual or possible adventures, and no one else's.

The notion that a predicate must be detachable from existence thus amounts to the idea that individuality is something added to qualities. And if by qualities is meant universal and limited ones, this is true. But absolutely particular qualities can hardly be found except as embodied in actual individuals, and absolutely unlimited properties, such as knowledge that is in no sense or respect less than knowledge, in no sense ignorance, can be found only in the unique and necessarily actual individual, God.

In arguing that there can be no contradiction in supposing a thing absent with all its predicates, but only in supposing a thing present with contradictory predicates, Kant is either asserting that when we conceive a thing we can conceive it as neither actual nor possible, or else he is asserting that we can conceive God as merely possible. Neither contention should be granted.

Also fallacious is Kant's attempt to prove the irrelevance of existence to perfection by arguing that if a possible thing had every perfection except one, the addition of existence would only make the thing exist with the same near-perfection which it had as possible. The point, of course, is, once more, that nothing merely possible has *any* perfection in the strict sense, and that the transition from any imperfect value, however great, to perfection is not to be attained by adding another finite value, or by any addition. That one could add value forever in thought to the imperfect without reaching existence is only an aspect of the fact that one would never in this way reach perfection either. Unless the perfect is presupposed all along as that which the imperfect lacks and is measured by, then no transformation of the imperfect will define the perfect, which, as Plato said, defines both itself and the imperfect. The holy is not merely that which is without sin, but that which fully appreciates all interests; and we know sin as the deliberate failure to appreciate the totality of interests because we have some sense of this totality, some sense, however weak, of the holy. We do not get to God by adding to the idea of something else, but we do get to something else by subtracting from what we intuitively know of God.

The strongest point in Kant's immensely influential but hardly too clear criticism of the argument is surely his contention that the argument's premise, the non-impossibility of God, is not to be accepted lightly. But it is only Kant's own subjectivistic system, generally rejected by those who in effect rely upon it as the base of his attack on the argument, that makes it seem sensible to him to suppose that a consistent idea might lack even a possible object.

One might of course hold that possibility depends on the constitution of the world, not on our thought. But then we have to ask, Would not another world constitution have been possible? The only ground for a negative reply must be that another world is inconceivable; so we come back to conceivability as ultimate criterion.

The fact that logicians have not elucidated these aspects of the theistic problem is certainly not a question of lack of ability, or of honesty. But logicians seem almost to have said to themselves: "We have, incidentally to our main concerns, disposed of the theologico-metaphysical proof par excellence. Nothing could be more satisfactory. Let us turn to more scientific concerns." But if mere disposing of an argument is less instructive than understanding it, and if philosophical interests are not identical with those of natural science, then something further is to be desired.

It is said by logicians to be absurd to say, "The such and such (or the perfect) exists." We must say, There is an x, an individual, such that it has a certain property. Thus: there is an x such that x is perfect (omniscient, etc.). Now the ontological argument merely holds that if this proposition is false, *then perfection is imperfection.* For if there is no perfect x, then perfection is either a meaningless term, or it means the mere possibility of perfection; but the mere possibility of perfection implies that perfection could come into being, or be produced or have its being derivatively from whatever it is that constitutes its " possibility," and this amounts to saying that perfection could come into being as imperfection.

Why have logicians denied that we could ever infer from a predicate that something embodies that predicate? The ground appears to be the inductive one that most predicates do not imply existence; therefore we may suppose that none do. Such an inference obviously could not be conclusive. To clarify the matter we should consider carefully the relation between essence and existence in the most widely contrasting cases. By considering " redness " alone we certainly never could discover what things in the world are in fact red. But it may be going too far to say that the predicate redness is conceivable in complete detachment from red objects. If we imagine red, at least our psychological, and perhaps our physiological, state is somehow qualified by redness, and it is a moot point in philosophy whether redness literally does ever qualify anything except minds-and-bodies endowed with color vision. The quantitative properties ascribed by physics to things which we experience as red are distinguishable from redness as given. To ask whether anything is really red means in science whether anything really has these quantitative properties. And while these properties do not in the mere conception imply the reality of external objects precisely embodying them, it is nevertheless true that if we know what we mean by wave lengths and the like it is because we have experiences, and are organisms, which do illustrate in principle though not necessarily in detail what such quantitative aspects are like. In other words, the more fundamental aspects of predicates are always actualized somehow in the experience which refers to them.

The problem is not, whatever logicians may sometimes like to imagine, that of getting from mere disembodied predicates to actualities, but of getting from actualities, such as actual experiences (which include some portions of the actual environment as experienced), to other real or possible experiences or portions of the environment. This is done by following the tracks of universals, generic features of actuality and possibility alike. By this means, predicates can be approximately (though only so) defined, even though they are not actualized. But if nothing like redness were actual here and now, say as the memory of a real red object, I could not here and now speak of the possibility of redness somewhere else. Nor could I do so unless the idea of a " place " were illustrated by the here and now. Logicians may claim that it is only a psychological, not a logical, necessity that essences should be illustrated in actuality. But the making of such a verbal distinction seems to correspond to no actual evidence.

The truth then seems to be that generic essences imply the reality of some instance or other, and that particular essences are only approximately identifiable apart from their instances. By combining a number of such approximate predicates one may conceive a possible something strikingly unlike anything actual. But simple and quite definite essences are apparently never knowable unless they are embodied.

Here lies a possibility of extending the ontological argument so as to overcome its hypothetical character. The basic paradox of the argument, overlooked by many of those who speak in generous terms about its paradoxicality, is that the inseparability of essence and existence in God seems to imply that it is no easier to know one than the other. As Aquinas, perhaps the best of all the critics of the argument, pointed out, to have an intuition of the nature of God would be to have an intuition of his existence, so that any experience which furnished the premise for the argument would also, without the argument, furnish its conclusion. But for second-type theists, who admit not only an identity between the divine essence and the divine existence, but also an identity between the essence of the universe and the divine, the cosmological argument is open to the same objection. And the objection amounts to this, that a necessary truth can be deduced only from a necessary truth, since to know the contingent *as such* is *ipso facto* to know the necessary.

All theological truth is one, except in emphasis. All argument for God seeks simply to show that even in denying him we know him, that the conclusion in question is only a clearer way of seeing the premises — any premises which state what at bottom we all believe, or which explicate the most general aspects of any man's thought. The experience from which we derive the premises for theological (or atheistic) argumentation must no less directly support the conclusion, but not for all that so clearly. We are seeing God in both cases if in either, but not in the same relations, and only when we have brought out a sufficient number of these relations will we see that it is really God that we are dealing with. Deductive transition among these relations is for the purpose of enabling us to judge whether the entire system of ideas we are operating with really expresses what we intuitively know in all our experience and thinking. It is the same with deduction everywhere in philosophy.

We have seen that impossible predicates are arbitrary complexes of predicates severally thrown together. Now the predicate of deity is not an arbitrary congeries of essences thrown together. As Descartes said in this connection, it is as extraordinary for its unity as for its richness. Yet the argument is here more complex than he recognized, since we have to consider the two aspects of God as brought out in second-type theory. Of the necessary or primordial aspect, what the older theologians said (as though it applied to God as a whole) needs only to be repeated. We can speak of a variety of properties, the usual divine attributes, but they turn out to be merely different ways of conceiving one unique property. Omniscience and omnipotence are not related like having hoofs and having horns. No sense can be made out of omniscience that does not imply omnipotence, any more than feeling can be explained apart from volition, or vice versa. The same applies to the relations of knowledge and goodness in God. To say God is good is only to say his action is decided in full awareness of all the interests affected, and this could no more be without omniscience than omniscience could be without it.

But the consequent or concrete nature of God is not simple in this fashion. It embraces all the positive predicates actualized anywhere. This follows from the primordial attributes themselves, since to be omniscient is to include in one's experience all that is, whatever it be. How can we be sure that all actual predicates are compatible together in such fashion that they could constitute the content of one experience? As Leibniz said, not all things that are possible are compossible. However, at this point second-type theism escapes a paradox of traditional theism. It does not hold that all possible values are included as actual values in the being of God, but only that all actual ones are included as actual and all possible ones as possible. Now all actual predicates are certainly compossible, or they could not all be actual. The notion of the togetherness of things in God is only the most intelligible notion of their togetherness in " existence," remembering that the togetherness we are most concerned with is togetherness of life, experience, values, not a togetherness — of no direct consequence to anyone, by definition — of mere dead matter or neutral entities. How can there be a contradiction in the idea of a knowledge of all actuality and of all possibility? Could we define all actuality, or all possibility, in any other way than as the content of experience as it would be if all vagueness or unconsciousness of reference were overcome with full and clear awareness? And how can the various lives in the world make one world unless the unity of the world is itself living and sensitive to value differences?

Thus it is hard to see how there can be any contradiction in the idea of God as conceived in second-type theism, though there are, as we have seen, plenty of contradictions in first-type theism, according to which God is a mind — without a body; a power — resisted and acted upon by no other power; a will — without change; a knower of the contingent — yet wholly necessary in all his nature; a love — totally unaffected by the fortunes of those it loves; and so on.

Of course, first-type theists may respond to such a challenge by asking if there is not a contradiction in the duality of natures ascribed to God by the new theism. It has been said that the primordial and the consequent natures are really two Gods. This I hold to be a complete misunderstanding. Do a man's character, so far as constant, and the man's concrete stream of experiences make two men? Then why should the distinction between the abstract identical aspect of God and his concrete diverse aspects (which are infinitely plural, except that one may speak of them all generically — as *the* "consequent nature" — when they amount merely to the necessity that there be some unique concrete nature for each moment of time) generate two Gods?

Yet the idea of God might be regarded as an arbitrary

and hence perhaps self-contradictory compound in another way. Perfect knowledge, it might be said, is the result of the uniting of the ideas of knowledge and of perfection, or, again, " knowing all " is the union of knowing and totality. But it is not so simple. Perfection would be meaningless without knowledge. Totality is already implied in the idea of knowledge. The knower has, by the meaning of knowledge, a world to know. He may know only a part of it, but this part as such belongs to the whole which omniscience would know. That the part is known without knowing the whole implies that the part as such is not known altogether as it is, or in other words that even the part is not known without qualification. But to qualify knowledge of the part we must understand what knowledge without qualification or in its simplicity would be. The complex idea here is that of partial or limited knowledge. Evidence of this is seen in the history of thought, in which the first version of assertions is in the absolute form, while the relativity of human truths is only very painfully and late appreciated. Thus omniscience is not the result of qualifying the idea of knowledge derived from our own knowledge but of removing the qualifications we have, still imperfectly, learned to make in our own knowledge by using the more or less subconscious vision of God. God is not fundamentally negative — the non-finite — but the non-imperfect, that is, the perfect knower, the knower *simpliciter,* the knower who is never less than knower, the righteousness which is never less than righteous.

But are there not ideal conceptions which measure existence, and yet whose literal actuality is not so much as possible? Thus perhaps " absolute equality," or " absolute circularity," are not even possible existents, but only abstract measures of what exists. Yet, though impossible, they are not self-contradictory. And may not absolute goodness, or perfect knowledge and power, be similar "regulative" ideas, without constitutive import?

This is the most persuasive way, so far as I can see, to formulate the atheistic hypothesis. It is plausible to say that an actual perfect circle is impossible, and yet the idea of perfect circularity is free from contradiction. It is also plausible to say that circularity is a general idea without intrinsic individuality, and hence it may be rather an implicit comparison of individuals than a reference to any one as it is or could be in itself. Perhaps the idea of an absolutely circular individual really is a contradiction, destroying the very idea of individuality which it presupposes. The idea of circles would still have objective reference through the fact that some things are more nearly circular than others, with sheer circularity the ideal limit of the series of more and more perfectly circular things.

But although geometrical ideas are perhaps ideals which it is the very nature of reality, as Plato thought, to embody imperfectly, there is a sense in which these ideas are literally actualized. Geometrical equality may never be absolute, but it is perfectly possible to experience precise equality in another form. There may be just two horses and just two cows in a field, and the number of horses is then exactly, not approximately, equal to the number of cows. Counting may be absolute, provided there is sufficient discontinuity between the units to be counted, as well as an unmistakable similarity between the units. In measurement of length the units are without such discontinuity, and there are all degrees of the similarity in question. We have then to treat as equal lengths which do not for our observation involve a different number of units. Absolute equality would have to mean that for no possible observation, or not for omniscience, would the number of equivalent units be different.

Again, a perfect circle could be defined as a line at every point equidistant from a given point, or as a self-returning line which has everywhere the same shape. Clearly the same sort of problem as those just considered is involved, the same mixture of algebraic and spatial ideas, the former quite capable of literal embodiment, the latter problematic, and in their absoluteness inseparable from the idea of omniscience, of God.

This idea itself seems to be of another order. True, the idea of "all" in omniscience can be got at algebraically. One may speak of all the letters in the equation $ax + bx = z$. But, as we have seen, omniscience is not the mere knowing of all things whereas we know only some, for not a single item of this all is known absolutely as it is except to omniscience. Omniscience is qualitative as well as quantitative. We know nothing with absolute distinctness. Yet our idea of things "as they really are" can apparently only be the idea of them as they are or would be to an ideally distinct experience, i.e., to God. Thus it is "God" that defines "actuality," not vice versa.

Something like the foregoing argument for the ultimacy of the idea of God is what Berkeley was perhaps trying, not very successfully, to formulate. The argument does not in the least depend upon supposing that what we immediately know is only our own ideas, only states of ourselves. The conclusion reached is not that all objects are merely ideas, or rather states, of God, but that they *are* such states, whatever else they may be. Nor is the argument one from the "egocentric predicament," for it reasons from the idea that one's own self, no less than every other, is relative to a measure of reality which our own half-unconscious awareness cannot furnish for itself any more than for anything else, and which only a clear consciousness could furnish. Thus the reasoning puts the center of things in the divine Other, not in the human ego. We do not fallaciously argue: Objects depend on us, for they are our ideas; but still, they do not really depend upon us, for we cannot produce ideas at will, hence we may suppose they depend upon God. The argument is rather: The immediate object, which is chiefly the life of the living parts of the body, does truly depend partly upon us; our control over it, by voluntary shifts of attention, is real, but very limited and imperfect. The cosmos is a cosmos because it is in all parts subjected to a control in principle like ours over the body but without the defects which express the fact that we are each the mind of a human body, not of the cosmos. Berkeley neglected the mind-body relation and hence did not see the element of dynamic interaction between subject and object, hence regarded the object as purely " passive," without life of its own, a mere idea of the subject, an egocentered entity. Hence he could find in immediacy no analogy for the power which his theory ascribed to God of producing ideas in the minds of his creatures. We immediately produce ideas, that is, states in the sentient units of our bodies, and they in us; that is, we are contributors to their states and they to ours. God is simply the maximal contributor or cause of ideas in all minds; he is not the sole cause, for he acts in partnership with all other individuals, but the supreme cause.

Nor is the argument that we know things only as known (by us). It is rather that we know them only as known *and* as self-known, that is, we refer all contents of experience to more than one center of awareness, or focus of individuality, in abstraction from which things are merely — abstractions, not concrete entities, dynamic units, given or thinkable as such. One's " own " individuality is only one of the foci in one's own experience, which is immediately, though in our case not very distinctly, social. The only focus which is necessary to the idea of reality is the divine, which is always present as the point of reference for our sense of our own reality on the same terms as for the reality of anything else.

Thus we define reality in terms of the divine as the experience which is distinct and in a sense complete where ours is vague and partial, hence an experience which confronts no unknown objects — the unknown being not absolutely so (or it could not be spoken of) but the vaguely, poorly known. Yet this definition must be formulated with care.

Simply to say a " complete all-perfect experience " is to raise all the paradoxes of immutable perfection and determinism we have so often pointed out. But our own experience, in its a priori aspects, as always, gives us the clue. There are two senses in which our experience is incomplete and disharmonized, and only one of them is responsible for the sense of ignorance. It is ignorance that I do not know just what I was doing at this moment yesterday, that my memory of that time is somewhat vague and fluctuating; it is ignorance that I do not know just what the possible or probable reader is feeling as I write these lines, that, in short, my idea of " the people in the world who some months from now could possibly read a book of this sort " is so vague. I may some day meet the reader and find out at least something of what he was doing at this very time. In the future I will find out what is already a part of the past, including the tendencies already established for the future. Or in the future I may find out what could be known at any time, such as some truth of mathematics. These are the only two sorts of ignorance, and both are discovered by finding that the incompletion of one moment's experience can be removed at another moment, although it is part of the meaning of the incomplete experience that its completion could have come earlier. Hence the ignorance. But the incompletion which consists in the fact that the thing to be known is itself future, is in the portion of time which is incomplete in essence and not accidentally — this incompletion is not ignorance, and its removal is an addition to knowledge which defines an addition to reality. Omniscience is simply that mode of knowledge in which only this kind of addition to knowledge is possible, the kind identical with the transition, for the object itself, from futurity to presentness. Nothing is vague in the perfect knowledge except as this vagueness coincides with futurity. In our knowledge there is much vagueness which we know is vagueness about the present and past, not about the future only. That this is so is an immediate datum. I not only am vague about what I shall feel, I also am unclear about what I have felt. Vagueness of memory is as immediately known as anything about memory. At any rate this vagueness will hardly be denied. But present perception in our case is vague also, not merely or essentially in that it does not tell what is going to happen, but that it does not tell with distinctness what is happening now. My several sensations, visual, auditory, and the others, have certain qualitative characters, alike or different with respect to each other, and these characters and relations are not as definite to my consciousness as I know they must be in themselves. This vagueness is both given and inferable from what is given.

All we have to do to conceive omniscience is to banish all such vagueness from the idea of experience, but leave that vagueness which defines the futurity of what is future. What I " shall " do tomorrow, that is not only vague now, it must ever be vague. For when tomorrow comes, what is then experienced cannot be what I " shall do " but what I then am doing, and the distinctness of this is compatible with the vagueness of the other. If I say, "I shall do *x*," and I do not do *x*, this contradicts my assertion; but if I merely say, "I shall do something or other within such and such vaguely defined limits, and what I do will not be vague but definite, though what definite thing it will be is vague," then my assertion is not refuted by the definite thing, within the specified limits, that I actually do when the time comes. If, however, I say that the limits specified are as definite as they could be made in advance, this assertion might be known to be false, either by discovery of a general law of behavior shown by probable induction to obtain, or by direct intuition into the determinate aspects of the future. Thus, if I knew the future to depend more upon my advance resolution than upon the resolutions or plans or past histories of any other being, and if I knew what these other plans or resolutions or past histories were, then this knowledge plus my consciousness of my own resolution, which would take account of all the other data mentioned, would be the future as given now, that is, as future. (And I should be God.) Yet I still would not know what the future would be when present, for the future is the "determined to be determined *somehow*" (within more or less narrow limits), not the "determined to be determined just precisely in such and such a way."

Thus an experience is conceivable which would be clear about its unclarities, and would have no unclarities except such as constituted the futurity of the future. There would be left for this experience something to find out about other experiences only in the sense that these other experiences themselves had their futures to find out, that is, to make, to actualize, to get into determinate present form. All beings other than God have to go into the future to find out not solely about the future but about what, for themselves or other beings, is already present or past.

That there are these other beings is part of what is vaguely given in the present. The non-ignorant knowledge goes into the future only to find out about the future, that is, it finds things where they are in time; those of its data that have the mark of pastness or presentness need no further experiencing to complete, but only those that have the mark of futurity.

In this way it seems possible without circularity to define omniscience as a certain completeness and clarity of experience, and reality as the content of such an experience. If this is correct, then the ideal by which imperfect knowledge is judged is the idea of perfect knowledge, of God, not the idea of mere reality. " Things as they are in themselves " only amounts to " things as they would be to a sympathetic intuition whose incomplete meanings were exclusively futuristic." When we complain that no one understands or knows us fully, not even we ourselves, do we not implicitly appeal to such a perfect sympathetic intuition as would enjoy all our feelings and experiences to date (most of which we ourselves have largely forgotten, or remember with almost infinite vagueness) and our future experiences just so far as these are implicated in the others but no further?

Does anyone think there is some perfectly mindless slate, called " truth," or " reality," or " the past," upon which all past experience that is incompletely defined in our present human experiences is distinctly inscribed? Yet what else can an atheist think (of course subconsciously, for, may I repeat it, the main difference between theists and atheists can lie only in the proportion of their thinking about cosmic matters which is conscious, and in the harmony or conflict between the conscious and unconscious portions) ?

A plausible counter-argument to the ontological is to

say that it is precisely the perfect which we should expect not to exist. Heroes with nothing but merits and virtues, like villains with no redeeming touch, are unconvincing. We know at once that they are fictitious. The ideal is the soaring of aspiration beyond the actual, enhancing the good and abstracting from the evil.

But we must beware of a fallacious induction of the form: all contingent realities are imperfect, therefore there is no perfect and necessary reality. Of course, no contingent thing embodies sheer perfection, and therefore conceptions of such a thing which ascribe perfection to it are fictions. And God is not a hero with nothing but merits, he is not the actuality of our aspiration to be as much as possible all that a human being may be. This aspiration is in ultimate truth a soaring beyond the actual. What we seek in regard to it God also seeks for us and himself, because of our freedom not altogether attaining it. But in another aspect God is the strictly superhuman being by reference to whose immutable essence the limitations and the possibilities of man can be measured. He is not what we ought to be, or should like to be, but what it is nonsense to suppose our being, except when his perfection is conceived as limited by certain human properties. The hero is he who trusts his friend or bravely faces his enemy even when he does not know what he is thinking and doing; God knows what all are thinking and doing.

Nor is it true that we reach the divine ideal by abstracting from evil. God is not the being whose life is sheer joy and beauty, but the cosmic sufferer, who endures infinitely more evil than we can imagine. What we abstract from in conceiving God is that which is itself a kind of abstraction, namely, ignorance, lack of interest in the interests of others. God is the concrete unity of the world, not the selected catalogue of its good aspects. This unity as such is purely good ethically, in that it is strictly all-inclusive and does face fully the evil as well as the good, does not evade anything or fail to realize the full quality of things. One may abstract the mere property of inclusiveness or catholicity of interest, the lovingness of God, but in so selecting this wholly good aspect (the primordial nature) we are omitting not only all particular evils but also all particular goods, the whole consequent nature of God, and have merely the fact that God always loves everything, without any of the things he loves. Thus the selection involved in isolating the holiness of God is fair as between the particular goods and evils, simply omitting both, and leaving a mere form of goodness as such, or in general, as holding of all possible states of God. This generic goodness is purely good only from an ethical standpoint, for from the aesthetic it is both good and evil, since the general form of love has the two sides of rejoicing with the joy and sorrowing with the sorrows of others, or of promoting their welfare, and in a manner loving what they love and hating what they hate.

The ethical absoluteness of God is hardly analogous to that fictitiously ascribed to the hero, for it is much more like that unfailing sympathy which a man has for at least some portion of his own body, the portion in the case of man shifting from moment to moment, since man's body is integral with a cosmos whose mind is not his. God is beyond this form of limitation, the whole cosmos being his body, so that all parts of it are alike his immediate associates in the mutuality which is the connectedness of things.

In any case sinlessness as applicable to man is not holiness as conceived of God, and the two are separated by an infinity. Yet the human holiness is indeed what remains as possible of the divine when we restrict the immediate and vivid sympathy for all to immediate and vivid sympathy chiefly for varying portions of that little part of the world which is a human body, and at most for other human or animal bodies and minds with which the given person's body is in effective, relatively direct interaction.

The ontological argument as no longer merely hypothetical is then as follows: Any predicate is either itself embodied in actuality or is a special case or combination of predicates that are so embodied; the predicate of deity (in its essence or primordial nature) is not derivable from other predicates, is not a special case or an arbitrary combination, but the most original or universal predicate, from which the others are derived by limitation or specialization. It is the unity of the underivable or generic predicates. Now the original unity of our generic concepts cannot be empty of meaning or self-contradictory, for all of our generic concepts depend upon it. Hence the idea of God is a genuine and self-consistent idea, and since it is consistent only when taken as referring to an actual deity, a merely possible one being the same as an undivine divinity, the predicate of deity must exist in a real God.

In this form, in which both the non-impossibility and thence the actuality of God are proved, the argument is no longer merely the ontological, but includes a form of the cosmological as the first step. But Kant showed that the converse relation is also true, that the cosmological is complete only if the ontological is valid. The cosmological proof shows that there must be a necessary (everlasting) being, but this proves God only if the religious idea furnishes the sole way of construing necessary existence. And if it does so, why can we not infer existence straightway from the idea? To this it has been objected that there is a difference between the direction of inference from perfection to existence in the two cases. The cosmological argument says, there must be a self-existent being, every self-existent being is perfect, is divine, therefore there is a perfect, a divine being; the ontological argument, on the contrary, says that every perfect being is self-existent, and according to ordinary logic, all *a* is *b* does not imply that all *b* is *a*. But the implication does hold provided it be shown also that there can be but one *b*. To say that all *a*'s (self-existent beings) are *b*'s (perfect beings), but some *b*'s are perhaps not *a*'s, is to imply either that *a* is a null-class (in which case the cosmological argument must be invalid) or else that there is a conceivable plurality of *b*'s (perfect beings) one of which may be *a* and another not *a* (not self-existent). But a plurality of perfect beings is not conceivable. Hence the cosmological argument cannot be valid unless the ontological is so.

A subtle objection here is that of Aquinas, who held that the ontological argument is indeed valid *per se* (or for God himself), but that it is not valid for our knowledge, since the ontological inference from perfection to existence proceeds from the (to us) unknown to the to-be-known, whereas the cosmological inference from contingent existence to necessary existence as perfect proceeds from the known to the provisionally unknown, and thereby follows the true order of finite knowing. But this is open to a double objection. Kant brought out one of the objections when he denied that we know contingent existence as such. How do we know that the world is not self-sufficient apart from God? How do we know that things really are contingent, that they could be otherwise than as they are? Scholastics will reply, because things change, and if a thing does not remain in the state in which it is, that state cannot be necessary. Its non-existence occurs, hence it must be possible. But Kant replied, it is possible when it occurs, but is it possible at any other time? Perhaps events are necessary when they occur? To answer this we must analyze what is meant by time and change, by past, present, and future. According to much recent thought at any rate, Aristotle was right, though not radical enough, in holding potentiality an essential aspect of time. The future is neither not-being nor actuality, but real potency.

This line of thought is incomplete until we have generalized beyond all open alternatives to reach the common features of all times, to which there is no alternative because they are presupposed by the very idea of alternation —as its universally common traits, involved on both sides of each and every choice. This non-alternative factor or factors can be understood, the cosmological argument shows, only as the perfection of God in his primordial nature. But who could reach this conclusion, or understand it, unless he had already some intuition, which needed only awakening, of the nature of God? Perhaps nothing could be derived from the cosmological argument by a mind wholly unable to see force in the ontological, for the two are the same relation read in opposite ways, and this relation is one of partial identity in the content of two experiences, the secular and the religious, an identity such that to have no appreciable degree (at least potentially) of the religious must mean that one has no appreciable degree of the secular.

The artificiality of the separation of the cosmological and ontological arguments (as in Aquinas) seems all the clearer in view of the fact that the idea of God which Aquinas (and apparently Anselm and Kant as well) wished to prove is in reality, as we have seen, by all available tests, self-contradictory and impossible, so that the valid ontological argument with respect to it is that God is as conceived impossible. Hence necessarily there is no such being. Truly the saint, and Kant with him, did well to insist that no man knows the possibility of such a God a priori.

That is compatible with one's knowing its impossibility a priori! But the very procedures which define this impossibility also show what qualifications suffice to remove it and to produce an idea which survives every test of conceivability, or at least, whose inconceivability, if it be so, must be of a radically different and more obscure order.

Kant appears to be right then in considering that if the ontological argument has no force the cosmological has none either. But he fails to see that the ontological argument, if valid, does more than furnish a required final step in the cosmological argument. Its validity implies the validity of all the steps in the other argument. (Indeed, all theological reasoning is of one piece. To be certain that it is right or wrong at any point would be to see its correctness or incorrectness at all other points. The difficulty, if not the impossibility, is to be quite certain at any point. We can only be as clear and certain as we are able to be, so to speak.) For if, as the ontological argument assumes, perfection is conceivable, and if, as the argument shows, conceivable perfection implies existent perfection, as that which all existence implies, then the cosmological reasoning, which holds that existence implies perfect existence, could not be invalid. This does not mean that the ontological argument, in its hypothetical form, presupposes for its validity the acceptance of the cosmological. On the contrary, the ontological argument shows that the mere consistency of the idea of God implies the validity of the cosmological argument. Hence, if one had rejected the latter argument but felt that the idea of God cannot be meaningless, one would be forced by the ontological to reconsider the cosmological argument. Thus the ontological supports the cosmological inference not only, as Kant says, by furnishing one necessary step in it, but also by implying that the cosmological argument as a whole is valid, that existence implies the existence of God, unless God is a self-contradictory idea.

Our only reason for any conclusion is some form of experience, and the harmony of secular experience with religious (as yielding the idea of God) is surely a reason for increased confidence in both. To construe this harmony as confirming religious experience by means of secular experience is the cosmological way — which shows that secular experience is incoherent in its generic aspects unless God is taken to exist; to construe the harmony as confirming secular experience (as interpreted by the cosmological argument) by means of religious experience is the ontological way — which shows that the religious experience is not even coherent in its chief conception or qualitative datum unless this quality belongs to an actual and not a merely imaginary being and the sort of being called for by the cosmological inference.

The cosmological argument says, the world is not even possible, and hence secular experience is nonsense, unless God is actual; the ontological says, God is not even possible, and religious experience is nonsense, not just illusion — and therefore by the cosmological inference (whose validity can be inferred from the ontological) all experience is nonsense — unless God exists.

Just as there are people who deny that "God" need have any rational meaning, so there are those who deny that "universe" or "existence as such" need have any rationally explicable content. In the one case the cosmological, in the other the ontological, argument fails. The final decision derives from the realization through reflective experience of the meanings in question, and of the impossibility of making skepticism in either direction a sincere philosophy. All men, it seems, must ultimately or at least obscurely feel the religious ideal as the referent of all comparisons between interests, presupposing an inclusive interest in interests which can only be God's and not any merely human interest. (The very ideal of universal tolerance which by a strange result of false religion has come to seem to some the privilege of the irreligious is really but a disguised form of the divine ideal. No one is really fully tolerant except deity, or could fully realize what is meant by the command to appreciate the various actual interests without prejudice.) Again, all men feel themselves parts of a whole, a universe. These two inevitable references have the same referent, as the two arguments show.

The relationship of the two arguments also means that religious experience warrants the theological enterprise. For if there is no possible inference from the world to God, then there can be no God and the very idea is nonsense. Conclusive refutation of the cosmological argument would invalidate the ontological, and vice versa. The arguments show that each mode of experience contains the same implicit affirmations as the other, but each with its own focus of greatest distinctness, the religious experience in its most perfect form containing the maximum all-round explicitness of outline.

The final argument is: the existential or cosmic ultimate — the key conception at which the search for knowledge of the real arrives — and the ethico-religious or value ultimate are one, and the character of this one is in both cases intelligible as deity. Or: experience is adequately guided for either practical or theoretical purposes only by the religious idea. The chief obstacle to agreement on this point has probably been the failure on both sides to distinguish between different dimensions of value, according as they do or do not permit an absolute maximum, with the resulting implication that the value ultimate means the complete actualization of the ideal in unimprovable perfection, whereupon the ideal loses its essential function, as Dewey so well insists — as did James and others before him.

It is hard to see how there could be any strict independence of the secular and the religious arguments. To reflect upon the idea of God is *ipso facto* to reflect upon its relation to existence and to other ideas. The idea of knowledge, even unqualified knowledge, implies something to know; the idea of power, something over which power is exerted; the idea of good will, that of other interests toward which good will can be extended. To know what one means by God without thinking of what one means by finite minds and a world which they constitute is impossible. Hence to think about God is the same as to think about the world, except in emphasis, and the cosmological and ontological arguments can only be two ways of seeing the same relationships.

To start with the idea of a being worthy of infinite or religious regard and loyalty is to end with, or never to have been wholly without, the idea of the world as integrated by an all-loving power. To start with the idea of the world as possessing necessarily some sort of unity and order is to end with, it is to have had from the beginning, the idea of an all-loving being as the full explication of this unity. The only " argument " is the identity of these two problems. God is " the world " understood, the world is " God " understood. In both cases we start with (1) the perfect being as vaguely given to intuition and (2) the perfect defined in a more or less definite concept; and we end by verifying the correspondence of the conception to the intuition. The agreement of concepts and percepts is of course the test of all truth. Religious experience provides at least a pseudo-percept of the world whole of which we are parts. So does secular experience, but with emphasis upon details or upon abstract aspects like geometrical pattern. Reflection shows that the two percepts describe the same object. This coincidence between world-intuition and God-intuition, secular and religious experience, is the only proof for God. We may trust our idea of what God is because it proves to be simply the full explication of what all our general or cosmic ideas imply, so that even to conceive the untruth of the idea is nonsense, for it would be the untruth of the ideas by which the conception of this untruth, and of any truth or untruth, is made meaningful. The only possible argument for God must show that doubt of God is doubt of any and all truth, renunciation of the essential categories of thinking.

If the theistic arguments are sound, no one is really without faith in God, any more than there are absolute skeptics; but some persons may be in a state of verbal confusion as to their basic beliefs. And certainly there are signs enough of confusion in atheistic writings. There are also many confusions in theistic writings, but they are (a theist will hold) lapses into verbal atheism, while the confusions of atheism are lapses into real, and not merely verbal, theism. The atheist really *believes* in the integrity of nature as permitting inductions, while the (first-type) theist only thinks he believes in the "timelessness" of deity, that is, by implication, in its non-purposive character, its lack of social passivity, etc. The negative character of atheistic beliefs, some of which are implied by first-type theism, explains how it is possible to confuse them with real beliefs. To deny something may only mean that we are pushing our belief in it down into the subconscious; but to assert a positive predicate we must have something positive in mind and be aware that we do. The atheist means to say that "deity" is a sound that fails to refer to any object; he is denying the significance of the word. But all the time there may be that in his thought to which the word could be attached, and which if redeemed from its obscurity in his mind would turn out to have the positive properties of which theists (in their more precise moments) talk. We need not repeat Descartes's mistake of supposing that beliefs and ideas which we have promised ourselves to suspend are really made inoperative in our thinking by that resolution, or that introspection can immediately disclose the depths of our own meanings.

The theist must maintain that a philosophy will eventuate in the affirmation of God, or in something either less definite than God or else theoretically incoherent and practically vicious.

Dewey, for example, comes fairly near to asserting theism. At times he does assert something vaguely like it. So does Santayana. Marx asserted something fairly definite, the dialectic of history and of the cosmic process, but this something was definitely wrong, at least in part, and when all that was wrong is removed, what is left is simply a vaguer equivalent of theism. There is no absolute presumption against vagueness. We may have to be vague. But there is a relative presumption against being vaguer than we have to be, and the only way to know the limits is to try more definite formulations until we are checked by disagreements, logical or experiential. Atheisms that are not really idolatry, a vicious form of theism, are deficient in clarity; theisms are often atheistic in some of their implications and hence deficient in consistency. The search for a more definite version of what atheists are trying to affirm, and a more coherent version of what theists have affirmed — these are the two lines of progress which do not imply hopeless stupidity in one side or the other, but admit that each party has been partially right, the one in refusing to regard almost utterly vague conceptions (or else obviously relative principles offered as absolute), the other in refusing to regard contradictions or ambiguities, as the best that man can do in clarifying his most general ideas.

CONCLUSION

(*Summary of the Arguments*)

THE ARGUMENTS advanced in the preceding chapters appear to justify a quite definite answer to the question, In what sense, if any, is there a supreme or perfect being? They point unambiguously to the AR conception, the second of the seven possible views defined in the first chapter, and diagrammed once more below.

	FIRST-TYPE THEISM	SECOND-TYPE THEISMS			THIRD-TYPE THEISMS AND ATHEISM			
A in	*all*		*some*			*no*		respects
	(A)		(AX)			(X)		
CASE	1	2	3	4	5	6	7	
	A	AR	ARI	AI	R	RI	I	

DEFINITIONS:

A, unsurpassable by anything, even by self
R, unsurpassable, except by self
I, surpassable, either by others or by self and others

The first view, or A (taken as sole property of God), being self-contradictory, is excluded by a negative ontological argument (chapter 3). It also conflicts with absolute requirements of ethics and aesthetics (chapters 4 and 6). It fails, finally, to furnish an ultimate or cosmic subject of change, or to afford any help in the explanation of time. Rather it denies time (chapters 7 and 8). The other five views, third to seventh inclusive, differ from AR in one or more of the following ways: (1) by introducing sheer imperfection into at least some aspect of God (ARI, AI, RI, I); or (2) by altogether denying absolute perfection to him (R, RI, I); or (3) by altogether denying relative perfection to him (AI, I). Against each of these three procedures there are decisive objections.

1. To introduce sheer imperfection into God is to contradict his unique status, to make him in so far just one more entity along with others without any essential functions peculiar to him. It means that the supreme being is inferior to some at least conceivable being (other than himself in another possible state) or that the supreme being is capable of falling into a position of inferiority. Such an unstable supremacy seems to meet no requirement of value or of ontology. It could not be the ultimate subject of change, for instance, for such a subject will always possess all positive predicates that are possessed by anything at a given time.

2. The complete denial of absolute perfection means that of all beings it is true that in each of their aspects they are surpassable, either by themselves alone or by others alone, or by both themselves and others. For instance, the ultimate subject of change must be less ultimate in this respect than it is capable of being, or than something else is capable of being. But this implies a possible change for which there would be no ultimate subject, thus contradicting the premise that all change is change of something. Ultimacy is not a matter of degree, unless of the absolute degree, and this is unsurpassable.

3. The complete denial of relative perfection is no less fatal. A being incapable of acquiring increased value is a being without intelligible relation to change, to ethical choice, or to the aesthetic value of variety (absolute variety being inconceivable).

In addition to all this, the ontological argument strongly tends toward the conclusion that AR, being free from inconsistency and having positive meaning which leads to valuable and experientially unforced interpretations at every point, can be construed only as descriptive of existence (since it cannot, in consistency with its own meaning, be taken as descriptive of potentiality, and since additional to existence and potentiality no third mode of being is available as the object of a meaningful conception). Thus AR is self-evidently true of an existent being, and the other six conceptions become at best superfluous.

But AR is of course a mere logical schema, not a full description of God. Our arguments have, however, indicated how the schema is to be made more concrete. We have seen that there is perfect agreement between the unforced interpretation of the religious idea of divine love and the meaning of AR when interpreted through the dimensions of existence as given even in secular experience. These dimensions so far as abstract and therefore independent of the distinction between possibility and concrete existence admit absolute perfection and indeed require it. The mere abstract correctness and adequacy of knowledge and of will in relation to the objects known and willed require as the measure of knowledge and will and also of their objects a perfect case, hence omniscience, omnipotence (meaning unsurpassable power, not all possible power in one, this being indeed impossible), and pure righteousness are validated. They are required to render the final subject of change really the final subject. One cannot conceive God as knowing a great deal, or nearly everything, and at the same time see in him the recipient of *all* actual predicates. All means all, not many or most. And if the will of God is merely remarkably catholic in its sympathies, then there are some events whose occurrence has nothing to do with him, and then he cannot really be the self-identity of time and change as such. Even more obviously, he will not furnish the ethical ideal, or the ultimate cause which all endeavor is to promote, even though it be through the glorious failure of lesser causes.

On the other hand, the dimensions of experience, where these are so concretely conceived as to depend upon actuality as such, do not admit perfection except in the relative or self-surpassing sense. To know what there is to know is cognitive perfection, but to find the known enjoyable to contemplate involves a dependence upon the variety and harmony of the known, and to this variety and harmony there is no absolute upper limit. Additions to the world to be known inevitably constitute additions to the aesthetic richness of the knowledge even though this be cognitively perfect at both the earlier and the later moments. Hence there is entire agreement between the requirements of metaphysics and the religious idea that God derives satisfaction, and varying degrees of displeasure, from our acts and fortunes.

Doubtless many will still feel that somehow the religious idea is richer than the mere metaphysical idea as justified by the arguments we have advanced. Two aspects of the problem must be distinguished.

1. In so far as the religious idea involves reference to the special nature of man, whose very existence is (so far as I can see) metaphysically contingent, philosophical theology in its purity knows nothing of the content of the idea. Sin, grace, forgiveness, as phenomena peculiar to the relations of God to man, are simply not discussed, though certainly not denied. The infinite fullness of the divine life is empirical not metaphysical. Empirical science and theology (revealed theology is in this sense empirical) are the sources for any knowledge we have of God beyond the bare outline of the dimensions of his being. *That* he has an infinitude of contingent features is metaphysical; what these features are is not. Yet apart from his contingent content God would be an absolute emptiness and futility, of no more value to himself than to us. The final, the highest knowledge is not metaphysical, but empirical in

that total sense in which both the generic or merely identical or universal features and also the inexhaustibly growing particularities of experience are included. Only philosophy, science, and religious theology, theology drawing upon special experiences of gifted individuals and groups, can together furnish man with his greatest measure of such total knowledge.

2. There is another sense, however, in which the metaphysical idea of God is more concrete than it is often thought to be. Taking " perfect love " in strict generality, without regard to what is loved and to what is peculiar to loving *this* rather than *that,* it is, I believe, true that this idea is at once the description of the generic nature of God, that nature which he always has, and the minimal fulfillment of metaphysical (and secular ethical) requirements. It seems to me clear that all conceptions of the cosmic factors of existence that stop short of this idea do so only by *failing to elucidate the meaning of abstractions in relation to experience in its general dimensions.* If the cosmos is not held together by love, it is held together by empty words, like " causality " for instance, whose referents in direct experience are never clearly detected and hence whose meaning is more or less undetermined. Between the complete emptiness of mere matter, mere something, mere being, and the love of God generically considered, philosophical history discloses no reasonable half-way point. Metaphysics evaporates into thin air, or it leads us to religion. And for it to evaporate into thin air is for us to treat our abstractions from experience as though experience could throw no light upon their meaning. The most general abstractions from experience are still experiential, they cannot refer to what is just not experience, to mere matter, mere being. Or, if one admits that experience is ultimate but denies that loving experience is anything but

a special case, the answer is that mere experience apart from any social-sympathetic character is just as unidentifiable as mere being apart from experience. Cosmic being is cosmic experience, is cosmic sociality or love. This much of philosophic idealism has been untouched by the criticisms of realists, which always focus upon some perversion or misunderstanding of the social conception of reality. This much of idealism is what secular and religious people alike, though not with the same degree of consciousness, intuit as the atmosphere of all existence and all striving.

EPILOGUE

Panentheism, Transcendental Relativity, and the Trinity

SOME READERS will feel the need for labels for the doctrines of this book, and since such expressions as Second-Type Theism, or AR, are colorless and have no familiar meaning, while familiar labels like pantheism, supernaturalism, and the like are laden with vague and conflicting associations, I shall here discuss some labels that seem to me suitable.

Pantheism is conveniently defined as the logical contrary of pure transcendental deism (the term theism, which is more commonly used for the contrary of pantheism, suggests that the doctrine conforms to religion, really describes the *theos,* the God of worship, and that is open to dispute). Deism here means that God is the super-cause taken as self-sufficient, a complete being, in abstraction from any and all of his effects. God thus excludes the world; he is only its cause; in no sense is he effect, of himself or anything else. Pantheism (better, " pandeism," for again it is not really the *theos* that is described) means that God is the integral totality of ordinary cause-effects, and that there is no super-cause independent of ordinary causes and effects.

God thus includes the world; he is, in fact, the totality of world parts, which are indifferently causes and effects. Now AR is equally far from either of these doctrines; thanks to its two-aspect view of God, it is able consistently to embrace all that is positive in either deism or pandeism. AR means that God is, in one aspect of himself, the integral totality of all ordinary causes and effects, but that in another aspect, his essence (which is A), he is conceivable in abstraction from any one or any group of particular, contingent beings (though not from the requirement and the power always to provide himself with *some* particulars or other, sufficient to constitute in their integrated totality the R aspect of himself at the given moment). Now the term which comes closest to saying all this is "panentheism," since it distinguishes God from the "all" and yet makes him include all. The apparent paradox dissolves when we see that the "all" which is in God, yet not all of God, is the ordinary totality of actual, contingent existence, while the all which *is* God is that totality (stretching through infinite past time, and nearly all unknown to us) as involving, *besides ordinary causes,* the whole as an inclusive agent acting on its parts, further a supreme, abstract causal factor which contains no particular within itself (see above, pp. 236 ff.). These distinctions make sense only when AR is assumed (hence Spinoza's failure, who assumed mere A).

Just as AR is the whole positive content of perfection, so CW, or the conception of the Creator-and-the-Whole-of-what-he-has-created as constituting one life, the super-whole which in its everlasting essence is uncreated (and does not necessitate just the parts which the whole has) but in its *de facto* concreteness is created — this panentheistic doctrine contains all of deism and pandeism except their arbitrary negations. Thus ARCW, or absolute-relative panentheism, is the one doctrine that really states the whole of what all theists, if not all atheists as well, are implicitly talking about. *ARCW has no contrary* (except the purely negative one of denying all cosmic conceptions and all conceptions of perfection, if not all conceptions whatever). You may contradict ARCW, but only by going from the center and sum of all meanings of " perfect " and " world " toward some half-meaning which cries aloud for its " other," some eccentricity which calls for its opposing eccentricity.

In both cases, AR and CW, one is not putting together concepts which contradict each other, but is avoiding contradiction by keeping abstract and concrete, eternal cause and *de facto* effects, where they belong, in relation to each other, as forming one inclusive (though not unchanging or in all ways symmetrically interdependent) being. It can even be shown that A and R are not simply two concepts, but rather two essential elements deducible from one concept; and the same is true of C and W. I cannot develop this here, but the single concept of perfection which says everything may be called Transcendental Relativity, or reflexive universal transcendence, and defined thus: T/T is the property of the self-transcender who in all general or categorical dimensions of value (not to all possible degrees) transcends all other beings. The single concept from which the cosmic ideas follow is that of " the self-changing whole which includes all other beings as its (more or less) self-changing parts." From the perfection concept (which is a generalization of R to make it apply, so far as " other beings " are concerned, to all dimensions), AR, as a unity in duality, follows; and from the single cosmic concept, CW, or panentheism, follows. And from the religious idea of " lover of all beings " both AR and CW, as two ways of saying the same thing, follow. (Of course, all this does not follow from the mere symbols, by pure formal deduction. It follows when we consult the generic experiences which give meaning to " better than," or " change," or " love," or " whole." But the reasoning could profitably be worked out on its formal side also.) When these relations are studied, it becomes almost completely self-evident that the dynamic or self-excelling aspect of perfection is not derivative from the mere absolute — the mere excelling of others than self, the sheer maximum of value — but rather the absolute is a phase of the self-excelling excelling of all others (if it is *all* others, *there* is the maximum, since no self-excelling or non-self-excelling being can excel more others than *all* others, yet this is an absolute only in a certain respect). Similarly, time is not derivative from eternity, but eternity is the element of integrity in the ever expanding variety which is time. As for ordinary imperfection, non-transcendental relativity, it is inherent in T/T, but is property of the perfect only as properties of parts are possessed by their wholes. Imperfect parts cannot make an absolute whole, but they can make a super-relative whole, an R, which is abstractly absolute even though concretely self-surpassing without limit.

T/T can be called, as we have just suggested, the super-relative, for it includes absoluteness on some dimension; and on all dimensions it negates transcendence of itself by any other being, as ordinary relativity does not. T/T is also the super-absolute, for it is absolute on all closed (abstract) dimensions, on which alone absoluteness means anything, and it is self-transcendently transcendent of all on the remaining dimensions — on which the mere absolute would be nothing. Thus we explain both absoluteness and relativity, without having to posit a merely relative world that somehow has the illusion of the absolute, or a merely absolute being that somehow has the illusion at least of relativity.

Since Reflexive Transcendence is relational, it is in a manner the relativists that triumph. Is it not time for theologians to consider the logic of relations? And is it not time for logicians to discover that the problems of theology are in part at least problems of relational structure, and so not exactly meaningless? How can the logical relations of ideas like " better than " (transcendence), " all," " self," " other," be meaningless? [1] Yet the whole problem is there. Until theologians become logicians (on a decent, modern level of precision and generality), or until logicians become theologians, how can the three-thousand-year-old problem of God be dealt with in terms satisfactory for our culture? (For example, Russell has said that the theory of types refutes the classical concept of God. The principle of self-transcendence of transcendence without any upper limit to the self-transcendence seems indeed connected with the theory of types, the veto on the class of all classes, that is, a final "all." But I suggest that atheism may also be guilty of an illegitimate use of "all" when it says, for example, that given any being an *other* superior to it is thinkable. For the universe is a being, and what could be superior to it, *except itself* in another stage or state? To treat the cosmic all as just one more thing involves, I am confident, just as hopeless difficulties as to treat it as all-perfect. AR perfection is just the recognition that the cosmic all is of another type, somehow incomparable, and incomparable by being more, even in terms of value, than anything *else* is or *can* be, because whatever may be, the cosmos will enrich itself with that.

Reflexive Transcendence throws some light, too, upon the idea of the Trinity. For T/T is in a manner the Father, and A and R are the Logos and Holy Spirit. This is not utterly fanciful. Part of what was said about the three persons agrees with the logic of T/T, A, and R. The three are in a sense equal, since all are necessary to God, yet T/T is the one from which the necessity of the other two can best be understood, and in this sense it begets the other two in a logical, not a temporal sense.

However, the three elements are apparently not at all "persons." Yet there are, in a manner, distinct persons in God, though unfortunately they are neither three in number nor equal to each other. I refer to the temporal series of self-states in God. The divine personality is concretely and in part new each moment, and each new divine self sympathizes with its predecessors and its (in outline) anticipated successors. It is even true that these persons in

God are immutable (though not eternal or ungenerated) for, as events, once they occur they are immortally there in the life of God. But each self is superior to all its predecessors, except in the abstract or A factor (which includes the requirement that there shall always be an R factor, a new state of self-transcendence, but includes no such state in particular), this factor being identical in all. Thus the Trinity seems not so much one idea as several, some of which may be profoundly true, especially as compared to the idea that God is sheer unity without inner distinction, and without any intelligible relations of self-love. The "mystery" of the Trinity, object only of faith, seems less impenetrable than the mystery of the philosophical absolute which was taken as an object of reason!

While theologians and logicians (with many exceptions) tend to enforce the cruel and fallacious dilemma — *either* a discredited, ill-generalized, inexact logic, *or* the abandonment of the belief that love is the highest wisdom and the most far-reaching power — while this happens, the world shows as never before the need of men to be able to retain and intensify this belief, and to do so with their intelligence, not in dangerous contempt of responsible, self-critical, cooperative thinking.

NOTE

1 On the positivistic view that metaphysical and theological conceptions are meaningless, see my article, "Anthropomorphic Tendencies in Positivism," *Philosophy of Science*, 1941. D. H. Parker's *Experience and Substance* (University of Michigan Press, 1941) is an able defense and exposition of a type of metaphysics roughly similar to that expressed in this book. See also A. C. Garnett's *Reality and Value* (Yale University Press, 1937); or Paul Weiss, *op. cit.;* or W. P. Montague, *op. cit.;* or the philosophical writings of A. N. Whitehead (The Macmillan Co., 1926 to 1938).

INDEX

ACKNOWLEDGMENTS

THE AUTHOR wishes to thank the following publishers for permission to quote from works published by them:

Harper & Brothers – from Booth Tarkington, *Seventeen.*

Harvard University Press – from *The Collected Papers of Charles Sanders Peirce,* edited by Charles Hartshorne and Paul Weiss.

Longmans, Green & Company – from William James, *Collected Essays and Reviews;* and from Rickaby, *General Metaphysics.*

Princeton University Press – from Paul Weiss, *Reality.*

The Religious Education Association – from *Religious Education.*

Charles Scribner's Sons – from Berdyaev, *The Destiny of Man;* from C. I. Lewis, *Mind and the World Order;* from Étienne Gilson, *The Spirit of Mediaeval Philosophy;* and from Jacques Maritain, *The Degrees of Knowledge.*

Yale University Press – from John Dewey, *A Common Faith.*

He wishes also to thank Mr. E. D. Kennedy for permission to quote his poem, published in the *New Republic.*